TAKE A WALK
SEATTLE

TAKE A WALK
SEATTLE

---

120 Walks through Natural Places in Seattle, Everett, Tacoma, and Olympia

4ᵗʰ EDITION

Sue Muller Hacking

SASQUATCH BOOKS
SEATTLE

To Chip and Angela for embracing the Vagabond Walkers

Printed in the United States of America

Published by Sasquatch Books

21 20 19 18 17   9 8 7 6 5 4 3 2 1

Editor: Gary Luke
Production editor: Em Gale
Cover design: Mikko Kim
Interior design: Bryce de Flamand
Cover photograph: Tere Sue Gidlof
Maps: Lisa Brower
Copyeditor: Janice Lee

Library of Congress Cataloging-in-Publication Data is available.

ISBN: 978-1-63217-090-3

Sasquatch Books
1904 Third Avenue, Suite 710
Seattle, WA 98101
(206) 467-4300
www.sasquatchbooks.com
custserv@sasquatchbooks.com

Photo Credits

Jason Costanza, https://flic.kr/p/e5EMx6, CC BY 2.0, converted to grayscale: page 31; Tobin Fitzthum for ThurstonTalk.com: page 224; Amanda Hacking: pages 133 and 135; Laura Jean Miller: page 64; Mike Miller: page 22; Eric Willhite: pages 20, 50, 52, 72, 93, 116, 133, 143, 146, 149, 157, 166, 175, 187, and 207

All other photos courtesy of the author.

CONTENTS

WALKS AT A GLANCE

EVERETT

Walk #	Trail/Park	Park Acreage	Miles of Trail	Connecting Trails	ADA Trail *	Dogs **	Bicycles **	Horses **	Restrooms
1	Jennings Memorial and Nature Parks	61	1.5		✓	✓			✓
2	Jetty Island	200	2 to 4						✓
3	Langus Riverfront Park	96	3.6	✓	✓	✓	✓		✓
4	Spencer Island	415	4	✓					✓
5	Centennial Trail	n/a	30		✓	✓	✓	✓	✓
6	Narbeck Wetland Sanctuary	50	1.3		✓	✓			✓
7	Howarth Park	28	1			OL			✓
8	Forest Park	190	1.5			✓			✓
9	Lowell Riverfront Trail	n/a	3		✓	OL	✓		✓
10	Meadowdale Beach Park	108	2.5		✓	✓	✓		✓
11	Southwest County Olympic View Park	120	1			✓	✓		
12	Yost Park	48	1.5		✓	✓			✓
13	Lynndale Park	40	1.5		✓	✓	✓		✓
14	Terrace Creek Park	60	3		✓	OL	✓		✓

n/a	Information not available, particularly concerning acreage of land surrounding converted railway trails
ADA Trail*	Sometimes only one trail or segments of a trail will be ADA compliant
**	May or may not be permitted on all trails
OL	Off-leash area in, or connected to, park/trail
Beaches***	These are checked only for walks that allow wading/swimming access to a lake or Puget Sound

Picnic Areas	Playground	Freshwater Beach ***	Saltwater Beach ***	Nature Preserve	Forest	Stream/River/Creek	Wetlands/Marsh	Meadow/Farmland	Mountain Views	Interpretive Trail	Best Birding	Salmon Run	Gardens	Sports Facilities	Art in the Parks	Campgrounds	Historical Site
✓	✓				✓	✓	✓	✓		✓			✓	✓			✓
✓		✓	✓				✓			✓	✓						
✓							✓		✓	✓							
			✓				✓		✓	✓	✓						
✓							✓		✓	✓							✓
✓			✓				✓			✓	✓						
✓	✓	✓			✓	✓			✓					✓			
✓	✓				✓			✓						✓			
✓						✓	✓	✓	✓								
✓		✓			✓	✓			✓								
					✓					✓							
✓	✓				✓	✓	✓			✓				✓			
✓	✓				✓									✓			
✓	✓				✓	✓								✓			

Walk #	Trail/Park	Park Acreage	Miles of Trail	Connecting Trails	ADA Trail *	Dogs **	Bicycles **	Horses **	Restrooms
15	North Creek Park	81	1.5	✓		✓			✓
16	Bob Heirman Wildlife Preserve	343	2 to 3						✓
17	Lord Hill Regional Park	1,463	6+			✓	✓	✓	✓
18	Paradise Valley Conservation Area	793	13			✓	✓	✓	✓

SEATTLE

NB   Bicycles allowed only in Shoreview Park

Walk #	Trail/Park	Park Acreage	Miles of Trail	Connecting Trails	ADA Trail *	Dogs **	Bicycles **	Horses **	Restrooms
19	Boeing Creek and Shoreview Parks	79	4		✓	OL	NB		✓
20	Hamlin Park	80	3		✓	✓	✓		✓
21	Carkeek Park	216	6.1		✓	✓	✓		✓
22	Golden Gardens Park	88	3.2		✓	OL			✓
23	Discovery Park	534	11.8		✓	✓	✓		✓
24	Green Lake Park	324	2.8	✓	✓	✓	✓		✓
25	Burke-Gilman Trail	n/a	16.5	✓	✓	✓	✓		✓
26	Ravenna Park	50	4.5			✓	✓		✓
27	Warren G. Magnuson Park and NOAA Art Walk	320	3	✓	✓	OL	✓		✓
28	Union Bay Natural Area	74	1.5		✓	✓	✓		✓
29	Washington Park Arboretum	194	4.5		✓	✓	✓		✓
30	Interlaken Park	52	1	✓		✓	✓		
31	The Grand Forest (Bainbridge Island)	240	7	✓		✓	✓	✓	
32	Gazzam Lake Nature Preserve (Bainbridge Island)	445	6.3	✓		✓	✓	✓	
33	Fort Ward Park (Bainbridge Island)	137	3.3	✓	✓	✓	✓	✓	✓
34	Schmitz Preserve Park	53	1.7	✓		✓			
35	Camp Long	68	3.2			✓	✓		✓

Picnic Areas	Playground	Freshwater Beach ***	Saltwater Beach ***	Nature Preserve	Forest	Stream/River/Creek	Wetlands/Marsh	Meadow/Farmland	Mountain Views	Interpretive Trail	Best Birding	Salmon Run	Gardens	Sports Facilities	Art in the Parks	Campgrounds	Historical Site
✓	✓			✓			✓			✓	✓						
✓		✓		✓		✓	✓	✓	✓		✓	✓					
✓	✓	✓				✓	✓	✓		✓	✓						
					✓		✓		✓	✓				✓			
✓	✓	✓			✓	✓	✓	✓			✓			✓			
✓	✓				✓	✓								✓	✓		✓
✓	✓		✓		✓	✓	✓		✓		✓	✓	✓				
✓	✓		✓		✓		✓			✓	✓	✓					✓
✓	✓		✓		✓		✓	✓	✓	✓			✓				✓
✓	✓	✓					✓			✓				✓	✓		
✓		✓			✓				✓				✓				
✓	✓				✓	✓								✓	✓		
✓	✓	✓				✓	✓	✓		✓			✓	✓	✓		✓
✓				✓		✓	✓	✓	✓	✓			✓				
	✓						✓			✓	✓	✓					✓
					✓	✓		✓									✓
✓					✓	✓	✓				✓						
		✓	✓	✓			✓				✓						
✓		✓		✓					✓	✓	✓					✓	✓
				✓	✓	✓											
✓					✓	✓	✓							✓		✓	

Walk #	Trail/Park	Park Acreage	Miles of Trail	Connecting Trails	ADA Trail *	Dogs **	Bicycles **	Horses **	Restrooms
36	Lincoln Park	135	5.3		✓	✓	✓		✓
37	Westcrest Park	80	4.4	✓	✓	OL	✓		✓
38	Luther Burbank Park (Mercer Island)	77	3		✓	OL	✓		✓
39	Pioneer Park (Mercer Island)	113	5		✓	✓	✓	✓	
40	Seward Park	299	5.7	✓	✓	✓	✓		✓
41	Kubota Garden	34	1.5			✓			✓

EASTSIDE

NB   Bicyles allowed only in Wilburton Hill Park

Walk #	Trail/Park	Park Acreage	Miles of Trail	Connecting Trails	ADA Trail *	Dogs **	Bicycles **	Horses **	Restrooms
42	Sammamish River Trail	n/a	9.4	✓	✓	✓	✓	✓	✓
43	Gold Creek Park	35	2.8			✓		✓	✓
44	Saint Edward State Park	316	7.5	✓	✓	✓		✓	✓
45	Big Finn Hill Park	220	9.5	✓		✓	✓		✓
46	O. O. Denny Park	46	1	✓		✓			✓
47	Juanita Bay Park	110	1.3		✓	✓	✓		✓
48	Puget Power Trail	n/a	3	✓		✓	✓	✓	
49	Farrel-McWhirter Farm Park	68	2	✓	✓	✓	✓	✓	✓
50	Watershed Preserve (Redmond)	800	7.5	✓	✓		✓	✓	✓
51	Watershed Park (Kirkland)	73	2.8			✓	✓		
52	Bridle Trails State Park	482	28	✓		✓		✓	✓
53	Marymoor Park	640	5	✓	✓	OL	✓	✓	✓
54	Ardmore Park	30	1.5			✓			
55	Evans Creek Preserve	179	2.6			✓	✓		✓
56	Bellevue Botanical Garden and Wilburton Hill Park	158	3.5	✓	✓	NB	NB		✓
57	Kelsey Creek Park	150	2.5	✓		✓	✓	✓	✓
58	Lake Hills Greenbelt	150	3	✓	✓	✓	✓		✓
59	Mercer Slough Nature Park	320	6.5	✓	✓	✓	✓		✓

Picnic Areas	Playground	Freshwater Beach ***	Saltwater Beach ***	Nature Preserve	Forest	Stream/River/Creek	Wetlands/Marsh	Meadow/Farmland	Mountain Views	Interpretive Trail	Best Birding	Salmon Run	Gardens	Sports Facilities	Art in the Parks	Campgrounds	Historical Site
✓	✓		✓		✓				✓					✓			
✓	✓				✓				✓				✓		✓		
✓	✓	✓					✓	✓	✓					✓	✓		✓
					✓												
✓	✓	✓			✓				✓	✓	✓				✓		
✓						✓	✓		✓	✓				✓		✓	✓

Picnic Areas	Playground	Freshwater Beach ***	Saltwater Beach ***	Nature Preserve	Forest	Stream/River/Creek	Wetlands/Marsh	Meadow/Farmland	Mountain Views	Interpretive Trail	Best Birding	Salmon Run	Gardens	Sports Facilities	Art in the Parks	Campgrounds	Historical Site
✓					✓	✓	✓	✓						✓	✓		
✓					✓	✓											
✓		✓			✓	✓					✓		✓	✓			✓
✓	✓				✓	✓	✓			✓				✓			
✓		✓			✓	✓			✓								
✓							✓			✓	✓						
					✓	✓		✓	✓								
✓	✓				✓	✓		✓									
				✓	✓	✓	✓			✓							
					✓	✓		✓	✓	✓							
✓					✓					✓			✓				
✓	✓				✓	✓	✓	✓	✓	✓	✓		✓	✓		✓	
✓	✓				✓	✓	✓										
✓				✓	✓	✓	✓	✓	✓								
✓	✓				✓		✓	✓					✓	✓	✓		
✓	✓				✓	✓	✓	✓									✓
					✓	✓	✓	✓			✓		✓				
			✓		✓	✓			✓	✓							✓

Walk #	Trail/Park	Park Acreage	Miles of Trail	Connecting Trails	ADA Trail *	Dogs **	Bicycles **	Horses **	Restrooms
60	Robinswood Park	60	1	✓		OL	✓		✓
61	Weowna Park	80	2.5	✓		✓			
62	Soaring Eagle Regional Park	600	13	✓		✓	✓	✓	✓
63	Hazel Wolf Wetlands Preserve	116	1.5	✓			✓		
64	Beaver Lake Preserve	57	1.2	✓	✓	✓			✓
65	Beaver Lake Park	82	2		✓	OL			✓
66	Coal Creek Natural Area	450	6	✓		✓			
67	Lewis Creek Park	55	3	✓	✓	✓	✓		✓
68	Lakemont Community Park	124	3	✓	✓	✓			✓
69	Cougar Mountain Regional Wildland Park	3,000	50	✓		✓		✓	✓
70	Squak Mountain State Park	1,545	13	✓		✓		✓	✓
71	Lake Sammamish State Park	512	5.2	✓	✓	✓	✓		✓
72	Tiger Mountain	4,430	20	✓	✓	✓	✓	✓	✓

SOUTH KING COUNTY

NB Horses and bicycles allowed only on the Green-to-Cedar Rivers Trail in Lake Wilderness Arboretum; picnic areas, playgrounds, and beach are available at Lake Wilderness Park

Walk #	Trail/Park	Park Acreage	Miles of Trail	Connecting Trails	ADA Trail *	Dogs **	Bicycles **	Horses **	Restrooms
73	Seahurst Park	182	2		✓	✓			✓
74	Gene Coulon Memorial Beach Park	57	1.5		✓				✓
75	Cedar River Trail (Northwest Section)	n/a	8	✓	✓	OL	✓		✓
76	Duwamish–Green River Trail	n/a	13.5	✓	✓	✓	✓		✓
77	Des Moines Creek Trail	156	2		✓	✓	✓		
78	Green River Natural Resources Area	300	1.3	✓	✓				
79	Spring Lake and Lake Desire Park	390	4.5	✓		✓	✓	✓	
80	Cedar River Trail (Southeast Section)	n/a	6	✓	✓	✓	✓	✓	✓
81	Clark Lake Park	130	2			✓	✓		
82	Soos Creek Trail	775	7.5		✓	✓	✓	✓	✓

Picnic Areas	Playground	Freshwater Beach ***	Saltwater Beach ***	Nature Preserve	Forest	Stream/River/Creek	Wetlands/Marsh	Meadow/Farmland	Mountain Views	Interpretive Trail	Best Birding	Salmon Run	Gardens	Sports Facilities	Art in the Parks	Campgrounds	Historical Site
✓	✓				✓		✓				✓			✓			
✓					✓	✓				✓							
					✓		✓			✓							
				✓	✓	✓	✓			✓	✓						
✓					✓	✓	✓	✓		✓							
✓	✓	✓			✓	✓	✓	✓					✓	✓			
					✓	✓											✓
✓	✓				✓	✓	✓	✓		✓	✓			✓			
✓	✓				✓	✓				✓				✓			
					✓	✓			✓								✓
✓					✓	✓				✓	✓						
✓	✓	✓			✓	✓	✓	✓		✓	✓			✓			
✓					✓	✓	✓			✓	✓						
✓	✓		✓		✓				✓								
✓	✓	✓					✓			✓	✓			✓			
✓					✓	✓							✓		✓		
✓	✓					✓			✓				✓	✓	✓		
✓	✓		✓		✓	✓			✓		✓	✓					✓
✓				✓		✓	✓	✓		✓							
					✓		✓		✓								
✓					✓	✓					✓	✓					
					✓	✓	✓	✓	✓	✓		✓				✓	
✓	✓				✓	✓	✓			✓	✓						

Walk #	Trail/Park	Park Acreage	Miles of Trail	Connecting Trails	ADA Trail *	Dogs **	Bicycles **	Horses **	Restrooms
83	Lake Wilderness Arboretum	42	3	✓	✓	✓	NB	NB	✓
84	Saltwater State Park	88	2			✓	✓		✓
85	Game Farm and Game Farm Wilderness Parks	120	4	✓	✓	✓	✓		✓
86	White River Trail	n/a	2.2	✓	✓	✓	✓	✓	✓

TACOMA

Walk #	Trail/Park	Park Acreage	Miles of Trail	Connecting Trails	ADA Trail *	Dogs **	Bicycles **	Horses **	Restrooms
87	Burton Acres Park	68	1.1			✓	✓		✓
88	Sehmel Homestead Park	98	4.4	✓	✓	✓			✓
89	Point Defiance Park	700	11		✓	✓	✓		✓
90	Dash Point State Park	398	11			✓	✓		✓
91	West Hylebos Wetlands Park	120	1.7		✓				✓
92	Titlow Park	75	2.5		✓	✓	✓		✓
93	Wright Park	27	1.5		✓	✓	✓		✓
94	Tacoma Nature Center	71	2.5		✓				✓
95	Chambers Bay Loop	900	3.5	✓	✓	OL	✓		✓
96	Chambers Creek Canyon Trail	n/a	1.5			✓			✓
97	Fort Steilacoom Park	340	10		✓	OL	✓	✓	✓
98	Wapato Park	80	1.4		✓	OL	✓		✓
99	Swan Creek Park	290	2			✓	✓		✓
100	Clarks Creek Park	55	4.5	✓		OL	✓		✓
101	Foothills Trail	n/a	26	✓	✓	✓	✓	✓	✓
102	Spanaway Park and Bresemann Forest	300	8		✓	✓	✓		✓
103	Nathan Chapman Memorial Trail	n/a	1.6	✓	✓	✓	✓		✓

OLYMPIA

Walk #	Trail/Park	Park Acreage	Miles of Trail	Connecting Trails	ADA Trail *	Dogs **	Bicycles **	Horses **	Restrooms
104	Frye Cove Park	86	3		✓	✓			✓
105	Burfoot Park	60	3.8		✓	✓			✓

Picnic Areas	Playground	Freshwater Beach ***	Saltwater Beach ***	Nature Preserve	Forest	Stream/River/Creek	Wetlands/Marsh	Meadow/Farmland	Mountain Views	Interpretive Trail	Best Birding	Salmon Run	Gardens	Sports Facilities	Art in the Parks	Campgrounds	Historical Site
NB	NB	NB			✓					✓	✓		✓	✓			✓
✓	✓	✓			✓	✓						✓				✓	
✓	✓				✓	✓		✓				✓		✓	✓	✓	
✓	✓					✓					✓	✓			✓		
✓		✓			✓												
✓	✓				✓		✓	✓					✓	✓	✓		✓
✓	✓		✓		✓			✓		✓	✓	✓	✓		✓		✓
✓	✓		✓		✓	✓		✓	✓	✓						✓	
✓				✓	✓	✓	✓			✓	✓						
✓	✓		✓		✓	✓	✓		✓	✓	✓			✓			
✓	✓						✓						✓	✓	✓		
✓	✓		✓	✓	✓		✓			✓	✓						
✓	✓		✓		✓			✓	✓								
					✓	✓						✓					
✓	✓						✓	✓		✓			✓				✓
✓	✓				✓		✓			✓		✓	✓		✓		
✓		✓			✓	✓						✓					
✓	✓				✓	✓	✓			✓		✓		✓			
✓						✓	✓	✓		✓	✓						✓
✓	✓	✓			✓	✓	✓			✓			✓				
✓	✓				✓		✓										
✓	✓		✓		✓				✓								
✓	✓		✓		✓	✓	✓		✓								

Walk #	Trail/Park	Park Acreage	Miles of Trail	Connecting Trails	ADA Trail *	Dogs **	Bicycles **	Horses **	Restrooms
106	Woodard Bay Natural Resources Conservation Area	870	3	✓	✓				✓
107	Chehalis Western Trail	n/a	21.5	✓	✓	✓	✓	✓	✓
108	Tolmie State Park	105	4.3		✓	✓	✓		✓
109	Nisqually National Wildlife Refuge	3,000	4		✓				✓
110	Sequalitchew Creek	38	1.5			✓	✓		✓
111	Priest Point Park	341	6			✓			✓
112	McLane Creek Nature Trail	150	2.7		✓				✓
113	Watershed Park (Olympia)	153	2.8	✓		✓			✓
114	Olympia Woodland Trail	n/a	2.5	✓	✓	✓	✓	✓	✓
115	Tumwater Historical Park and Capitol Lake Interpretive Trail	35	1.5	✓	✓	✓	✓		✓
116	Tumwater Falls Park	15	1	✓		✓			✓
117	Pioneer Park (Tumwater)	85	1.5		✓	✓	✓		✓
118	Mima Mounds Natural Area Preserve	625	3		✓				✓
119	Millersylvania State Park	843	8.6		✓	✓	✓		✓
120	Yelm to Tenino Trail	n/a	14	✓	✓	✓	✓	✓	✓

Picnic Areas	Playground	Freshwater Beach ***	Saltwater Beach ***	Nature Preserve	Forest	Stream/River/Creek	Wetlands/Marsh	Meadow/Farmland	Mountain Views	Interpretive Trail	Best Birding	Salmon Run	Gardens	Sports Facilities	Art in the Parks	Campgrounds	Historical Site
✓				✓	✓		✓			✓	✓	✓					
✓					✓		✓	✓			✓						
✓			✓		✓		✓		✓		✓						
				✓	✓	✓	✓		✓	✓	✓	✓					
			✓		✓	✓	✓		✓	✓							✓
✓	✓		✓		✓	✓			✓	✓	✓						
✓				✓	✓	✓	✓			✓	✓	✓					
					✓	✓	✓					✓					
✓					✓	✓											
✓	✓					✓	✓		✓	✓		✓					✓
✓	✓					✓				✓			✓	✓			✓
✓	✓					✓		✓	✓						✓		
✓			✓						✓	✓	✓	✓					✓
✓	✓	✓			✓	✓	✓				✓					✓	
✓					✓	✓		✓	✓	✓	✓						✓

INTRODUCTION

Walking has always been my favorite way to exercise. Being out-
doors, even on cloudy Northwest days, refreshes my soul, clears my
mind, and lets me feel truly alive. When my family was younger, taking a walk often meant going to the mountains for long day hikes or
squeezing in a short stroll in a park between family errands. Now that
my time is freer, I love to walk for health and exercise, and as a way
to catch up with friends or family. But I don't want just any walk—I
want cathedral-like forests, open meadows, tranquil ponds, mountain
and water views, birds and other wildlife. And I have found—nestled
in the seemingly endless urban bustle from Everett to Seattle and
Olympia, and east to Issaquah and Bellevue—more than a hundred
small sanctuaries of nature just a few minutes from home. What
glorious freedom, if only for an hour or two, to step from the car and
immerse oneself in the gentle pace of foot travel.

How These Walks Were Chosen

These 120 walks lie along the shores of Puget Sound and the lowland
forests and meadows beneath the Cascade Foothills. They are accessible year-round and mostly child- and dog-friendly, and the majority
are easy, short walks just minutes from your home or workplace, be it
in Olympia, Seattle, Everett, Issaquah, or any of the cities in between.

Increased traffic congestion over the past 20 years has challenged
our goal of offering walk choices within 30 minutes' drive of the urban

centers, but many new greenbelt trails and parks have been created, resulting in an ever-increasing number of trail options.

My criteria for a good walking trail are that it be at least a mile in length, be surrounded by greenery or close to water, and allow no motorized vehicles. Most trails in this book meet that one-mile minimum, and others are part of a larger system of trails within a park where you are limited only by your energy and time. A few small parks, such as Tumwater Falls, Hazel Wolf Wetlands Preserve, and Seattle's Schmitz Preserve may fall a bit short on trail length but equal others in beauty. All walks are on public land, with the exception of Tumwater Falls and Narbeck Wetlands Sanctuary, which are open to the public daily. All the trails in this book are free for walking, although those on state and Department of Natural Resources (DNR) land require vehicles to have a Discover Pass.

Most important is that every walk travels through natural places— everything from lakeshores and saltwater beaches to meadows and forests.

Keeping Updated

Since the third edition of this book, maintenance crews and trail volunteers have paved old trails and created new ones. Landslides and floods have closed or diverted others. More railroad right-of-ways have been and are being acquired and converted to trails, and new nature preserves now add green spaces to the local maps. I've tried to stay up to date with changes and improvements, but nature and politics rule. Because of this constant growth and change, things may not be as I have portrayed them by the time you take some of these walks. You should always visit park websites and stay informed about any closures before making the trek. With luck, the changes will be for the better. How lucky we are to live in a place where the number of parks, trails, and walks has increased over the years!

What about Regional and Sidewalk Trails?

The Puget Sound region is crisscrossed with many long regional trails, which are usually converted from abandoned railway lines and are extremely popular with bicyclers. Some of these regional trails have always been included in this book: the very popular Burke-Gilman and its extension, the Sammamish River Trail, for example. Others, such as the Centennial Trail and the Chehalis Western Trail, made the cut because, though they are long, they include many short stretches that appeal to walkers.

To keep this book true to its goal of nearby walks, we've eliminated regional trails that are too far afield, such as the Snoqualmie Valley and Preston-Snoqualmie Trails, and others that are just not natural enough, such as the East Lake Sammamish and Interurban Trails.

Popular urban walks such as Everett's North View and South View Parks; Seattle's Alki Beach Trail, Lake Washington Boulevard, and Myrtle Edwards Park; Tacoma's Wright Park and Ruston Way; and Olympia's Capitol Lake don't meet our definition of walks in natural places. But they are wonderful places to walk: some of them right alongside the Sound with the scent of sea air, the call of gulls, and views out over the water. An Internet search will direct you to the nearest trailhead or park address.

Thoughts on Safety

Not every trail is as safe as a suburban sidewalk. Despite maintenance efforts, mudslides obliterate paths, rain erodes them, and fallen trees block them. Walking in natural places can be risky. Wear appropriate footgear and try to walk with someone else, especially in the more remote parks. Be aware that wildlife, such as coyotes and bears, are occasionally seen on some of the trails that connect by greenbelts to the foothills. For their safety, keep dogs on leashes. Take common sense, a cell phone, and anything else you need. You're on your own.

Trails and Parks Belong to Everyone

I've had people beg me, on hearing that I was writing this book, not to reveal "their" special trail or park. One hiker told me, "We don't want a lot of folks overrunning the trails, picking the flowers, and not picking up after their dogs." No one wants that, whether they come from nearby or afar. But the more users a park has and the better it's known, the more likely that it will be protected and cared for.

My experience is that most people who share the trails respect the natural areas and understand the need for preservation and care. When parents feel that way, they encourage the same feelings in their children. There is no "my park" or "your park." These are all our parks.

Whether parks are signposted or not, the same minimal courtesies are asked of all visitors:

1. Stay on the trail. As one sign in a Bellevue park says, "Plants grow by the inch, and die by the foot."
2. Keep pets on a leash unless in a designated off-leash area. Always clean up after your dog.
3. Keep children and pets out of salmon-spawning creeks.
4. Don't feed the waterfowl, squirrels, or other wildlife.
5. Don't pick the flowers or forage for mushrooms.
6. Take only memories and pictures. Leave only footprints.

With everyone's cooperation, we can preserve our trails for ourselves and as a heritage for generations to come.

Consider Volunteering

Every weekend, year-round, hundreds of volunteers work on the trails and parks we love. They clear fallen branches, repair drainage, restore the natural habitat, and build new trails. Others volunteer as docents or citizen patrols to inform and aid other walkers. Without volunteers, our region's parks, wetlands, shorelines, and trails would not be what they are today.

Why volunteer? It's healthy, fun, and outdoorsy. It's companionable and educational, and it builds teamwork. It's great for the economy and helps the environment!

Learning about park and trail volunteer opportunities is as easy as clicking on your city or county website, or asking at your favorite park office. Even the State of Washington needs volunteers for its parks and public lands. Private organizations include the very active Washington Trails Association and Issaquah Alps Trails Club. There is so much that needs doing!

A GUIDE TO THIS BOOK

These 120 walks are arranged roughly from north to south, grouped in chapters according to six urban hubs: Everett, Seattle (including Mercer Island and Bainbridge Island), the Eastside (including Bellevue, Redmond, and Issaquah), South King County (including Des Moines, Renton, and Kent), Tacoma (including southern Vashon Island), and Olympia.

Each chapter begins with a locator map and a list of walks so you can easily choose where to go.

Each walk begins with a brief location description that places the walk very generally in reference to an urban center. Distances given are in driving miles (not as the crow flies) from an approximation of the city's downtown area.

Then follows a brief description line that includes the size of the park or trail area, the setting, and special attractions of the walk.

The address provided is the street location of the park or trailhead, not a mailing address. You may be able to use this address for an Internet map search. If a park doesn't have a specific street address, we have stated that the one provided is approximate.

A summary of the walk follows, with these headings:

TRAIL	Approximate length in miles; type of surface (boardwalk, gravel, natural surface, or paved).
STEEPNESS	Level (flat or nearly so), gentle (easy ups and downs), moderate (gets the heart rate up), or steep (stairs or equivalent steepness).
OTHER USES	Who shares the trail with you, the pedestrian. This might be bicycles or horses. Although not explicitly noted, expect to share paved trails with skaters. None of these walks allow motorized vehicles (with the exception of park maintenance vehicles).
DOGS	Three possibilities—on leash, not allowed, or off leash. (Designated off-leash areas may or may not include the trail.) Dog-friendly areas may be restricted.
CONNECTING TRAILS	Other trails (both included in this guide and not) that intersect the walk.
PARK AMENITIES	Restrooms (including freestanding facilities), interpretive walks, picnic tables, playgrounds, playing fields, et cetera. (Refer to maps and driving directions for parking information.)
DISABLED ACCESS	Americans with Disabilities Act (ADA) access, for the trail and/or park. (Call the listed office for details; their definition of "accessible" and yours may differ.) Some trails are barrier-free but don't meet ADA requirements.

A walk may have more than one setting, characterized by the following icons:

FOREST . . . .

RIVER/STREAM . . . . . .

LAKE/WETLAND. . . . . .

MEADOW/FARMLAND.

NATURE PRESERVE . . .

PUGET SOUND . . . .

MOUNTAIN VIEWS. . . .

WALK DESCRIPTIONS: May include ecological, historical, and scenic information. They are not intended to be step-by-step trail guides; the goal is to entice and invite you to discover the pleasure of the walk on your own.

GETTING THERE: Driving directions in this book are basic and brief, and start from either the closest downtown or major freeway; they will be of little help if you take a wrong turn. There may be public transport available to the trailhead or park. Most parks and trails are open daylight hours only, but some urban parks stay open later. Check park websites for seasonal hours.

CONTACT: Contact numbers may be for the individual park's office or a central parks department office. If there is an opportunity to volunteer at this park, it may be noted here.

MAPS: The map shown for each walk is intended to give a general sense of the layout of the park and trail. Do not rely on these to locate yourself in complex parks such as Cougar Mountain, Lord Hill, Paradise Valley, Soaring Eagle, and others with extensive trail systems. We have tried to show the major trails within each park, but there may be secondary paths that are not shown. Please follow guidelines and signs when walking as there may be problems with erosion and other hazards.

Map orientation is with north up, and the scale is approximate. The difference between paved, gravel, and natural surface trails is not indicated due to constantly changing conditions.

Map Legend

Symbol	Label	Symbol	Label
═══	ROAD	╴ ╴	TRAIL
▬▬	DOCK/BOAT LAUNCH	Ⓟ	PARKING
ℝ	RESTROOM	⊼	PICNIC AREA
⋀	CAMPSITES	╫╫╫	RAILWAY
▬▪▬	PARK BOUNDARY	⊟	BRIDGE
🌲	FOREST	⩉	WETLAND/MARSH
⬮	WATER (RIVER, LAKE, SOUND)		

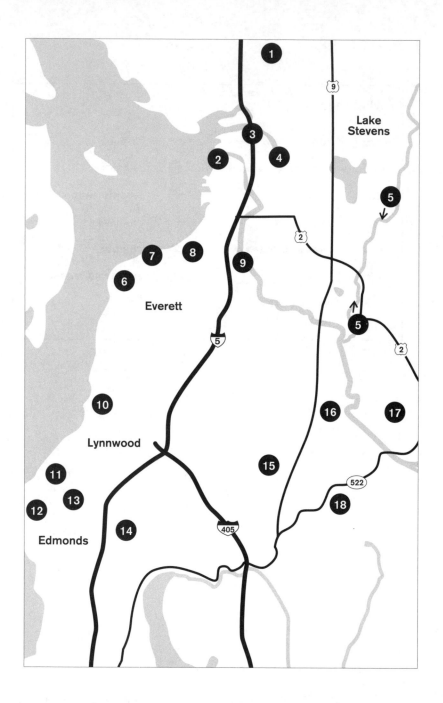

EVERETT

1 JENNINGS MEMORIAL AND NATURE PARKS

Marysville, 7.5 miles north of Everett

Explore 61 acres of meadow, forest, and wetland in these twin parks.

TRAIL	1.5 miles; paved, natural surface
STEEPNESS	Level to gentle
OTHER USES	Bicycles
DOGS	On leash
CONNECTING TRAILS	None
PARK AMENITIES	Picnic area, restrooms, playground, demonstration garden, interpretive signs, fishing pond, ball fields, historical displays and museum
DISABLED ACCESS	Restrooms, garden

Stroll the undulating hills of these two parks from passive forest and meadows to an active park with ball fields, a children's fishing pond, playgrounds, and a Master Gardener demonstration garden. In the wetlands, cattails make homes for marsh wrens and red-winged blackbirds. Raptors overhead reveal the presence of the tiny, secretive voles and mice that seek shelter in the grasses.

These twin parks are so closely aligned it's hard to know when you walk from one to the other. The Armar Road entrance is for the Memorial Park, and here you'll find the city parks office, where you can stop in for more information. History buffs will be intrigued by the 1901 steam donkey engine on display and enjoy a visit to the Marysville Historical Society museum.

A half-mile paved path leads from one park to the other and around the fishing pond. After that the trails are natural surface through the western red cedars and into the meadows and the wetland. Boardwalks and bridges allow you to navigate over the sensitive wetlands and next to softly flowing Allen Creek, which bisects the parks.

The themed demonstration garden invites you to experience an English cottage garden and a meditation garden. You can learn techniques for growing your own flowers, fruit trees, vegetables, and herbs. In summer the park rings with the sounds of children, and you'll find classes, movies, and fishing derbies, but the wetlands and sensitive natural areas will still beckon dedicated walkers.

ADDRESS: 6915 Armar Road, Marysville

GETTING THERE: From I-5 southbound, take exit 199 (WA 528). Drive east on WA 528 for 0.7 miles. Turn left on 47th Avenue NE. Continue 0.5 miles, bearing right at the fork onto Arlington-Marysville Road/Armar Road. The park entrance is on the right.

CONTACT: Marysville Parks and Recreation Department, (360) 363-8400, www.marysvillewa.gov

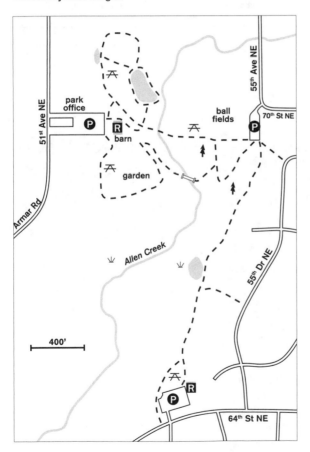

2 JETTY ISLAND

1.5 miles northwest of downtown Everett

Walk and bird-watch in these 200 acres of salt marshes, beaches, and sand dunes along Port Gardner Bay.

TRAIL	2 to 4 miles, depending on tide; natural surface
STEEPNESS	Level
OTHER USES	Pedestrians only
DOGS	Not allowed
CONNECTING TRAILS	None
PARK AMENITIES	Open summer only; free ferry mid-July to Labor Day; restrooms, boating, picnic tables, classes, guided interpretive walks
DISABLED ACCESS	None

Built almost a hundred years ago at the mouth of the Snohomish River to create a freshwater harbor in Puget Sound, this man-made island has succeeded in ways its creators probably never imagined. A southerly breeze cools the western shore, carrying the scent of seaweed and the barks of California sea lions. Sandpipers sprint on the mudflats; ospreys soar above. Around the Scotch broom, swallows dart and dive for their insect meals. Near the shore, crabs scurry for shelter under rocks. In the salt marsh, salt crystals glisten on the stems of the pickleweed.

Measuring 2 miles long and 0.5 miles wide, this wildlife preserve just 3 minutes from the Everett marina is the city's summer pride. For 7 or 8 weeks each summer, Wednesday through Sunday, the eighty-passenger ferry run by the Mosquito Fleet fills to capacity to take families, walkers, and bird lovers across the Snohomish River channel to the dock on Jetty Island. From there they disperse, though the majority cluster around the picnic tables on the western shore. To find solitude, walk either north or south for 3 or 4 minutes. You'll think you're on a deserted island—just you and the terns, herons, swallows, and shimmering, slippery, pungent sea lettuce that lines the beach.

At low tide you can circumnavigate the island on the mudflats, though you have to be willing to get your feet squishy with mud. On the western side, a berm built by the Army Corps of Engineers has created a new salt marsh. Here you are likely to see many of the more than forty species of birds that visit or nest on the island. In early summer, expect to be dive-bombed by protective mother gulls warning you away from their nests.

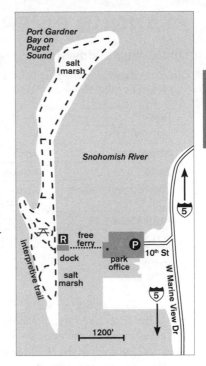

ADDRESS: 10th Street Boat Launch, Everett

GETTING THERE: From downtown Everett, follow Everett Avenue west to W Marine View Drive. Turn right (north) and go 1.75 miles. Turn left (west) at 10th Street into 10th Street Boat Launch and Marine Park.

What Is That?

Find out by joining a naturalist-led walk. Most are free. Call your city or county parks department for information. Parks also offer classes in outdoor-related topics such as gardening, birding, geology, animal care, naturalist studies, and science. Fees may vary.

Parking fee is $3 on Friday and weekends. Ferry reservations can be made by Everett residents or groups of over eight people 48 hours in advance. Call (425) 257-8304. Other visitors can ride the ferry on a first-come, first-served basis.

CONTACT: Everett Parks and Recreation Department, (425) 257-8300, www.everettwa.org/parks

<u>3</u> LANGUS RIVERFRONT PARK

6 miles east of downtown Everett

Cascade views and bird-watching abound along these 96 acres of the Snohomish River and Union Slough.

TRAIL	3.6-mile loop; gravel, paved
STEEPNESS	Level
OTHER USES	Bicycles
DOGS	On leash
CONNECTING TRAILS	Spencer Island (Walk #4; no bicycles or pets allowed)
PARK AMENITIES	Restrooms, picnic tables
DISABLED ACCESS	Trail, restrooms, picnic area

Old barges docked forever against the bank of the smooth-flowing Snohomish River recall days gone by when rivers and lakes, not roads, united the Northwest. Well-tended lawns and a paved walkway seem so genteel compared to the stalwart pilings of old docks. Great blue herons and belted kingfishers feed from the river—one on foot, the other on wing—and migrating waterfowl rest in the reeds along the shore.

Enjoy Langus Riverfront Park with a civilized promenade along the riverfront, a hefty mile out and back, from the northern end—or with a 3-mile triangular loop walk along the Snohomish River and Union Slough. For the longer loop, continue south after the pavement ends, passing under the imposing I-5 freeway bridge. The first stretch follows the river, where fishing boats, tugs, tourist boats, and an occasional log boom float by. At the southernmost spot, Picnic Point, views open to grasslands, the Cascades, and on clear days, Mount Rainier.

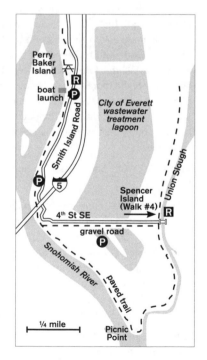

From Picnic Point the trail heads north along Union Slough, where a variety of deciduous trees line the pathway on a dike above the tidal trough. Across the water (if it's high tide) or mud (if it's low tide) lie the marshes, ponds, and dikes of Spencer Island, a nature preserve (Walk #4). Jackknife Bridge ahead spans Union Slough, serving as an entrance to the preserve. From the bridge, you can retrace your route to stay on the paved trail, or complete the loop by walking west on the gravel maintenance road (4th Street SE) back to the river. Along the road you walk between waste treatment ponds, where waterfowl abound. With binoculars you can see a palette of colors: the distinct black-and-white plumage of the hooded merganser, the orange bill of the scoter, or the blue bill of the male ruddy duck in late spring.

ADDRESS: 400 Smith Island Road, Everett

GETTING THERE: From I-5 southbound, take exit 198 (WA 529 S/WA 99). Go south on WA 529 and turn right onto 34th Avenue NE/Frontage Road. Follow the road left under WA 99, then stay right for Smith Island Road, which leads to Langus Riverfront Park.

From I-5 northbound, take exit 195 (E Marine View Drive). Continue on E Marine View Drive. Turn right on WA 529/WA 99 N. After crossing the Snohomish River, turn right on Smith Island Road and follow it to the park.

CONTACT: Everett Parks and Recreation Department, (425) 257-8300, www.everettwa.org/parks

4 SPENCER ISLAND

6.5 miles east of downtown Everett

Union and Steamboat Sloughs surround these 415 acres of bird-watchers' wetland paradise.

TRAIL	4 miles; natural surface
STEEPNESS	Level
OTHER USES	Pedestrians only; hunters from mid-October to mid-January on the north end; no pets
DOGS	Not allowed
CONNECTING TRAILS	Langus Riverfront Park (Walk #3)
PARK AMENITIES	Restrooms, interpretive signs, bike rack near footbridge
DISABLED ACCESS	None

Spencer Island is a birder's paradise and a frequent destination for National Audubon Society field trips. On bright days the ruddy ducks and American wigeons appear to be floating on top of their upside-down twins as they paddle across the mirrorlike surface of the pond. Northern harriers and red-tailed hawks hunt overhead. In the still waters by the marsh grasses, you might see river

otters flipping and diving for fish. Nesting boxes for wood ducks and swallows dot numerous islets in the marsh, and on the southern loop bat boxes make welcome homes for these flying mammals.

But even without binoculars and a passion for birds, the miles of trail along dikes above the estuary are inviting for their hours of strolling and gazing at the scenery. After entering the preserve over Jackknife Bridge, turn either north or south on the wide wood chip–lined paths. On clear days, Mount Pilchuck dominates the skyline to the east, and to the north, Mount Baker may stand, white and craggy.

Early settlers created dikes and sloughs to remove the tidal influx of salt water and to protect their farmlands. When Washington State, Snohomish County, and the City of Everett joined forces in the early 1990s to return this area to its natural state, they breached the dike wall with culverts and bridges. Now the wetland is an estuary again, responding to the ebb and flow of the tides from Puget Sound. This combination of salt water and freshwater from the Snohomish River provides a habitat for hundreds of species of birds and mammals.

From mid-October to mid-January the northern trails (administered by the state Department of Fish and Wildlife and signposted) are open to hunting, so most walkers go south during those months. Interpretive signs provide information on the area's history and its natural history. Benches and viewing platforms add a human touch to this otherwise wild and beautiful estuary.

ADDRESS: 4th Street SE, Everett (east end)

GETTING THERE: From I-5 southbound, take exit 198 (WA 529 S/WA 99). Go south on WA 529, and turn right onto 34th Avenue NE/Frontage Road. Follow the road left under WA 99, then stay right for Smith Island Road. Turn left on 4th Street SE (gravel road). Parking is on the right in a few hundred yards. Walk east on 4th Street SE to Jackknife Bridge, which leads to Spencer Island.

From I-5 northbound, take exit 195 (E Marine View Drive). Continue on E Marine View Drive. Turn right on WA 529/WA 99 N. After crossing the Snohomish River, turn right on Smith Island Road and proceed as above.

CONTACT: Snohomish County Parks and Recreation Department, (425) 388-6600, www.snohomishcountywa.gov/parks

5 CENTENNIAL TRAIL

8 miles southeast of Everett (Snohomish Trailhead) or 8 miles east of Everett (Machias Trailhead)

Walk portions of this 30-mile trail along the Pilchuck River for Cascade views in pastoral Snohomish Valley.

TRAIL	30 miles one way; paved rails-to-trails conversion
STEEPNESS	Level
OTHER USES	Bicycles; horses on separate equestrian trail
DOGS	On leash
CONNECTING TRAILS	None
PARK AMENITIES	Restrooms, picnic tables
DISABLED ACCESS	Trail access, restrooms at Pilchuck and Machias Trailheads

Just minutes east of the I-5 corridor lies the fertile Snohomish Valley with its pastures, dairy farms, and picturesque barns. You've probably driven through it countless times en route to the Cascades or Eastern Washington. Now, the Centennial Trail lets you slow the pace and walk this valley, breathing the clear, fresh air (and, yes, sometimes the aroma of cows). Views are expansive, from the dairy-farm pastures to the peaks of the Cascades.

Like other paved converted railroad grades, this trail is great for distance walking, stroller pushing, or bicycling. There are twelve trailheads, so you can choose to walk either north or south.

From historic downtown Snohomish, the trail parallels Maple Avenue and the Pilchuck River. Soon, vistas

open to embrace the pastures and farms. In the 1880s settlers cleared trees and drained the swampy land to leave rich, fertile soil. Now, as then, it is prime dairy land. Cows and horses graze in the lush fields.

In the small town of Machias, a replica of the old railroad station now serves as a rest area and rental facility. Near the trail's midpoint, on the outskirts of Lake Stevens, you'll cross several country roads and driveways, so be sure to keep kids in close check. The trail continues to ever more rural areas as it approaches Arlington.

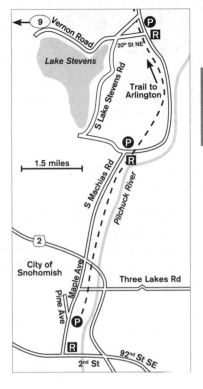

ADDRESS: *Snohomish Trailhead:* 402 2nd Street, Snohomish; *Pilchuck Trailhead:* 5801 S Machias Road, Snohomish; *Machias Trailhead:* 1624 Virginia Street, Machias; *Lake Stevens/20th Street NE Trailhead:* 13205 20th Street NE, Lake Stevens. For details about eight other trailheads to the north, visit www .centennialtrail.com.

GETTING THERE: *Snohomish Trailhead:* From I-5 take exit 194 onto US 2. Head east on US 2 for about 8 miles. In Snohomish, exit US 2 at 88th Street SE. At the first light turn right onto Pine Avenue and follow Pine to the intersection with Maple Avenue for limited parking.

Pilchuck Trailhead: Proceed as above, continuing on Maple Avenue through Snohomish. Maple becomes S Machias Road. The trailhead is in about 2 miles on the right.

Machias Trailhead: Proceed as above, to the stop sign past the Pilchuck Trailhead. Turn right and follow S Machias Road to the old fire station. Turn left onto Division Street and go 2 blocks to the trailhead on the right.

Lake Stevens/20th Street NE Trailhead: From I-5 take exit 194 onto US 2. Head east on US 2 and exit left onto WA 204. Go north 2.7 miles, following signs to Lake Stevens. Turn left onto WA 9. Go 1.7 miles, then turn right onto WA 92 (Granite Falls Highway). After 2.8 miles turn right onto N Machias Road. The trailhead is in 1 mile on the right with parking for a hundred cars.

CONTACT: Snohomish County Parks and Recreation Department, (425) 388-6600, www.snohomishcountywa.gov/parks

<u>6</u> NARBECK WETLAND SANCTUARY

7 miles southwest of downtown Everett

Walk a wetland trail and see wildlife flourish in this 50-acre man-made sanctuary.

TRAIL	1.3 miles; natural surface, boardwalk, paved
STEEPNESS	Level
OTHER USES	Pedestrians only
DOGS	On leash
CONNECTING TRAILS	None
PARK AMENITIES	Restroom, picnic tables, interpretive trail
DISABLED ACCESS	Restrooms, paved trail; some sections of gravel trail

Spring and summer are the prime times to visit a Northwest wetland, when the new green shoots are coming up, goslings and ducklings abound, and the blackbirds return to sing in the cattails. But year-round, a small wetland such as Narbeck offers level walking, a glimpse of life in a beaver pond, and the poetic shape of deciduous branches against a blue sky.

Narbeck is the story of success in wetland mitigation banking, a process whereby a new wetland is created in advance of destroying another. When Boeing needed to expand its facilities, it worked with federal and state governments to create a large man-made wetland that serves to control flooding and provide habitat for wildlife, and is specifically created to offset any future wetland destruction in the area.

Over a 7-year timeline, the land was transformed. Earth berms were constructed to retain water in the ponds created by Narbeck Creek, and hundreds of native plants were restored to the area. Today, Narbeck is a sanctuary for many animals, including ring-necked ducks, mallards, rabbits, raptors, crows, and songbirds. An interpretive trail invites strolling and reading, or you can sit in the cave-like wildlife blind and watch for beaver and bird action on the pond.

ADDRESS: 7007 Seaway Boulevard, Everett

GETTING THERE: I-5 northbound, take exit 189 (WA 527). Immediately follow signs to WA 526/Mukilteo. Go west on WA 526 for 2.9 miles, then turn right on Seaway Boulevard. Stay in the middle lane to avoid being swept into Boeing. After the light at 75th Street SW, go 0.25 miles to the park entrance on the right.

CONTACT: Snohomish County Parks and Recreation Department, (425) 388-6600, www.snohomishcountywa.gov/parks. To volunteer, contact Friends of Narbeck Wetland Sanctuary at 425-388-5108 or visit www.narbeck.org.

7 HOWARTH PARK

2 miles southwest of downtown Everett

This 28-acre tri-level park offers views, play areas, and a forested ravine leading to beaches and an off-leash area on Possession Sound.

TRAIL	1 mile round trip; boardwalk, natural surface
STEEPNESS	Level to steep
OTHER USES	Pedestrians only
DOGS	On leash on trails; designated off-leash area on beach
CONNECTING TRAILS	None
PARK AMENITIES	Restrooms, bridge over railroad tracks, picnic and barbecue area, playground, tennis courts
DISABLED ACCESS	Restrooms

Beachcomb, swim, or cavort with your dog—free of its leash!—while harbor seals frolic in the waters of Possession Sound and drift logs entice children to clamber. Howarth Park offers one of the few beach-access trails in the city of Everett. Nestled almost secretly behind suburban lawns and homes, this community park welcomes forest walkers, beach explorers, or just casual strollers.

Near the tennis courts at the western end of the park you'll find restrooms, picnic areas, and a playground. Dropping steeply from the lawn to the ravine below, a staircase trail ends at a boardwalk, which meanders above a stream. Following this trail does not lead to the beach, however, but to a T-junction with a narrow, steep trail bordering the railroad tracks. In dry weather, you can ascend the natural-surface path back to the playground and parking or return along the ravine walk. Unauthorized trails lead onto the railroad tracks, but crossing is illegal and, given the frequent passage of trains, extremely dangerous.

To reach the beach safely, either walk or drive to the eastern end of the park. From the eastern parking area you'll find a trail that follows Pigeon Creek in a young scrub forest, and another that traverses a small wetland, then climbs to a pedestrian overpass above the railroad tracks. This is a favorite place to stand when the train whistle shrills and the locomotive and cars rumble beneath you. At the beach end is a lookout tower with panoramic views of Port Gardner Bay and the navy ships. Just north of the tower is the off-leash area, where dogs are free to romp in the sand and salt water or play tag with their human companions among the drift logs and boulders. A short walk south takes you to the public beach.

ADDRESS: 1127 Olympic Boulevard, Everett

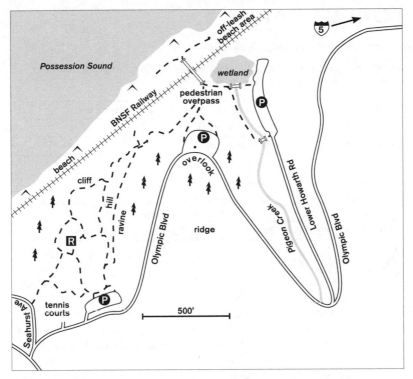

GETTING THERE: From I-5, take exit 192 (41st Street/Broadway/Naval Station). Turn right (if southbound) or left (if northbound) on 41st Street and continue through two traffic lights. The road turns up a hillside and becomes Mukilteo Boulevard. Go west on Mukilteo Boulevard past the traffic light at Dogwood Drive and around the first curve of the road after the intersection. Just after the intersection with Seahurst Avenue, enter the park by turning right on Olympic Boulevard.

CONTACT: Everett Parks and Recreation Department, (425) 257-8300, www.everettwa.org/parks

<u>8</u> FOREST PARK

1 mile south of downtown Everett

Leave the playgrounds and petting farm behind, and explore the quiet forest in this 190-acre city park.

TRAIL	1.5 miles; natural surface, paved utility road
STEEPNESS	Moderate to steep
OTHER USES	Pedestrians only
DOGS	On leash
CONNECTING TRAILS	None
PARK AMENITIES	Restrooms, animal farm, picnic shelters, playground, pool, sports fields, water playground
DISABLED ACCESS	Restrooms, animal farm, picnic shelters, pool

When you've hauled the kids off the massive playground (which is fully fenced to keep them from wandering into the steep forest), look for the wooden gate and trailhead between Cedar Hall and the picnic shelter. Here, in the largest of Everett's city parks, forest tranquility beckons. Wide, wood-chipped paths lined with logs welcome you into the big-leaf maple and cedar forest on the ridge above a deep ravine. Look for old snags decorated with fungus and old-growth stumps with springboard notches still visible, like eyes peering out from the sometimes-charred wood. You can stroll the ridge awhile, then rest on a bench overlooking the fern-filled ravine and out to the sunny baseball diamond beyond. Though the forest looks wild, an occasional rhododendron bush and a proliferation of English ivy tell of a more cultivated past when the park housed a full-fledged zoo.

For a gentle stroll, follow the contoured trails that wind through open forest to the old utility road to the west. If you want heart-pumping exercise, head east on the staircase trails that lead down to the east entrance road and back up again. Next to a lawn, the road, lined with rock walls—and, in summer, the bright colors of foxglove in bloom—makes its way toward Mukilteo Boulevard. You can climb back to the main park grounds through the forest or on the ridges on either side of the ravine. If you choose the ridge west of the utility road, you'll find the fern- and cedar-filled forest. Just below the playground fence are open cedar groves, perfect for warm-weather picnics. Be sure to pack out all that you pack in, as there are no trash receptacles on the trails.

Another forest walk begins at the end of Pigeon Creek Road (just across Mukilteo Boulevard from the west entrance). Drive about 0.5 miles north to the parking lot by the railroad tracks. There is no beach access, and crossing the

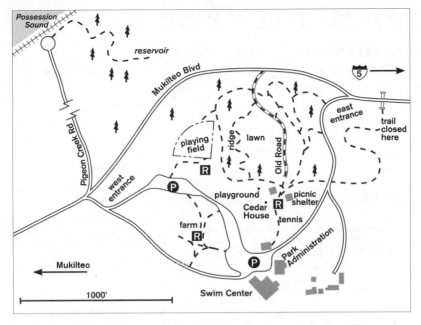

tracks is prohibited. The wooded trail that begins here climbs the hill toward a reservoir in about 0.5 miles. Eagles nest high in the branches of the 80-year-old fir trees.

For those with kids, don't miss the animal farm and a chance to pet, and maybe feed, the resident rabbits, ducks, pigs, goats, ponies, and llamas. The farm is open late spring through September.

ADDRESS: 802 Mukilteo Boulevard, Everett

GETTING THERE: From I-5, take exit 192 (Broadway/41st Street). Follow signs for 41st Street W. After crossing WA 99 (Evergreen Way), follow 41st Street uphill as it becomes Mukilteo E Boulevard. The park is on the left in about 1 mile.

CONTACT: Everett Parks and Recreation Department, (425) 257-8300, www.everettwa.org/parks

9 LOWELL RIVERFRONT TRAIL

2.5 miles southeast of downtown Everett

Walk a 3-mile loop along the Snohomish River, where wetlands and meadows give views of birds and the Cascades.

TRAIL	3-mile loop; paved
STEEPNESS	Level
OTHER USES	Bicycles
DOGS	On leash; short connecting walk to Lowell Park off-leash area
CONNECTING TRAILS	Lowell Park off-leash area on S 3rd Avenue, west of railway line (use overpass)
PARK AMENITIES	Restrooms, picnic tables, viewpoint
DISABLED ACCESS	Trail, restrooms

This strip of manicured trail on the banks of the Snohomish River offers intimate river-edge walking and dramatic views of the Cascades. A late-afternoon visit reveals the Cascades set in bright relief to the east and a sheen of slate blue and mauve on the glassy Snohomish River. In contrast to the manicured park, the river is lined with old tumbledown shacks and craggy remains of piers. Pilings bound by cable still stand, resisting the unrelenting push of the water.

A bustling private industrial site for the past century, this area is now being restored to its natural state of meadow and wetland. From the parking lot, head either north or south. The walk to the south is more sylvan, with cottonwoods, alders, and blackberry thickets by the river. Across the water a barn, now softened by weathering, winds, and climbing vines, squats on its old foundation. It was here that E. D. Smith

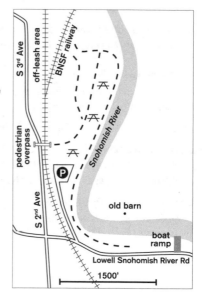

ran a sawmill and a logging camp, with a store, post office, and blacksmith shop, from the 1860s to the 1880s. For decades, the river was active with boats and log barges making their way to the Everett mills.

If you walk north from the parking lot, you'll find a more parklike setting, with lawns, benches, and picnic tables. When the trail turns west into a sandy meadow, you can loop back to the parking lot on one of the myriad access roads or return on the pavement by the river's edge, completing a 3-mile walk.

ADDRESS: 3084 Lowell Snohomish River Road

GETTING THERE: From I-5, take exit 192 (Broadway/41st Street). Follow signs for 41st Street W. Turn right onto S 3rd Avenue, which becomes Junction Avenue. Continue onto 2nd Avenue, then in 0.5 miles turn left onto Lenora Street. Continue onto Lowell Snohomish River Road to the parking area.

CONTACT: Everett Parks and Recreation Department, (425) 257-8300, www.everettwa.org/parks

10 MEADOWDALE BEACH PARK

Lynnwood, 14.5 miles southwest of Everett

Follow Lund's Gulch Creek through forest to reach a Puget Sound beach in this 108-acre park.

TRAIL	2.5 miles round-trip; natural surface, paved (in lower meadow)
STEEPNESS	Moderate to steep
OTHER USES	Bicycles
DOGS	On leash
CONNECTING TRAILS	None
PARK AMENITIES	Restrooms, picnic tables
DISABLED ACCESS	Paved trail, restrooms, picnic area—call (206) 339-1208 to request disabled parking pass for beach and picnic area

A gracefully curved descent on a wide graveled trail brings you into the aromatic forest. By keeping your eyes low on the huge bases of the Douglas fir and cedar stumps, you can envision these giants as they were a hundred years ago, before they were cut for the mills. Robins and rufous-sided towhees hop slowly from the trail.

This upland-to-beach park was created with walkers in mind. Although the beach is accessible by car for those who need to drive, the layout forces all others to take the 1.25-mile walk from the upper parking lot to the beach. Allow walking time (about 30 minutes) to return to the parking lot from the beach in daylight.

Small mileposts help you keep track of the distance traveled. At 0.5 miles a washout shows the power of water and the need to preserve soil-retaining plants

on steep hillsides. Beside the trail, Lund's Gulch Creek cuts a swath in the forest and whispers its wet sounds on its way to Puget Sound. At the footbridge, you can choose to cross to the picnic area, lawns, and lower parking lot or continue straight, still in the woods, to arrive at the tunnel to the beach. You may hear a train

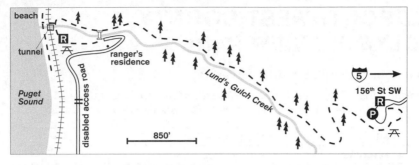

whistle blow, then watch a long freight chug past on the tracks that separate the forest from the sand.

To reach the water, pass beneath the tracks through the echo-filled tunnel. After the narrow ravine, the view feels exceptionally expansive. The snowy, hazy forms of the Olympics rise in the west, ferries from Mukilteo and Edmonds ply the Sound, and at low tide the beach beckons you to explore its rippled sand.

If the beach is your goal, call ahead to learn the status of the sometimes impassable tunnel to the shore.

ADDRESS: 6026 156th Street SW, Edmonds; disabled access (call ahead for gate PIN): 15433 75th Place W, Edmonds

GETTING THERE: From I-5, take exit 183 (164th Street SW). Travel west on 164th Street SW and go 1.7 miles to the intersection of 168th Street SW and WA 99. Cross WA 99 and continue west for 2 blocks. Turn right on 52nd Avenue W. Turn left on 160th Street SW, then right onto 56th Avenue W. Turn left onto 156th Street SW and continue until you reach the park entrance at the end of the road.

CONTACT: Snohomish County Parks and Recreation Department, (425) 388-6600, www.snohomishcountywa.gov/parks

---

Bring a Bucket and Shovel

Many Puget Sound beaches are open for clamming. Some are seasonally closed; others are permanently closed due to pollution or natural marine toxins. For information, call the individual park or the Washington State Marine Biotoxin Hotline at (800) 562-5632.

11 SOUTHWEST COUNTY OLYMPIC VIEW PARK

Edmonds, 16 miles south of Everett

Inviting trails meander through 120 acres of mature forest that border Perrinville Creek as it flows to Browns Bay on Puget Sound.

TRAIL	1 mile total; natural surface
STEEPNESS	Gentle to steep
OTHER USES	Bicycles
DOGS	On leash
CONNECTING TRAILS	None
PARK AMENITIES	Interpretive trail
DISABLED ACCESS	None

Immerse yourself in the natural sounds of bickering squirrels and cheerful birdsong just minutes from the Edmonds–Kingston ferry and the I-5 corridor. This park (known as Olympic View Park because of its location, not for views!) is the largest tract of forest within Edmonds city limits and a haven for wildlife, and with a mile of trail, it is an inviting respite from the bustle of traffic and commerce. While touted to have two nature trails, at present only the walk to the south of Olympic View Drive is fully developed as an interpretive trail. For those with little time or a desire for an easy, wide trail, the south side is where you'll find a mini-arboretum with trees bearing Latin and local names, benches for resting weary feet, and an easy gradient for walking.

Across the road, to the north, the park is less developed but entices with steeper hills and numerous less-defined neighborhood trails. Here you can wander among remnants of old-growth forest where five-foot-wide stumps now nurture young saplings,

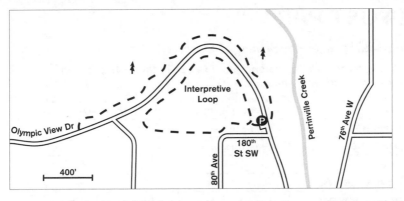

and small trails lead to children's forts and rope swings. For a good workout, head down the hill to the west and back up, but be careful with your footing!

Like most of the land bordering Puget Sound, this parcel was logged more than a hundred years ago, and evidence of the old-growth forest remains today in the form of springboard notches cut in the sides of huge stumps. These 120 acres were later donated to the University of Washington, and when the land was transferred to Snohomish County in 1971, it came with the condition that the parcel be forever managed as a passive woodland open space.

ADDRESS: Olympic View Drive and 180th Street SW, Edmonds

GETTING THERE: From I-5 southbound, take exit 181 (196th Street SW/WA 524) and merge onto 196th Street SW. After 2.6 miles turn right onto 76th Avenue W. Turn left at Olympic View Drive. The parking lot is on your left after you pass 180th Street SW.

From I-5 northbound, take exit 179 (220th Street SW). Turn left onto 220th Street SW. Turn right at 76th Avenue W, then left onto Olympic View Drive. The parking lot is on your left after you pass 180th Street SW.

CONTACT: Snohomish County Parks and Recreation Department, (425) 388-6600, www.snohomishcountywa.gov/parks

12 YOST PARK

Edmonds, 17 miles southwest of Everett

Explore interpretive trails along Shell Creek in these 48 acres of forested ravine and wetlands.

TRAIL	About 1.5 miles total; natural surface, paved
STEEPNESS	Gentle to steep
OTHER USES	Pedestrians only
DOGS	On leash
CONNECTING TRAILS	None
PARK AMENITIES	Playground, tennis court, interpretive trail; summer only: restrooms, picnic tables, pool
DISABLED ACCESS	Ridge Trail, restrooms, pool area

Despite its well-trodden trails, this ravine of wooded wildness in a neat residential area of Edmonds may be unknown to folks who come for the more obvious pleasures: swimming and picnicking. Deep in the greenery below the pool, Shell Creek cuts a path through a second-growth red-alder forest.

To walk in this sylvan wonderland, leave the parking lot by the yellow maintenance gate and stroll Ridge Trail (the paved maintenance road) east along the rim of the gulch. From here you can look into the upper branches of alders, maples, and firs as though you were an owl perched nearby, surveying your entire domain. There are several places where you can descend to the natural trail, letting the shouts of playing children fade above you. Listen instead for the high, tinkling warble of the winter wren or the *dee-dee-dee* of the black-capped chickadee.

Wooden bridges and walkways cross Shell Creek and its tributaries (some dry by late summer). The eroded banks of these streams show evidence of winter flooding. To prevent erosion, stay on the trails in this steep forest. Old stumps, long dead themselves, now provide life to cedar saplings and red huckleberry. Numbered posts correspond to notes on an informal nature guide that is available at the pool or the city parks office at 700 Main Street.

A loop trail encircles the base of the ravine. Feeder trails branch off, some rising steeply up the hillside and then petering out, others emerging on Main Street to the north. To the west, the trail crosses bogs and ends at the remains of an old concrete dam. Backtrack a short way to where the trail climbs again to rejoin the Ridge Trail near the parking area.

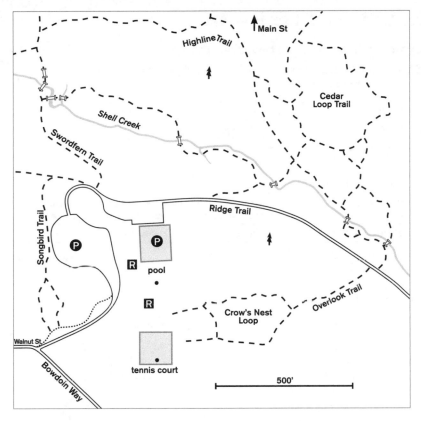

ADDRESS: 9535 Bowdoin Way, Edmonds

GETTING THERE: From I-5 southbound, take exit 179 (220th Street SW/Mountlake Terrace). Turn right on 220th Street SW. Go about 1.9 miles and turn right onto 92nd Avenue W. Go 0.5 miles and turn left onto Bowdoin Way. The park entrance is on the right, on the corner of Bowdoin Way and 96th Avenue W.

From I-5 northbound, take exit 177 (WA 104/Edmonds). Follow WA 104 toward Edmonds. Go about 2.8 miles and turn right on 100th Avenue W. This becomes 9th Avenue S. Go about 1 mile and turn right on Walnut Street, which becomes Bowdoin Way.

CONTACT: Edmonds Parks, Recreation, and Cultural Services Department; (425) 771-0230; www.edmondswa.gov/parks-recreation-departments/explore -parks.html

<u>13</u> LYNNDALE PARK

Lynnwood, 15 miles southwest of Everett

Stroll this 40-acre enclave of quiet second-growth forest just minutes from suburbia.

TRAIL	1.5 miles total; natural surface, paved
STEEPNESS	Level to steep
OTHER USES	Bicycles on paved trails
DOGS	On leash
CONNECTING TRAILS	None
PARK AMENITIES	Restrooms, playground, picnic shelter, amphitheater, basketball courts, ball fields, tennis courts, skate park
DISABLED ACCESS	Paved trail, restrooms, picnic shelter

Like many other community parks, this one hides its best features behind sports courts and picnic shelters. Very accessible to wheelchairs, strollers, and little feet in skates, 0.5 miles of paved trails lead from the easternmost parking lot west past an amphitheater, and from there another mile of trail winds through the quiet second-growth forest. Here bigleaf maples form a cool canopy in summer or create graceful frames around a pale winter sky. Autumn paints the forest orange, red, yellow, and brown.

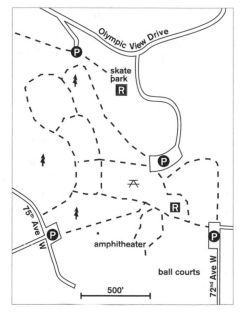

The paved trail crosses wide gravel trails and narrow natural trails, all hinting at the possibilities for exploration. Venture onto the natural trails and find the ravine (an old gravel pit, long ago reclaimed by nature) and the new wooden steps, the latter courtesy of the local Boy Scouts. The park boundaries are clear, so wander at will.

ADDRESS: 18927 72nd Avenue W, Lynnwood

GETTING THERE: From I-5 southbound, take exit 181 (WA 524). Merge onto 196th Street SW. In 2 miles turn right onto 68th Avenue W. Turn left onto 189th Place SW, then left onto 72nd Avenue W.

From I-5 northbound, take exit 179 (220th Street SW). Turn left on 220th Street SW. In about 0.5 miles turn right onto 66th Avenue W. In 0.8 miles turn left onto 208th Street SW then right onto 68th Avenue W. After 1 mile turn left onto 189th Place SW. Go 0.3 miles and turn left onto 72nd Avenue W. A northern parking lot is reached via Olympic View Drive.

CONTACT: Lynnwood Parks, Recreation, and Cultural Arts Department; (425) 670-5732; www.lynnwoodwa.gov/playlynnwood/parks.htm

<u>14</u> TERRACE CREEK PARK

Mountlake Terrace, 16 miles south of Everett

A streamside trail wanders through 60 acres of playing fields and forested ravine.

TRAIL	3 miles round-trip, plus spurs; paved, gravel
STEEPNESS	Gentle to steep
OTHER USES	Bicycles
DOGS	Off-leash near the Recreation Pavilion, otherwise on leash
CONNECTING TRAILS	None
PARK AMENITIES	Restrooms, playground, picnic areas, disc-golf course, ball fields
DISABLED ACCESS	Paved trail, restrooms

In this small neighborhood park, the trail gently ascends a peaceful strip of forest in a ravine below suburban Mountlake Terrace. Beginning as a paved walkway by the playground lawn, the trail soon changes to more rugged gravel and climbs moderately into the stately second-growth forest. Deep in the wooded ravine, the air is still and quiet. Winter wrens hop from bush to bush and woodpeckers tap old snags for their beetles and bugs. This suburban forest is home to opossums, raccoons, and other small forest critters.

Lyon Creek murmurs softly alongside the trail. Side trails lead to ridgetop homes invisible behind summer growth, but one trail, heading sharply west, will lead to the Mountlake Terrace Recreation Pavilion, and just north of that, a large off-leash dog park between 53rd Avenue W and 52nd Avenue W. The main north–south trail ends when it reaches 222nd Street SW, but there are numerous side trails to explore along the way.

The strange-looking objects that resemble open metal trash containers throughout the park are in fact holes for disc golf, a game of skill for those adept at tossing Frisbee-like discs long distances. Most of the disc-golf course is along spur trails on the sides of the steep ravine. It's interesting to imagine the contortions necessary to retrieve stray discs from the thickets of blackberry and nettle.

ADDRESS: 23200 48th Avenue W, Mountlake Terrace; *Recreation Pavilion and off-leash area:* 5303 228th Street SW, Mountlake Terrace

GETTING THERE: From I-5 southbound, take exit 179 (220th Street SW/Mountlake Terrace). Turn left onto 220th Street SW. Turn right on 56th Avenue W, then left on 236th Street SW. Go about 0.8 miles and turn left on 48th Avenue W. The park is on the left at the corner of 48th Avenue W and 233rd Street SW.

From I-5 northbound, take exit 178 (236th Street SW/Mountlake Terrace). Turn right on 236th Street SW and proceed as above.

CONTACT: Mountlake Terrace Recreation and Parks Department, (425) 776-9173, www.cityofmlt.com/530/recreation-parks

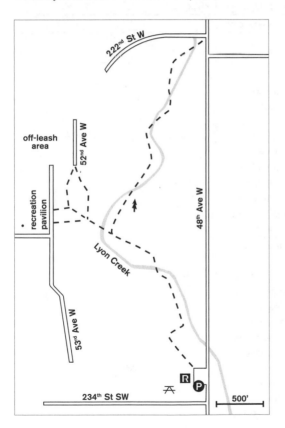

<u>15</u> NORTH CREEK PARK

Mill Creek, 12 miles south of Everett

Interpretive boardwalks cross 81 acres of wetlands for bird-watching and nature study.

TRAIL	1.5 miles round-trip; boardwalk
STEEPNESS	Level
OTHER USES	Pedestrians only
DOGS	On leash
CONNECTING TRAILS	North Creek Trail
PARK AMENITIES	Restrooms, interpretive signs, picnic tables, playground, viewpoint
DISABLED ACCESS	Restrooms

Step from the pavement to a sturdy boardwalk rimmed by waving cattails. Overhead, red-tailed hawks may soar, and in the hardhack Virginia rails may cackle. This enclave of open wetlands is excellent for bird-watching or studying the wetland habitat. Although surrounded by suburban homes, the reed canarygrass and beaked sedge grow tall enough to give you a sense of solitude. But you are most definitely not alone: not only is the wetland home to dozens of species of birds, including great blue herons, song sparrows, common snipes, marsh wrens, and many species of ducks, but beavers dwell here as well.

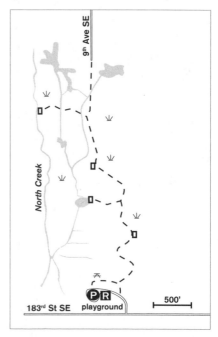

This level boardwalk trail meanders north for more than 0.5 miles over what is technically called Mukilteo muck (really!), which refers to the water-logged soil of the wetland. Interpretive signs and benches border the trail; two spurs lead west to ponds and viewpoints near the creek.

Caught in the Web

Late-summer and fall walks on little-used trails mean web-in-the-face hiking. Two options: wave a (dead) fern frond in the air in front of you as you hike, or generously offer to take place number two in line. Feign innocence when your companion turns round to glare at you with a spider on her nose. The upside to webs: damp with mist or morning dew, they glisten like silver necklaces on the branches. Undoubtedly one of nature's finer works of art.

Nestled between rolling hills, this land was once owned by the Bailey family of Mill Creek. When the county purchased the land, it recognized its value as a natural storm-water retention area. Luckily, they also saw its value as a natural classroom and park.

ADDRESS: 1011 183rd Street SE, Mill Creek

GETTING THERE: From I-5, take exit 183 (164th Street SW). Go east on 164th Street for 1.8 miles. Turn right (south) on the Bothell-Everett Highway (WA 527) and go 1.3 miles. Turn right on 183rd Street SE and go 0.2 miles. The park is on the right.

CONTACT: Snohomish County Parks and Recreation Department, (425) 388-6600, www.snohomishcountywa.gov/parks

<u>16</u> BOB HEIRMAN WILDLIFE PRESERVE

12 miles southeast of Everett

Meander through 343 acres of wild wetland and meadow out to cobble beaches on oxbows of the Snohomish River.

TRAIL	2 to 3 miles round-trip; gravel, natural surface
STEEPNESS	Level
OTHER USES	Pedestrians only; no pets
DOGS	Not allowed
CONNECTING TRAILS	None
PARK AMENITIES	Restroom (portable), picnic tables, fishing access
DISABLED ACCESS	None

A crisp winter day is a good day to step off the manicured trails and tackle the wildness of Bob Heirman Wildlife Preserve, also known to local anglers as Thomas' Eddy. With the deciduous trees spiking the blue sky with slender branches, the views to Mount Baker and the Cascades are unparalleled. It's easier, too, to get good views of the hundreds of overwintering birds on Shadow Lake and Robins Pond. Mallards, grebes, and buffleheads make mottled dark spots on the gray-blue lake, but it is the trumpeter swans, white, graceful, and huge, that stand out from the flock.

These 343 acres were saved from development by fisherman and activist Bob Heirman, who worked with the county to preserve this habitat for wildlife and fishing access. Today, this wildlife preserve on Thomas' Eddy is being left to return to nature without much interference from county maintenance crews. This means the paths stay clear because of constant use, not mowers and blowers, and when the seasonal floods sweep debris onto the riverbanks, the trails to the water will change.

From the well-kept lawns and picnic area near the parking lot, a short gravel path leads to two viewpoints over Shadow Lake for some great birding. From there, walk east toward the river, through high grass in summer but on a clearer trail in winter.

Wetlands stretch both north and south of the trail. Near the river's edge, a natural berm creates a dry pathway to lead you either up- or downstream. There may be downed trees to negotiate and trunks to crawl over, so this is not a trail for those seeking an easy stroll. Kids will probably love it, though, as there is a game of finding the best pathway through the flood debris. The goal is to arrive on the expansive, ever-changing cobble beaches of the Snohomish River.

When the steelhead run in winter and summer, this is a great fishing area, and you'll likely see fishing skiffs making their way up and down the river. Don't be surprised if the parking lot is full! In the dry season, the river takes on a languid motion and meanders slowly over sand and pebbles, making a possible swimming or wading hole. In winter, though, the river moves with a ferocious current, and it's best viewed from the safety of the cobbled banks.

ADDRESS: 14913 Connelly Road, Snohomish

GETTING THERE: From I-5 take exit 186 (WA 96 E/128th Street SW). Go east on WA 96 for 3.3 miles, then veer left onto Seattle Hill Road. After 1.5 miles, turn right onto WA 96/Lowell-Larimer Road. Continue for 2.7 miles (it becomes Broadway Avenue) and bear left onto Connelly Road. In 0.8 miles the preserve will be on your left.

CONTACT: Snohomish County Parks and Recreation Department, (425) 388-6600, www.snohomishcountywa.gov/parks

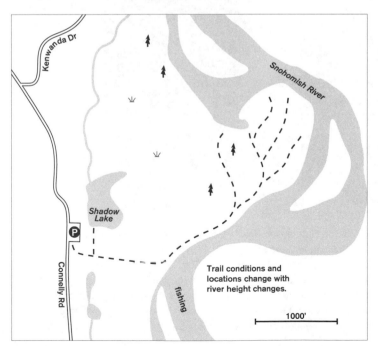

17 LORD HILL REGIONAL PARK

15 miles southeast of Everett

Snohomish River beaches, ponds, and mountain views highlight this 1,463-acre multiaged forest and wetland habitat.

TRAIL	More than 6 miles total; gravel, natural surface
STEEPNESS	Gentle to moderate
OTHER USES	Bicycles, horses
DOGS	On leash
CONNECTING TRAILS	None
PARK AMENITIES	Restrooms, interpretive signs, picnic areas, playground, viewpoints
DISABLED ACCESS	None

In the middle of the Snohomish River valley, a single hill rises 600 feet above the floodplain, welcoming walkers and horses to its wild and shaded forest paths. A remnant of long-ago volcanic outcroppings, Lord Hill derives its name from home-steader Mitchell Lord, who had a dairy farm on the flat land below the hill in the 1880s. By the 1930s the last old-growth timber had been cut, and in the 1980s the Department of Natural Resources cut patches of second-growth forest, pro-ducing today's multiaged forest and wetland habitat.

From the parking lot, head down the fragrant wood-chip path deep into the fir, hemlock, and maple forest. Where the trail levels, you'll be glad of sturdy puncheon bridges that span the miniature wetlands along the horse-trodden trail. Soon the wood chips and puncheons give way to a wide graveled path leading to a T-junction. To the left you reach one of the park's nine ponds. Turning right takes you up a rise in dense forest from which several trails branch off.

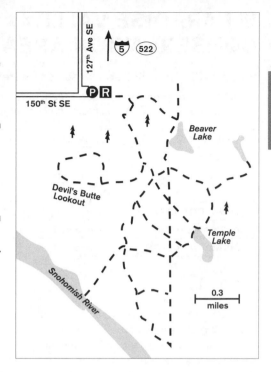

The map at the parking lot can be confusing, and until the signage and trails are completed, keep your internal compass working and ask equestrians the way out if you're not sure. With luck, you'll find one of the ponds with active beavers, or evidence of the resident deer or occasional bear or bobcat. A trek to the pipeline trail or Devil's Butte Lookout affords grand views of Mount Baker to the north and the Olympics to the west.

ADDRESS: 12921 150th Street SE, Snohomish

GETTING THERE: From I-5, take exit 194 (US 2/Wenatchee). Stay right at the end of the trestle and go about 2.5 miles. Turn right onto WA 9. At the Snohomish/Riverview Road/2nd Street exit, turn left on 2nd Street, then right onto Lincoln Avenue S (which becomes the Old Snohomish Monroe Highway). Go 2.7 miles and turn right on 127th Avenue SE. Go 2 miles to 150th Street SE. Turn left into the parking lot.

CONTACT: Snohomish County Parks and Recreation Department, (425) 388-6600, www.snohomishcountywa.gov/parks

18 PARADISE VALLEY CONSERVATION AREA

Woodinville, 20 miles southeast of Everett

In 793 acres of fern-filled forest, follow miles of well-signed trails to Cascade views and down into lush wetlands.

TRAIL	13 miles; natural surface
STEEPNESS	Gentle to moderate
OTHER USES	Bicycles, horses
DOGS	On leash
CONNECTING TRAILS	None
PARK AMENITIES	Restrooms, interpretive trail, map signs
DISABLED ACCESS	Restrooms

Step back in time to a land bedecked in soft and rustling sword ferns, a land green with salal and Oregon grape undergrowth, shaded by young deciduous trees. Imagine small dinosaurs lurking about in the brush. Such is the luxuriant beauty of Paradise Valley Conservation Area. This almost 800-acre park was part of the 1887 homestead of the Lloyd family and remained in the family until its purchase by Snohomish County in 2000. Logging roads crisscrossed the land and form the basis for some of today's trails through the almost 100-year-old secondary forest. The ridge trails remain green throughout the year under their canopy of Douglas fir and western hemlock, while the valley's cottonwoods, willows, and dogwoods glow with color in autumn. The park's extensive wetlands are home to beavers, frogs, and salamanders, while the forest provides habitat for coyotes, bears, and cougars. Just outside the current park boundary (but part of the next phase of development), Cottage Lake Creek abounds in resident trout and is graced by migrating salmon in spawning season.

Well-developed and maintained multiuse trails testify to the park's appeal to a variety of users and its strong support in the hiking, mountain biking, and equestrian communities. There are miles of hiking-only trails, and with extensive signage, walkers can choose to avoid the popular (and sometimes muddy) biking trails if they wish. The gentle Whispering Firs Interpretive Trail is a great starter hike for young families.

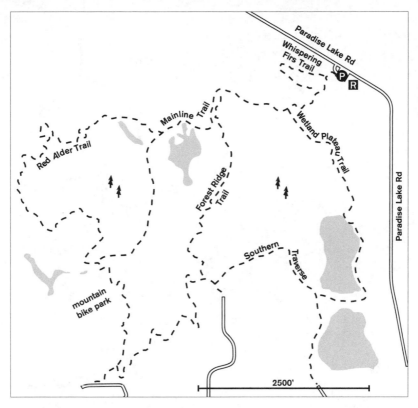

ADDRESS: 23210 Paradise Lake Road, Woodinville

GETTING THERE: From I-5, take exit 182 merging onto I-405 S. Take exit 23A to WA 522 east. Go left at the fork merging onto WA 522 E. Turn right at Paradise Lake Road. Go 1.7 miles to the parking lot, which is just north of the Lloyd family farm on the west side of the road.

From I-405 northbound, take exit 23 (US 2) toward Woodinville/Wenatchee, then merge onto WA 522 E. Go 5 miles and turn right at Paradise Lake Road. The parking lot is 1.7 miles down the road on the right.

CONTACT: Snohomish County Parks and Recreation Department, (425) 388-6600, www.snohomishcountywa.gov/parks

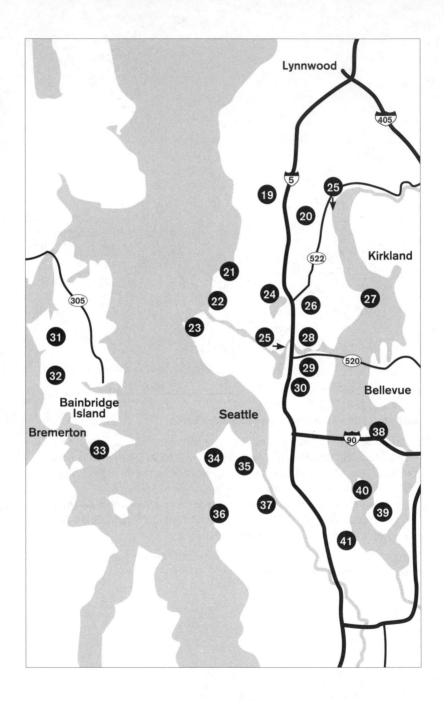

SEATTLE

19 BOEING CREEK AND SHOREVIEW PARKS

Shoreline, 17 miles north of downtown Seattle

79 acres of neighboring parks offer urban amenities and pristine nature where a clear stream fills a hidden lake.

TRAIL	4 miles; natural surface, paved
STEEPNESS	Level to steep
OTHER USES	Boeing Creek: Pedestrians only; Shoreview: Bicycles
DOGS	Off-leash area in Shoreview Park, otherwise leash and scoop
CONNECTING TRAILS	None
PARK AMENITIES	Boeing Creek: Benches, picnic area; Shoreview: Restrooms, playground, picnic area, ball fields, lake access (no lifeguard)
DISABLED ACCESS	Paved trails and restrooms in Shoreview Park

Follow serpentine trails deep into the ravine and then up onto the ridge of this green gem of a forest in the heart of Shoreline. Watch for pileated woodpeckers on the snags and cedar waxwings in the meadows in summer. Rated one of Puget Sound's finest urban forests by the scientists at EarthCorps/Seattle Urban Nature, Boeing Creek Park has a corps of volunteers who have put in many hours rejuvenating the trails and removing invasive plants from the waterway. The park is home to mountain beavers, raccoons, and red foxes, as well as a number of unusual trees such as a 200-year-old western yew. Both eastern gray squirrels and Douglas squirrels frolic among the branches.

From the northern parking lot, you can walk around the detention pond or dive straight into the forest. Going southwest (right) into the forest, the trail follows the streambed, crossing over a bridge of concrete steps placed there by a Girl Scout troop and replaced each

---

Trees Wanted–Dead or Alive

When you see a downed log or an old snag or stump, think of all the years the tree lived before it fell or burned. And look at all the life it supports now that it's dead. Old logs (usually Douglas fir) with young trees growing out of them are called nurse logs. Stumps can also host the new growth of other plant species. As the late Californian biologist Tony Hacking used to say, "A tree is arguably more alive after it's dead."

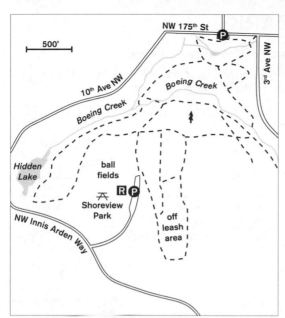

year when the stream floods. The sandy soil is especially vulnerable to erosion, so it's important to stay on the trail and not be tempted to take shortcuts up the steep ravine sides. Coming round a corner brings you to Hidden Lake with its glass-clear water and usually a family or two of ducks. If you're lucky, you may see them dive and skim the algae off the bottom of the lake. Wading is allowed, but there is no lifeguard.

From Hidden Lake, the trail climbs through the forest to emerge in an open space of broom and berries, madrona, and cottonwood. Although the boundary isn't marked, you've now crossed into adjoining Shoreview Park, an active recreation area with tennis courts, sports fields, restrooms, playground, and ADA-accessible walkways. Above the tennis courts is a large off-leash area with a track for running your canine friend through his or her paces. Back to the north, into the forest again, the trail stays high on a traverse above the creek and then angles down to meet the streambed once again in Boeing Creek Park.

ADDRESS: *Boeing Creek Park:* 17229 3rd Avenue NW, Shoreline; *Shoreview Park:* 700 NW Innis Arden Way, Shoreline

GETTING THERE: *Boeing Creek Park:* From I-5, take exit 176 (NE 175th Street). Go west on 175th Street. Continue 0.8 miles and turn left on Aurora Avenue N. Go 0.8 miles and turn right onto N 160th Street. For Boeing Creek Park, turn right on Dayton Avenue N. Go 0.3 miles and make a slight left onto Carlyle Hall Road N. Continue about 0.5 miles onto 3rd Avenue NW. The park is on your left. There is street parking here. Further parking is ahead and to the left on N 175th Street.

Shoreview Park: Follow the directions above to N 160th Street. Continue on N 160th Street until it becomes Innis Arden Way. Drive about 0.5 miles to Shoreview Park on the right.

CONTACT: Shoreline Parks, Recreation, and Cultural Services Department; (206) 801-2600; www.shorelinewa.gov/government/departments/parks-recreation -cultural-services

20 HAMLIN PARK

Shoreline, 11 miles north of downtown Seattle

Walk in 80 acres of towering, open forest with wide paths and open ravines, or stroll the perimeter of sunny ball fields.

TRAIL	3 miles; paved, natural surface
STEEPNESS	Level to steep
OTHER USES	Bicycles
DOGS	On leash
CONNECTING TRAILS	None
PARK AMENITIES	Restroom, picnic tables, playground, ball fields, art, orienteering course, historic canons
DISABLED ACCESS	Paved trail bordering ball fields

Step from your car and inhale air redolent with the scent of cedar wood chips. Follow wide, well-maintained trails into a dream forest of open glades, rolling hills, ravines with stairs cut into them, and fern-decorated slopes. A stroll in Hamlin Park can be an easy meander along almost level paths or a heart-stimulating walk up and down the three 50- to 80-foot-deep ravines that divide the park under glades of pines, hemlock, dogwood, and cedar. The wood-chip pile is testimony to the ongoing efforts of the Shoreline maintenance crew to keep this beautiful forest accessible to foot traffic by clearing downed trees and branches.

In our Northwest of dense, dark forests with tangled undergrowth, Hamlin is unprecedented for its lack of understory beneath towering trees. But beautiful as it is, the parks people would prefer an even more natural setting, and to this end they are experimenting with reintroducing native herbs and shrubs in a large fenced-off regeneration area. Elsewhere, salal and sword fern grow in comely bunches between log-lined trails

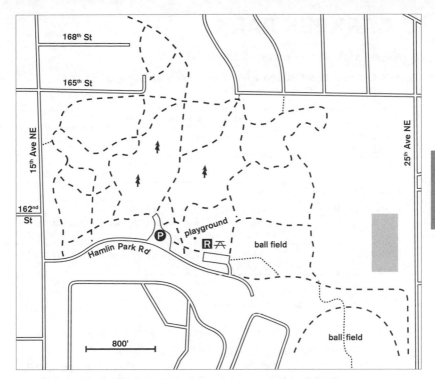

and next to wood-rimmed steps, giving this park a feeling of a manicured forest, a place where it seems bright even on the darkest days.

Out of the forest, in the park's southern region, you'll find a strange couple of historic relics: two eight-inch naval canons from the Spanish-American War, said to have fired the first shots in Manila Bay in 1898. Just how and why they were taken off the USS *Boston* and transported to Seattle (before Shoreline was Shoreline) seems a bit of a mystery. Hamlin has the requisite playground and restrooms as well as a sculpture that visitors can sit on (*Dew Beads*, glass and concrete balls evoking dewdrops in the forest) and playing fields, ready for shouts and cheers in baseball season.

ADDRESS: 16006 15th Avenue NE, Seattle

GETTING THERE: From I-5, take exit 175 (NE 145th Street). Go east on 145th for 0.5 miles to 15th Avenue NE. Turn left onto 15th and go 0.9 miles to 160th Street. The park entrance is on your right.

CONTACT: Shoreline Parks, Recreation, and Cultural Services Department; (206) 801-2600; www.shorelinewa.gov/government/departments/parks-recreation-cultural-services

21 CARKEEK PARK

8 miles north of downtown Seattle

Piper's Creek winds through 216 acres of forest to Puget Sound and views of the Olympic Mountains.

TRAIL	6.1 miles; natural surface, paved
STEEPNESS	Gentle to moderate
OTHER USES	Bicycles
DOGS	On leash
CONNECTING TRAILS	None
PARK AMENITIES	Restrooms, picnic shelters, playgrounds, Environmental Learning Center, model airplane field, demonstration garden
DISABLED ACCESS	Salmon-to-Sound Trail, Wetland Trail, part of Piper's Creek Trail, restrooms

Leave commercial Seattle behind as you wind down either a road or a footpath into this verdant ravine, where moss clings to the big-leaf maples and old logs straddle Piper's Creek. Like other ravines along Puget Sound, this one enchants with the steady downward flow of several small streams, the surprising gurgles of miniature waterfalls, and the profuse undergrowth of the forest. Salmon still spawn in this urban stream.

In spring the trailside is lush with salmonberry bushes, the fruit still yellow and orange, awaiting the summer sun. Incredibly large stumps, too big to hug, provide nutrients for young salal bushes and Douglas firs. But all is not wild here. The old orchard remains as testimony to the early settlers, A. W. Piper and his wife, Minna, who supplied produce to downtown Seattle from this homestead in the late 1800s.

A beautiful demonstration garden is now flourishing thanks to the ministrations of a score of volunteers. Look for this horticultural gem near the upper entrance to the park.

In the lower parking area, look for the stairs leading up to the footbridge that crosses over the train tracks to the watery world of Puget Sound. The sound of whinnying robins is replaced by the call of gulls, and your eyes are no longer drawn to branches overhead but farther away to the lofty Olympics in the west, or to your feet, where the sand ripples under the retreating tide.

ADDRESS: 950 NW Carkeek Park Road, Seattle

GETTING THERE: From I-5, take exit 173 (Northgate Way/1st Avenue NE). From southbound, go right on N Northgate Way (which becomes N 105th Street). From northbound, turn left on 1st Avenue NE, then left on N Northgate Way and go under the freeway. Drive west and turn right on Greenwood Avenue N. Go 2 blocks and turn left on NW 110th Street (which becomes Carkeek Park Road and winds down to the lower parking lot). Gates close at 9:00 p.m.

To access the trail at the southeast end of the park, stay on N 105th Street as it veers left to become Holman Road NW. Turn right on 3rd Avenue NW. Go 1 block and turn left on NW 100th Place to reach the small picnic and parking area.

CONTACT: Seattle Parks and Recreation Department, (206) 684-4075, www.seattle.gov/parks

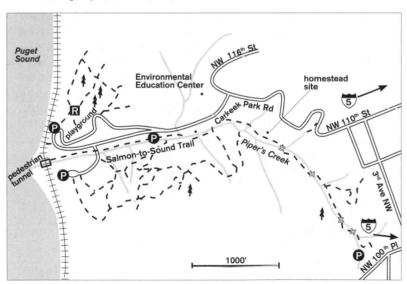

22 GOLDEN GARDENS PARK

11 miles northwest of downtown Seattle

With 88 acres over Puget Sound, you can traverse level forest trails, descend from a fern-filled forest to the beach, or peruse the beach and wetlands.

TRAIL	3.2 miles; natural surface
STEEPNESS	Gentle to steep
OTHER USES	Pedestrians only on upper trails
DOGS	Off-leash area in the upper park, otherwise leash and scoop
CONNECTING TRAILS	None
PARK AMENITIES	Picnic tables, restrooms, playground, interpretive signs
DISABLED ACCESS	Lower parking lot trail

Traverse gently sloping forest trails where ferns line the hillside and big-leaf maples stand tall above the soft dirt pathway. Here, more than 120 feet above Puget Sound, you can almost sense the Seattle of old, before the regrades and hill sculpting tore down the steep wooded slopes. From the off-leash area at the upper parking lot, you can walk back and forth on gentle slopes or take one of several steep staircases built into the hillside either up to the neighborhood above or down to the lower parking lot and beach.

Known mostly as a summer play park, with beaches, lawn, and playground, Golden Gardens has so much more to offer. In winter, the spindly branches of the alders frame the brilliant white of the Olympic Mountains to the west, and through

clear openings you can watch the ships and occasional courageous sailor on the Sound. In summer, the forest trails provide seclusion above the clamor of the playground, and you can hear the calls of the wrens and robins.

Near the lower parking lot, small wetland ponds create habitat for wintering birds such as gadwall, buffleheads, and mallards. And there is always the beach to wander, where the fresh salt air is a tonic for office-weary minds.

The Burlington Northern Santa Fe Railway runs through the park, and it is dangerous and illegal to cross the tracks. A pedestrian underpass is provided for safe passage from the upper and lower parking lots. Unlike other city parks, which close at sunset, Golden Gardens is open year-round until well after dark (see park signs, or call for hours), and beach fires are allowed.

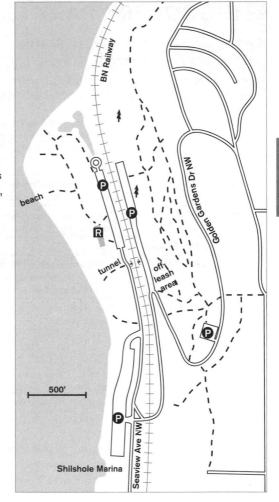

ADDRESS: 8498 Seaview Place NW, Seattle

GETTING THERE: From I-5 northbound, take exit 172 (N 85th Street) toward Aurora Avenue N. Drive west on NW 85th Street for 3.2 miles. Turn right onto 32nd Avenue NW. Wind down the hill on Golden Gardens Drive NW. The forest trails and off-leash parking will be on your right. For the beach and lower trails, continue to the bottom of the hill and turn right on Seaview Place NW and into the parking lot.

CONTACT: Seattle Parks and Recreation Department, (206) 684-4075, www .seattle.gov/parks/. To volunteer at a Seattle park, call (206) 684-8028.

23 DISCOVERY PARK

6 miles northwest of downtown Seattle
(Magnolia neighborhood)

Walk 534 acres of meadows, wetlands, forest, and beaches for views, bird-watching, art, and a historical lighthouse.

TRAIL	11.8 miles (including the 0.5-mile Wolf Tree Nature Trail and the 2.8-mile Loop Trail) plus 200-foot beach; gravel, natural surface, paved
STEEPNESS	Gentle to steep
OTHER USES	Bicycles on paved roadways only; pedestrians only on Loop Trail, Wolf Tree Nature Trail
DOGS	On leash; no dogs on Wolf Tree Nature Trail or the beach
CONNECTING TRAILS	None
PARK AMENITIES	Restrooms, classes, playground, picnic areas, sports courts, interpretive signs, maps, Daybreak Star Indian Cultural Center
DISABLED ACCESS	Restrooms, buildings, paved trail, pass available to drive to beach

Walk a windswept bluff by a grassy meadow, hunt ghost shrimp on the Puget Sound beach, or search the treetops for an eagle's nest. With more than 11 miles of trails to tread, Seattle's largest park presents a variety of Northwest habitats to explore just minutes from downtown.

Start at the visitor center (east gate) for maps, then set off on the Loop Trail to the west. Crossing the flower-strewn meadow, watch for violet-green swallows in summer, or listen for the screech of hawks in winter. The old buildings

are what remain of Fort Lawton, now recently converted to private homes with gated access.

From the sandy bluff, listen for foghorns and the barks of sea lions, and watch the vessels ply the Sound far below. If the wind is from the south, head down the forested trail to South Beach (the goal being to stay upwind of the Metro sewage treatment plant on

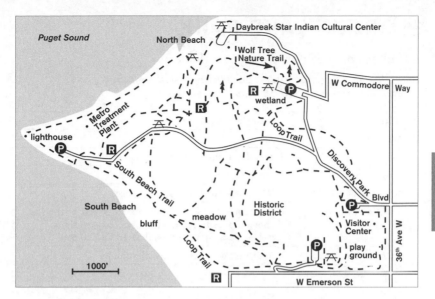

the headland). The trail is steep, with steps and observation platforms. Geology buffs can study the 300-foot cliffs for clues to our region's glaciated past.

Back on the Loop Trail, stick to the larger, marked trails. Later, as you become familiar with the large park's layout, you can explore the shortcuts and side trails with confidence. The Loop Trail takes you past the south entrance's picnic area and playground before returning to the visitor center. At the north parking lot, leave time for the 0.5-mile Wolf Tree Nature Trail, which features interpretive signs and peaceful walking.

ADDRESS: 3801 W Government Way, Seattle

GETTING THERE: From I-5, take exit 169 (NE 50th Street/NE 45th Street). Turn west on NE 50th Street and go about 1.7 miles (past the zoo) until it merges right onto NW Market Street; continue west. Turn left on 15th Avenue NW, cross the Ballard Bridge, and take the first exit on the right (Fisherman's Terminal/ Emerson). Emerson merges to the right onto Gilman Avenue W; continue west. At W Fort Street, bear left; it becomes W Government Way and leads to the park's east entrance.

Organized groups and cars with children under 7 or people over 62, or those with a state disabled permit, may be able to drive to the beach on the park's access road; inquire at the visitor center.

CONTACT: Seattle Parks and Recreation Department, (206) 684-4075, www.seattle.gov/parks. For information on volunteering, visit www.friendsdiscoverypark.org. For information on the Daybreak Star Indian Cultural Center, call (206) 285-4425.

<u>24</u> GREEN LAKE PARK

4.5 miles north of downtown Seattle

Green lawns and landscaping border the paved trail that circumnavigates placid 260-acre Green Lake.

TRAIL	2.8-mile loop; paved
STEEPNESS	Level
OTHER USES	Bicycles, in-line skaters (in designated lane)
DOGS	On leash
CONNECTING TRAILS	Woodland Park trails (south of lake)
PARK AMENITIES	Restrooms, picnic area, playground, beach, boating (nonmotorized), community center, concessions, fishing piers, sports fields, theater, wading pool
DISABLED ACCESS	Trail, restrooms, buildings, playground

Circle this peaceful urban lake on a defined 2.8-mile paved trail and meet a cross section of Seattle life. Year-round, Green Lake attracts families, dog walkers, joggers, bicyclists, the old, and the young—all out to enjoy this strip of greenery in the 324-acre park. In spring, walk beneath flowering cherry and dogwood trees. In fall, look for the red berries on the hawthorns.

No matter the time of year, there is activity on the lake: in summer the paddle-boaters, small sailboats, and windsurfers; in winter the wind kicking up whitecaps. Two nature-preserve islands provide shelter for many birds but are inaccessible to walkers except through the magic of binoculars. Fall, winter, and spring are the best times to see the migratory birds such as buffleheads and white-fronted geese. Throughout the year, the omnipresent mallards and Canada geese forage in the reeds by the lake's edge, and red-winged blackbirds add a splash of color to the scene.

Because of the paved trail's popularity, traffic flow on it is regulated: walkers (including those with baby strollers) take the inside half and can travel either direction, while those on wheels must stick to a counterclockwise direction

on the outer half. A crushed-gravel trail parallel to the paved path allows joggers and walkers to circle without encountering bicyclists.

ADDRESS: 7201 E Green Lake Drive N, Seattle

GETTING THERE: From I-5, take exit 169 (NE 45th Street/NE 50th Street) and head west on NE 50th Street. Go about 0.8 miles to Green Lake Way N, turn right, and park along the street by the lake or in lots farther north. Alternatively, continue west on NE 50th Street to park near the tennis courts (on the right). This also allows easy access to the wooded trails and hillsides of Woodland Park.

CONTACT: Seattle Parks and Recreation Department, (206) 684-4075, www.seattle.gov/parks

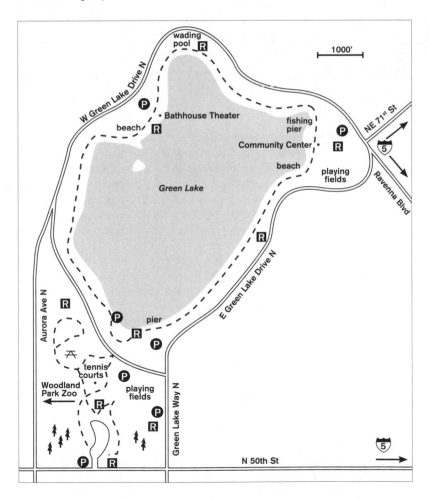

25 BURKE-GILMAN TRAIL

4 miles north of downtown Seattle (Ballard neighborhood) to
Kenmore, 12 miles north of Seattle

*Walk from park to park along Lakes Union and Washington via an
old railroad grade.*

TRAIL	16.5 miles one way; paved
STEEPNESS	Level to gentle
OTHER USES	Bicycles, in-line skaters
DOGS	On leash
CONNECTING TRAILS	Warren G. Magnuson Park and NOAA Art Walk (Walk #27), Sammamish River Trail (Walk #42)
PARK AMENITIES	Restrooms, beaches, picnic areas
DISABLED ACCESS	Trail, restrooms, picnic areas

Beginning in the Ballard neighborhood of Seattle and snaking along the shore of
Lake Washington to Kenmore, this 16.5-mile paved corridor of off-road walking
meets the needs of those who seek the freedom of the trail just blocks from home.

This wide, paved, multiuse trail follows the original grade of the Seattle, Lake
Shore, and Eastern Railroad, which, after almost a century, was abandoned in
1971 under the ownership of Burlington Northern. Seven years later, Seattle
opened the Burke-Gilman (named in honor of the original railroad's founders)
as an off-road multiuse trail. Near the western end, the trail passes Gas Works
Park, a miniwalk in itself, with views of Lake Union and downtown Seattle, then
continues east through the University of Washington campus and north past
Warren G. Magnuson Park (Walk #27). Enjoy the fall colors of the hazelnut trees
and big-leaf maples along this stretch.

North from here, increasing greenery lines the trail,
which often runs between
backyards that are well landscaped with both native and
exotic trees and shrubs. You
get peekaboo views of Lake
Washington, but the best
is saved for the far north.
Blackberries line the trail,
providing spring color and

fragrance and summer snacking. Two miles past Log Boom Park (Tracy Owen Station) in Kenmore, the trail changes to the Sammamish River Trail (Walk #42). Here you can enjoy a beach, a green lawn, and views south across Lake Washington.

One warning: the trail is heavily used by bicyclists and in-line skaters. Always walk on the right—in single file if it's a busy weekend. Toddlers and impatient children might do better on a quieter trail.

ADDRESS: *Access at Warren G. Magnuson Park:* 7400 Sand Point Way NE, Seattle; *Access at Log Boom Park:* 61st Avenue NE, Kenmore

GETTING THERE: The best access with parking: Warren G. Magnuson Park (see Walk #27), or Log Boom Park, Kenmore. Trail brochure shows other access points.

Log Boom Park: From I-5 northbound, take exit 171 (WA 522/Bothell/Lake City Way). Go north 6.5 miles, and in Kenmore turn right on 61st Avenue NE. The park is on the right.

From I-405 northbound, take exit 23 (WA 522 W/Bothell); southbound, take exit 23B (WA 522 W/Bothell). Go west on WA 522 about 4.4 miles, and turn left on 61st Avenue NE. The park is on the right.

CONTACT: Seattle Parks and Recreation Department, (206) 684-4075, www.seattle.gov/parks

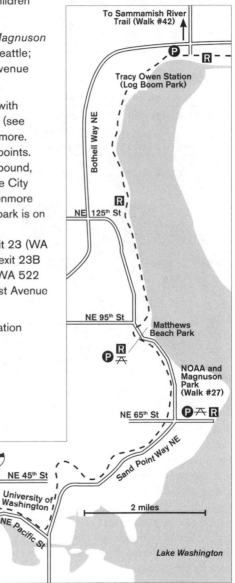

SEATTLE

<u>26</u> RAVENNA PARK

5 miles northeast of downtown Seattle

Explore 50 acres of tranquil forest trails in a stream-cut ravine hidden from urban bustle.

TRAIL	4.5 miles total; natural surface
STEEPNESS	Level to steep
OTHER USES	Bicycles on 5-foot-wide paths only
DOGS	On leash
CONNECTING TRAILS	None
PARK AMENITIES	Restrooms, picnic tables, playground, tennis courts, wading pool
DISABLED ACCESS	Restrooms, playground at Cowen Park

This secret cleft of choice greenery in the midst of urban Seattle offers some of the quietest, most treasured walking in the city. In fair weather, the steep side trails, the paths along the rims, and the wide trail in the ravine are filled with hikers, joggers, and dog walkers. Even in winter, when a dusting of snow coats the trail, footprints still tell of dedicated Ravenna-lovers out to enjoy their park despite slippery trails and a partially frozen stream.

One of Seattle's oldest parks—acquired before the 1909 Alaska-Yukon-Pacific Exposition—Ravenna has seen bad years and good. Known at midcentury as a squatter's haven, it was later cleaned up and has now become a magnet park for Seattleites.

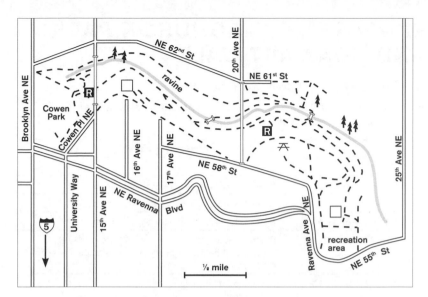

From the massive footbridge (at 20th Avenue NE) over the ravine and the rim trails where wild roses and berry bushes bloom, you look out into the canopy of immense red alder and maple. As you descend the angled trails that traverse the hillside, the vegetation changes to a mix of native and ornamental trees (yew, redwood, Pacific dogwood, Douglas fir) sheltering an undergrowth of fern and salal. Leaning madrona trees form intricate patterns with their peeling bark branches.

Once in the ravine, you have no sense of city, no sight of houses. The stream flows from west to east, heading for Lake Washington. Working its way around boulders and logs, it brings nutrients to the skunk cabbages and stream creatures that live in its water and along its banks.

ADDRESS: 5520 Ravenna Avenue NE, Seattle

GETTING THERE: From I-5, take exit 169 (NE 50th Street/NE 45th Street) and head east on NE 50th Street. Turn left (north) onto 11th Avenue NE, then, in 4 blocks, turn right onto (divided) Ravenna Boulevard. Go 3 blocks to Brooklyn Avenue NE and park on the street near Cowen Park; walk up Cowen Place NE to the western edge of Ravenna Park. You can also continue east on NE Ravenna Boulevard to the recreational end of Ravenna Park.

Alternatively, from I-5 northbound only, take exit 170 (Ravenna Boulevard/NE 65th Street) and go right on Ravenna Boulevard to Cowen Park.

CONTACT: Seattle Parks and Recreation Department, (206) 684-4075, www.seattle.gov/parks

27 WARREN G. MAGNUSON PARK AND NOAA ART WALK

8 miles northeast of downtown Seattle

Enjoy 320 acres of beaches, meadows, Cascade views, art, and an off-leash area along Lake Washington.

TRAIL	About 3 miles total; gravel, natural surface, paved
STEEPNESS	Level
OTHER USES	Bicycles; NOAA trail is pedestrians only
DOGS	Off-leash area, otherwise on leash
CONNECTING TRAILS	Burke-Gilman Trail (Walk #25) via streets
PARK AMENITIES	Restrooms, art, boat launch, picnic areas, playground, ball fields, tennis courts, wading pool, off-leash area
DISABLED ACCESS	Shoreline trail in Magnuson Park, restrooms, picnic areas

Still called Sand Point from its former days as a naval station, Magnuson Park is one of the brightest parks in the Seattle area, with miles of open meadows and lakeshore walking. Purchased from the navy in 1975, the park has seen years of improvement since the bleak days when it smelled of aviation fuel. To increase the greenery, the city originally planted trees, many of which died from lack of water. Now the park's pastoral setting is part of its allure, and any future plantings call for native shrubs, not trees. Only the southern end has a forested hillside with dirt trails; elsewhere, be prepared for sun and wind.

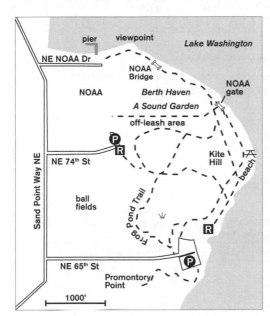

pier viewpoint Lake Washington

NE NOAA Dr

NOAA
Bridge

NOAA   NOAA
             gate
NOAA   Berth Haven
        A Sound Garden
        off-leash area

P
R

Sand Point Way NE

NE 74ᵗʰ St   Kite
                    Hill
                        beach
ball
fields

Frog Pond Trail

R

NE 65ᵗʰ St   P
Promontory/
Point
1000'

Blustery days offer entertainment as you walk the wide aggregate trail from south to north. Windsurfers and wakeboarders race from the headland onto the wind-whipped lake, and kite-flying aficionados wrestle with their colorful winged creatures from the hillock.

If you come with a dog, follow signs to the northwestern border of the park, where the designated off-leash area is rimmed by luscious summer blackberry thickets. This trail meanders past the playing fields and rejoins the paved aggregate walkway where it meets Lake Washington.

North of the off-leash area a fence marks the boundary of the National Oceanic and Atmospheric Administration (NOAA). Due to heightened security the gate on the northeast corner is opened to the public from 11:30 a.m. to 1:30 p.m. Monday through Friday only, or you can walk into NOAA grounds via the main gate from 9:00 a.m. to 5:00 p.m. Monday through Friday. To enter, you need to show a valid ID and undergo a security check (no picnic baskets or large containers are allowed). Dogs are allowed on-leash. Five art-in-the-parks projects here enhance the waterside graveled walk. Stroll across two bridges inscribed with quotes from *Moby-Dick*, enjoy views over the lake at *Berth Haven* and *Viewpoint Terrace*, guess the artist's intentions for the conical *Knoll for NOAA*, and walk through a haunting, moaning, otherworldly symphony of wind in *A Sound Garden*.

ADDRESS: 7400 Sand Point Way NE, Seattle

GETTING THERE: From I-5, take exit 169 (NE 45th Street/NE 50th Street). Drive east on NE 45th Street past the University of Washington, down the viaduct, and another 0.5 miles. Bear left onto Sand Point Way NE. Turn right on NE 65th Street or NE 74th Street into Magnuson Park. The NOAA Art Walk extends north from Magnuson Park.

CONTACT: Seattle Parks and Recreation Department, (206) 684-4075, www .seattle.gov/parks. To volunteer, contact Magnuson Environmental Stewardship Alliance: www.magnusonstewardship.org. For more information on the NOAA Art Walk, visit www.wrc.noaa.gov.

<u>28</u> UNION BAY NATURAL AREA

5 miles northeast of downtown Seattle

Resident and migrating birds abound among 74 acres of meadows, wetlands, and ponds on Lake Washington.

TRAIL	1.5 miles total with loops north and south; gravel, natural surface
STEEPNESS	Level
OTHER USES	Bicycles except on Yesler Swamp Trail
DOGS	On leash
CONNECTING TRAILS	None
PARK AMENITIES	Restrooms (weekday only), picnic tables, botanical garden, interpretive signs
DISABLED ACCESS	Trails, Yesler Swamp, restrooms (weekday only)

This swath of untamed greenery between the University of Washington's Husky Stadium and the Center for Urban Horticulture is a stopover for thousands of migrating waterfowl and other birds on the Pacific Flyway. Come during fall, winter, or spring, when the ponds may host ruddy ducks, hooded mergansers, and green- or blue-winged teals. The trees and bushes may be dotted with goldfinches, vireos, and waxwings. In summer the meadows are bright with yellow Scotch broom and blue chicory. All year long, mute swans glide on the calm waters of Union Bay, while Swainson's hawks hunt overhead and muskrats make their homes in Shoveler's Pond.

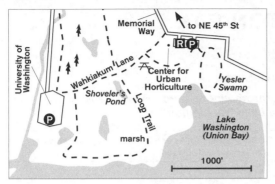

Before 1916 this was another cove of Lake Washington, but when the ship canal was built the water receded and the land slowly adapted to its dry status. It's now an ecological research area, and walkers are welcome provided they keep pets on a leash and walk only on established paths.

From Wahkiakum Lane, take the first left onto a wood-chip trail, which passes the seasonal Shoveler's Pond (dry in summer) and then crosses the meadow to the lakeshore. Stay alert for ring-tailed pheasants in the grass and the shadow of eagles overhead. Several small paths weave through the cattails at the water's edge. In summer these are practically impassable due to blackberry invasion, but in winter you can find tiny clearings from which you can watch the lake-loving waterfowl.

Continue on the paths around the other ponds, where you may see plovers and bitterns. New plantings of dogwood and other trees enhance the seclusion and help ensure the repeated return of the seasonal migrants. To the east of the parking lot Yesler Swamp is now ADA compliant. Boardwalks lead you to viewpoints in the wetlands by the lake. Union Bay is a walk for nature observers and for those who find pleasure in the wildlife surprises that each walk brings.

ADDRESS: 3501 NE 41st Street, Seattle

GETTING THERE: From I-5, take exit 169 (NE 45th Street/NE 50th Street). Drive east on NE 45th Street and go past the University of Washington and down the viaduct, staying on NE 45th Street. Turn right on Mary Gates Memorial Way following signs to the Center for Urban Horticulture (CUH). The longer preserve walk starts to the west of the parking lot, and Yesler Swamp Trail to the east.

From WA 520 westbound, take the exit for Montlake Boulevard NE and go north. Stay right, passing Husky Stadium and merging with NE 45th Street heading east. Turn right on Mary Gates Memorial Way and proceed as above.

CONTACT: University of Washington Center for Urban Horticulture, (206) 543-8616, http://depts.washington.edu/uwbg/visit/cuh.php. For information on volunteering, visit www.yeslerswamp.org.

<u>29</u> WASHINGTON PARK ARBORETUM

4 miles east of downtown Seattle

Birds and botanical treasures abound in gardens and wetlands in this 194-acre park along Lake Washington.

TRAIL	Waterfront 0.5 miles one way, garden paths at least 4 miles; natural surface
STEEPNESS	Level to gentle
OTHER USES	Bicycles on paved roads only
DOGS	On leash; not allowed in Japanese Garden
CONNECTING TRAILS	None
PARK AMENITIES	Restrooms, playground, classes, flower shows, gift shop, interpretive trail, Japanese Garden (admission fee), visitor center
DISABLED ACCESS	Azalea Way (when dry), restrooms, visitor center

With each season, color lures you deeper into the graceful elegance of the arboretum. Spring and summer bring an explosion of pink and white cherry blossoms; red, purple, and yellow rhododendrons; pink and white camellias; and an artist's palette of other perennials. Fall's warm tones of orange and yellow brighten the trails. Even in winter, the myriad colors of bark, foliage,

and winter berries contrast cheerfully with the drab days; as you walk, look for the striped maples, the tiger bark of the cherry trees, and the sinewy shapes of trees and shrubs.

First-time visitors may want to get a free map of this 194-acre park from the Graham Visitors Center and then set off on Azalea Way, taking small side trips into specialized gardens such as the Winter Garden, the Rhododendron Glen, and the Woodland Garden. Meander over paths on hillsides planted with exotic trees and shrubs. Cross the old stone bridge to the Pinetum for the pungent scent of fir and pine.

Along the Waterfront Trail bordering Lake Washington, birds abound. Here you'll find mallards, coots, and grebes. In spring the tree swallows swoop and dive for insects above the marsh and in the evenings return to their nesting boxes along the trail. Canada geese nest on the hummocks beneath the reeds and cattails. Test your knowledge of marsh plants with the self-guiding tour booklet that illustrates many of the common plants seen here. Whatever your reason for walking, this mature and well-loved park, dating back to 1934, provides constantly changing botanical treasures on its interlacing trails.

ADDRESS: 2300 Arboretum Drive E, Seattle

GETTING THERE: From I-5, take exit 168B (WA 520/Bellevue). Take the first exit (Montlake) from WA 520. Cross Montlake Boulevard NE and wind down the hill to the junction with Lake Washington Boulevard E. Turn right onto the boulevard and then left onto Foster Island Road. As you wind past several parking areas, Graham Visitors Center is on your left; free park maps are available.

From WA 520 westbound, take the Lake Washington Boulevard exit. The ramp turns left over the freeway; at the junction with Lake Washington Boulevard E, turn left. Take the next left onto Foster Island Road and proceed as above.

CONTACT: The Graham Visitors Center, (206) 543-8800, www.uwbotanicgardens.org. Call for volunteer opportunities.

<u>30</u> INTERLAKEN PARK

4.5 miles east of downtown Seattle

Find 52 acres of forested ravines teeming with birds and astounding views from Volunteer Park.

TRAIL	About 1 mile round-trip; natural surface, paved
STEEPNESS	Gentle (paved trail) to steep (natural trails)
OTHER USES	Bicycles
DOGS	On leash
CONNECTING TRAILS	Via short road walk, pathways in Volunteer Park and, when open, Lake View Cemetery
PARK AMENITIES	Benches
DISABLED ACCESS	Paved road (closed to vehicles)—caution: may not meet ADA requirement for a slope of less than 10 percent

Listen for the drumming of pileated woodpeckers or the chatter of squirrels as you stroll a historical greenbelt in the heart of Seattle. Interlaken is a birding hot spot hosting robins, bald eagles, osprey, juncos, pine siskins, flickers, owls, humming-birds, and more. A bird list is posted at the trailhead.

Recommended by the Olmsted brothers for preservation in 1903, Interlaken's forest and ravines boast remains of the region's original evergreen forest. You can walk the gently inclined paved road or climb one of several steep renovated footpaths. Crossing streams, ravines, and hillsides, these paths with an occasional bench for resting offer good exercise and reward hikers with expansive city views.

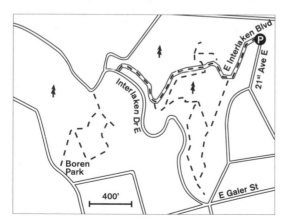

One primitive side trail joins the road at the corner of 19th Avenue and Interlaken Drive E, with more trails in Boren Park.

The Friends of Interlaken Park have been working to restore the trails and remove invasive plants such as English ivy, blackberry, and clematis. They request that hikers stick to the main trails and avoid the

> ## Thank the Visionaries
>
> "We want a ground to which people may easily go after their day's work is done, where they may stroll for an hour, seeing, hearing, and feeling nothing of the bustle and jar of the streets." Building upon the words uttered by their father, Frederick Olmsted Sr., in 1870, Frederick Olmsted Jr. and John Olmsted created public parks and boulevards in Seattle at the dawn of the twentieth century. Many of the parks you walk today, including the Washington Park Arboretum and Interlaken, Ravenna, Lincoln, Myrtle Edwards, Discovery, Schmitz Preserve, and Seward Parks owe their existence to the vision and energy of the Olmsted brothers.

shortcuts. Separated by lush forest from the traffic of Interlaken Drive E, this hillside greenbelt offers silence and nature study with views over Husky Stadium and the Montlake Cut.

Although maps show a continuous greenbelt running west from Washington Park Arboretum (Walk #29) to Volunteer Park, the best walking is from the trailhead at the corner of Interlaken Place E and 21st Avenue E to the junction with Interlaken Drive E. Turn left on the drive and follow the road for 0.5 miles to the historical marker and trailhead for Boren Park. Leave the road and switchback up a shrub- and forest-covered hill to tiny Boren Park with its tall sculpture, benches, and great views.

If you want to extend your walk, cross 15th Avenue E and enter serene Lake View Cemetery. Perched atop Capitol Hill, with views in all directions, this pioneer cemetery welcomes the public during daylight hours. If the cemetery walk is not your thing, go south a block to Volunteer Park for another mile of strolling.

ADDRESS: 2177 E Interlaken Boulevard, Seattle

GETTING THERE: From I-5, take exit 168 (WA 520). Take the Montlake Boulevard exit off WA 520. Turn right onto Montlake Boulevard and go south. It becomes 24th Avenue E. Go 0.5 miles and turn right on Interlaken Boulevard. The trailhead is on the right in about 3 blocks, where the road turns sharply left at 21st Avenue E.

CONTACT: Seattle Parks and Recreation, (206) 684-4075, www.seattle.gov/parks. For information on volunteering, visit www.greenseattle.org, call (206) 684-8028, or e-mail parksvolunteer@seattle.gov.

<u>31</u> THE GRAND FOREST

Bainbridge Island, 12.5 miles west of Seattle (with ferry ride)

A maze of quiet forest trails in three sections offers bird-watching and streamside solitude in these 240 acres.

TRAIL	7 miles; natural surface
STEEPNESS	Gentle to steep
OTHER USES	Bicycles, horses
DOGS	On leash
CONNECTING TRAILS	1.5-mile Forest to Sky Trail to Battle Point Park
PARK AMENITIES	Picnic area, limited parking
DISABLED ACCESS	None

Soft dirt trails quilt this open forest of Douglas firs in large, easy loops. Silence is broken by the sudden birdlike chatter of the tawny Douglas squirrels that patrol the tree trunks and branches like overzealous guardians of the woods. Three separate areas compose Bainbridge's Grand Forest, acquired from the Department of Natural Resources in 1990.

In the Mandus Olson block, called Grand Forest East, map signs along the trail with "You Are Here" dots help steer you around the loops. If your sense of direction is anything less than that of a migrating bird, you'll be glad they're there. So uniform is this forest that without the guidance of low, slanted sunshine it is easy to get turned around. In the southeastern corner a shallow ravine, a deep cradle of fern and shrub, extends to the east. Elsewhere, the understory shrubbery is low enough to give a clear view of the middle layer of pole-like trunks, characteristic of a farmed forest. Above it all spreads the upper story of Douglas fir boughs. With the openness comes great bird-watching possibilities: easy viewing to the tops of shrubs and a chance to see woodpeckers, nuthatches, and brown creepers on the trunks.

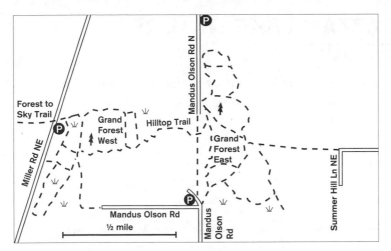

The Hilltop Trail now connects Grand Forest East to the trail system in the Grand Forest West section off Miller Road, just less than a mile away. Here in the west section you can explore a spiderweb of loops in a denser, more varied forest. Big-leaf maple and red alder mix with Douglas fir and western red cedar, and the eastern part is highlighted by a small stream and surrounding wetland. Two parallel trails lead north and south, with tributary paths joining them. Next to the westernmost one is a picnic table. Huge stumps border the trail, doing their work as nurseries for saplings.

The third section, known as Grand Forest North, has another 0.8 miles of trail to explore.

ADDRESS: Mandus Olson Road and 9752 Miller Road NE, Bainbridge Island

GETTING THERE: From the Bainbridge ferry head north out of Winslow on WA 305. To reach the Mandus Olson section, go 1.6 miles north and turn left on Sportsman Club Road. After the school, turn right on New Brooklyn Road. Go 1.3 miles and turn right on Mandus Olson Road. There is limited parking where the road makes a sharp left turn.

To reach the Miller Road section from New Brooklyn Road westbound, go 0.75 miles and turn right on Miller Road. Just past the Bainbridge Gardens nursery (on the left), at the top of a rise, look on the right for a sign for the Grand Forest. Two pullouts provide limited parking.

For the Grand Forest North section, there are several trailheads without parking. Head north on Miller Road; the first trailhead is just north of the northern parking area for Grand Forest West. Continue north to Koura Road, where there are a couple more trailheads.

CONTACT: Bainbridge Island Metro Park and Recreation District, (206) 842-3343, www.biparks.org

32 GAZZAM LAKE NATURE PRESERVE

Bainbridge Island, 14 miles west of Seattle (with ferry ride)

445 acres of towering mature forest surrounds placid Gazzam Lake, and trails lead to beaches on Puget Sound.

TRAIL	6.3 miles; natural surface
STEEPNESS	Gentle to moderate
OTHER USES	Bicycles, horses; pedestrians only on Peters Trail and Close Property
DOGS	On leash
CONNECTING TRAILS	Trails lead to Schel Chelb Park and southwest to the shore
PARK AMENITIES	Two small parking areas, information kiosks, trail signs
DISABLED ACCESS	None

The buffering effect of near-pristine upland forest shields you from the sound of vehicles and allows the chirping, twittering, and chattering noises of small forest animals to resound. The logging history of the region is revealed in the immense moss-softened stumps, still scarred with ax cuts. The quiet, cushioned earth yields beneath your feet, like walking on the soft belly of Mother Earth. Sword ferns create a green and bushy understory. From either of the two trailheads, the path undulates gently, staying wide, and welcoming you near the edge of 13-acre Gazzam Lake,

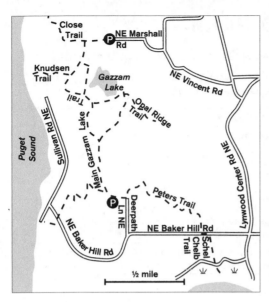

where a few spur trails lead you to the water's edge. Swallows dive and swoop for mosquito meals, and in summer the native yellow water lilies burst forth. Closed to swimming, boating, and fishing, the lake remains an unspoiled habitat for beavers, muskrats, and river otters.

South of the Deerpath Lane parking area, the trail enters an extension of the Gazzam Lake Trail on Peters Property, heading south and downhill to meet the trail leading to Rich Passage. The newer almost 1-mile trail spur, the Gazzam to Veterane Trail, leads west to the sound. Back by the lake, a new spur trail heads up to a ridge. And north of Marshall Road the trail joins the Close Property, a 49-acre addition to the preserve. Well-engineered switchbacks lead down to a

Eagle Food, Not Dog Food

Dead salmon make a tasty meal for hawks and eagles, but don't let your dog near that carcass. Dead salmon can carry a poison called rickettsia, which is not harmful to birds but can be deadly to dogs.

secluded beach on Puget Sound. Before the water comes into view, the forest's scent changes from sweet, fresh water to the bite of salt air.

ADDRESS: Deerpath Lane NE or 6105 NE Marshall Road, Bainbridge Island

GETTING THERE: From the Bainbridge ferry, follow Winslow Way E 0.3 miles and turn right on Madison Avenue N. Take the first left onto Wyatt Way NW. Go 1 mile and turn left on Eagle Harbor Drive NE. Go 0.2 miles and take a slight right onto Bucklin Hill Road NE. This becomes Blakely Avenue NE. Go 1 mile and turn right at NE Baker Hill Road. Go 1.2 miles and turn right on Deerpath Lane NE, where you will find a trailhead on the left. No facilities.

For the Marshall Road trailhead, proceed as above, but after turning onto Bucklin Hill Road, take the first right (a continuation of Bucklin Hill Road). Go 1 mile and turn left at Fletcher Bay Road, then immediately right onto NE Vincent Road. Go 0.5 miles and turn left on NE Marshall Road. Limited parking.

CONTACT: Bainbridge Island Metro Park and Recreation District, (206) 842-3343, www.biparks.org

<u>33</u> FORT WARD PARK

Bainbridge Island, 16 miles west of Seattle (with ferry ride)

Beaches and forest trails on 137 acres provide historic sites, bird-watching, and views of the Olympic Mountains.

TRAIL	3.3 miles; natural surface, paved
STEEPNESS	Level to steep
OTHER USES	Bicycles on paved shoreline path only, horses
DOGS	On leash
CONNECTING TRAILS	1.25-mile Fort Ward to Blakely Harbor Trail
PARK AMENITIES	Restrooms, boat launch, campground, gun battery ruins, interpretive signs, picnic tables, underwater park, viewing blinds
DISABLED ACCESS	Paved shore trail (Pleasant Beach Drive), restrooms, picnic area, upper parking lot

Although it was an extensive military holding in the early 1900s, not much remains of the original Fort Ward except the ruins of two gun emplacements. Today, the appeal of this Bainbridge Island park lies in its sylvan tranquility and water's-edge walking, rather than its military history. In the dense second-growth Northwest forest, the ferns and towering big-leaf maples enclose walkers in a green cocoon.

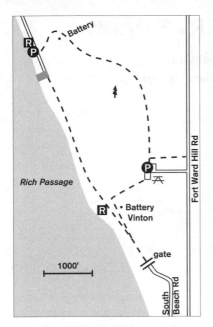

If you park at the boat launch at the northern end of the gated Pleasant Beach Drive, you can warm up with a stroll along the 4,300-foot paved trail bordering Rich Passage. To one side, sword ferns and horsetail vie for space beneath the hulking limbs of big-leaf maples and western red cedars. By the water, delicate white snowberries and wild roses line the path in late summer. Short spur trails lead to the water's edge and blinds for observing herons, cormorants, loons, and maybe harbor seals.

At high or low tide, the best walking may be along the almost-mile-long beach, from which you can more easily smell the fresh salt air, watch ferries negotiate the narrow Rich Passage, and observe the antics of the double-crested cormorants as they stretch and preen on the offshore pilings.

At the southern end of the road, past the bird blind, you can ascend the steep paved trail to the upper picnic area. From here, if the ground is not too muddy, head down the 0.5-mile natural-surface trail back to the lower parking lot where you started. Along the way, you can search the forest trees for Steller's jays and winter wrens. Don't leave the trail, though; poison oak, an uncommon plant in the Northwest, lurks in the undergrowth—green in summer, red in fall.

ADDRESS: 2241 Pleasant Beach Drive NE, Bainbridge Island

GETTING THERE: From the Bainbridge ferry, head north out of Winslow on WA 305. Go 1 mile and turn left on High School Road. Follow the brown state park signs south. In summer, you can enter the upland picnic area (Fort Ward Hill Road) or the boat launch area (Pleasant Beach Drive). In winter, only the boat launch area is open for parking.

CONTACT: Bainbridge Island Metro Park and Recreation District, (206) 842-3343, www.biparks.org

<u>34</u> SCHMITZ PRESERVE PARK

4 miles southwest of downtown Seattle

53 acres of old-growth forest reveal Seattle's roots amid birdlife and a small stream.

TRAIL	1.7 miles; natural surface
STEEPNESS	Gentle
OTHER USES	Pedestrians only
DOGS	On leash
CONNECTING TRAILS	Alki Beach Trail
PARK AMENITIES	Parking lot, interpretive signs
DISABLED ACCESS	None

To stroll in Schmitz Preserve in West Seattle is to sense how the Puget Sound region looked before the arrival of the logging mills. Towering, massive western red cedar, western hemlock, and Douglas fir create an ancient ambience all around. Although it is not pristine—nonnative English ivy invades from the neighborhoods, and a few old stumps reveal the ravages of the logger's saw—most of the forest remains untouched.

Walking the fir needle–lined path, you can hear birds singing, calling, moving about, and seeking food. Listen for the tapping of the pileated woodpecker, the largest North American woodpecker, with its bright-red crown, black-and-white neck, and black body. Nuthatches and brown creepers reside here, as does the less frequently seen or heard western screech owl.

As you meander along a small stream, notice the amount and variety of life that comes from fallen trees. Saplings of alder, hemlock, and Douglas fir send fine

roots into the decaying wood of ancient logs. Shrubs, too, such as red huckleberry and salal, find nutrients and moisture in these downed giants. Tall-standing snags house myriad insects that help supply the avian feeders. Removal of this downed wood and stumps would quickly destroy much of the life of the old forest, where the floor is often too thickly covered by needles and leaves to allow young saplings to grow.

For a more extended walk, stroll Schmitz Boulevard (closed to vehicles) north out of the parking lot. This old paved road leads through a deep ravine under Admiral Way, ending at a neighborhood park and playground.

ADDRESS: 5551 SW Admiral Way, Seattle

GETTING THERE: From I-5 southbound, take exit 163A (West Seattle Bridge/Columbian Way) and stay right. From I-5 northbound, take exit 163 (West Seattle Bridge/Columbian Way) and stay left to get on the West Seattle Bridge. Exit onto SW Admiral Way, following it uphill past a commercial district, then down a hill to SW Stevens Street. Look on the left for the park sign just before crossing a ravine. Turn left on SW Stevens Street, then bear right into the parking lot.

CONTACT: Seattle Parks and Recreation Department, (206) 684-4075, www .seattle.gov/parks. To volunteer, call (206) 684-8028 or e-mail parksvolunteer @seattle.gov.

Forest Playground?

Downed logs, stumps, and springboard holes are not gymnastics equipment. These dead trees might look big and tough, but they're not. Scrambling feet and grabbing hands break off the moss and bark, which harbor the insects that birds eat. Many young saplings can grow only on nurse logs. Teach your children to respect what has taken a long time to grow but takes only a moment to kill.

35 CAMP LONG

5 miles southwest of downtown Seattle

Interpretive trails explore 68 acres of wild forest and ponds; a rock-climbing wall and high ropes invite challenge.

TRAIL	3.2 miles; natural surface, paved
STEEPNESS	Gentle to moderate
OTHER USES	Pedestrians only
DOGS	On leash
CONNECTING TRAILS	None
PARK AMENITIES	Restrooms, brochure, camping, classes, maps, picnic shelters, rock climbing, rustic cabins to rent
DISABLED ACCESS	Rolling Hills Trail, restrooms, cabins

Walking in Camp Long is like finding wildlands in West Seattle. The air is fragrant with earth and greenery and sweet forest smells. Although this city park offers overnight camping (the only public camping in Seattle), these 68 acres hold more than cabins and a lodge. They are, for the day hiker, a place of tranquility and adventure. Beginning at the rustic 1940s lodge, walk left past the cabins to the beginning of the Animal Tracks Nature Trail. This 0.5-mile loop leads past ancient cedar stumps to a newer forest of alder and willow. Plaster casts of raccoon, heron, skunk, coyote, red fox, and squirrel tracks are displayed at the trailhead.

The longer Middle Loop Trail veers off from the nature walk, leading downhill through second-growth forest to the boundary near the golf course. This is a wet trail in winter, but board walkways provide some relief from the mud. Due east of the lodge, you come to Polliwog Pond, where turtles bask, salamanders slither, and water insects hatch. If you're lucky, you may see hawks, owls, or great blue herons.

The park offers classes on wetlands ecology, forest and pond ecology, and forest dwellers. Special park features include a high ropes challenge course, a climbing rock (on which instruction is given by prearrangement), and the "glacier," a concrete and stone structure with handholds and toeholds for climbing and rappelling.

ADDRESS: 5200 35th Avenue SW, Seattle

GETTING THERE: From I-5 southbound, take exit 163A (West Seattle Bridge) and stay right. From I-5 northbound, take exit 163 (West Seattle Bridge), and stay left to get on the West Seattle Bridge. Follow it to its end, staying left. At the first light off the freeway, turn left onto 35th Avenue SW. Go 1 mile and turn left on SW Dawson Street to enter the park. Closed Mondays and holidays year-round, as well as Sundays in January.

CONTACT: Seattle Parks an Recreation Department, (206) 684-7434, www .seattle.gov/parks. To volunteer, call (206) 684-8028 or e-mail parksvolunteer @seattle.gov.

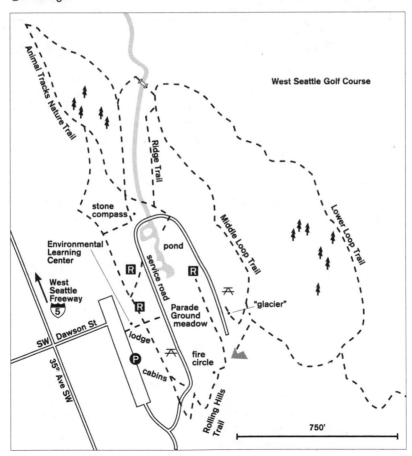

36 LINCOLN PARK

8 miles southwest of downtown Seattle

Bluffs and beaches along Puget Sound offer views of the Olympic Mountains from this 135-acre park.

TRAIL	5.3 miles, including 1 mile on a beach; gravel, paved
STEEPNESS	Level to steep
OTHER USES	Bicycles
DOGS	On leash
CONNECTING TRAILS	None
PARK AMENITIES	Restrooms, picnic shelters, playgrounds, sports fields, wading pool, swimming pool (summer only)
DISABLED ACCESS	Paved beach walk, restrooms, picnic areas

From high on the bluff at Lincoln Park in West Seattle, the barges and ferries look like large bathtub toys on the smooth water below. Madrona trees arch their vibrant red-barked limbs over the trail, and offshore an eagle may glide. These 135 acres of parkland offer lawns, views, beach, and water's-edge walking.

From the parking lots along Fauntleroy Way SW, choose any of the wide, smooth, and graveled paths, and walk west to wander between large old western hemlock and Douglas fir trees. Open lawns and picnic shelters with playgrounds attract many of the park's users, but for a walk, continue west to the bluff. Sloping gently to the south, the paved trail gives views out onto Puget Sound and Vashon Island. Curve around and down to the shore, where fresh breezes from the south stir the water and create waves that clatter the pebbles on the beach.

Wide, paved, and level, the mile of beach walk invites either a slow stroll or a heart-pumping power walk. Winter storms bring waves that crash against the seawall and throw mighty drift logs high on the beach. In milder weather, the shoreline begs for exploration. At the northern end, past the swimming pool, the walkway narrows to a seawall under the branches of a slope of mixed conifers, maples, and red alder. Choose a nonthreatening path up (one that slopes rather than climbs) to return to the upper park.

ADDRESS: 8011 Fauntleroy Way SW, Seattle

GETTING THERE: From I-5 southbound, take exit 163A (West Seattle Bridge/Columbian Way) and stay right. From I-5 northbound, take exit 163 (West Seattle Bridge/Columbian Way), and stay left to get on the West Seattle Bridge. Follow it to its end, and continue straight as it becomes Fauntleroy Way SW and curves left. In about 2 miles, the park is on the right.

CONTACT: Seattle Parks and Recreation Department, (206) 684-4075, www.seattle.gov/parks. To volunteer, call (206) 684-8028 or e-mail parksvolunteer @seattle.gov.

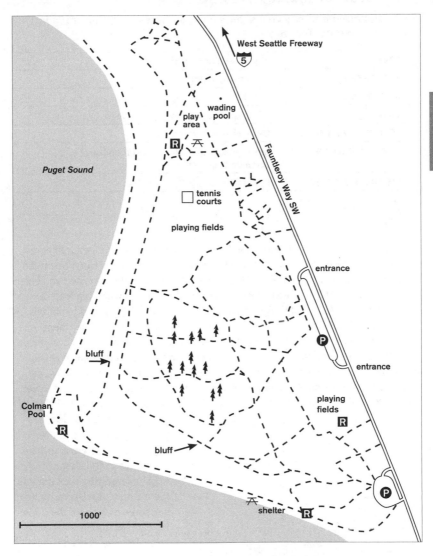

37 WESTCREST PARK

7 miles south of downtown Seattle

Enjoy mountain and city views, then walk 80 acres of sylvan trails in Seattle's largest forest.

TRAIL	4.4 miles; natural surface, paved
STEEPNESS	Level to moderate
OTHER USES	Bicycles
DOGS	Off-leash area, otherwise on leash
CONNECTING TRAILS	Duwamish Watershed Trail
PARK AMENITIES	Restrooms, picnic tables, playground, art, community garden
DISABLED ACCESS	Paved trail

Laid out like a green carpet atop south Seattle, Westcrest Park entices with acres of green lawn, paved trail, and wonderfully innovative playgrounds. But step off the hilltop into the sloping forest of the Duwamish Watershed to the east, and you enter a sylvan land of manicured trails under a canopy of hemlock, fir, and big-leaf maples.

The original Westcrest Park was wrapped squarely along three sides of the West Seattle Reservoir, but in 2011 the reservoir was lidded, and later these 20 acres were included in the park. Artful renovation and construction, completed in 2015, has turned a reservoir lid into beautiful lawn and paved walkways. The play area is particularly interesting, with a modified zip line and an innovative set of slides to help the smallest walkers descend from the upper lawns to the lower paths. Of aesthetic interest are the airplane-like kinetic sculptures by David Boyer,

called *Flyers*. On a clear day you get great views of the Olympics to the west and the Cascades to the east.

The large dog park attracts the majority of walkers, as there are acres of land for the pups to roam, including a separate small and shy dog enclosure. Once they've run their fill, put the dogs back on leash and enjoy the shaded trails to the east that crisscross through

Seattle's largest standing forest, the Duwamish Watershed. Well-maintained trails lead through high-canopy evergreen forest, and trail signs help keep you oriented.

ADDRESS: *South parking lot:* SW Henderson Street, Seattle; *Park location:* 9000 8th Avenue SW, Seattle

GETTING THERE: From WA 99 southbound, merge right onto WA 509. Continue 1.2 miles and take the Myers Way/White Center exit. Stay right to merge onto Olson Way SW. In 0.4 miles turn right onto SW Roxbury Street. Turn right onto 8th Avenue SW. In 0.2 miles turn right onto SW Henderson Street into the park.

From I-5 northbound, take exit 154 (WA 518/Burien) and head west on WA 518. Go 3.2 miles and exit onto WA 509 toward Seattle. In 1.2 miles turn left onto S 128th Street. Go 0.6 miles and turn right onto 4th Avenue SW. Continue 2 miles and turn left onto SW Roxbury Street and proceed as above.

CONTACT: Seattle Parks and Recreation Department, (206) 684-4075, www.seattle.gov/parks. Volunteering is welcome.

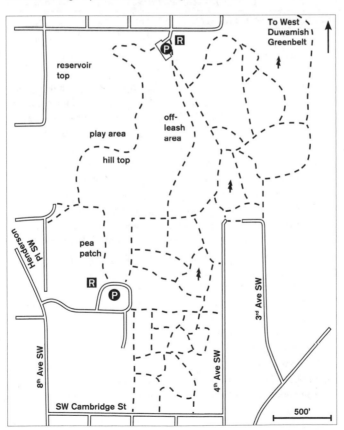

38 LUTHER BURBANK PARK (MERCER ISLAND)

Mercer Island, 6 miles southeast of Seattle

A historical setting with 77 acres on Lake Washington offers wetlands, meadows, and unusual art.

TRAIL	3 miles; natural surface, paved
STEEPNESS	Level to gentle; some steps to lake
OTHER USES	Bicycles
DOGS	Off-leash area, otherwise on leash
CONNECTING TRAILS	None
PARK AMENITIES	Restrooms, picnic areas, boat docks, playground, swimming beach, tennis courts, art
DISABLED ACCESS	Paved trails, restrooms, picnic areas

You can almost imagine the vast hand of the Lake Washington spirit reaching over this northeastern corner of Mercer Island and holding back the surrounding suburbia to preserve this stretch of land. With its grassy meadows, neatly tended lawns, pockets of berries, and bogs, Luther Burbank Park offers breathing space and expansive views across the lake to Bellevue and Seattle.

Once the grounds of a home for wayward Seattle boys, these 77 acres retain a few reminders of days past. Two sturdy brick buildings are all that remain intact of the Boys Parental School (later renamed Luther Burbank School). When you walk north from the building past the elegant poplar and cottonwood trees, stop and explore the ruins of the old barn. For more than 50 years, Holstein cows grazed where boat watchers sit today on the gentle hills of Luther Burbank Park.

At Calkins Point on the northern tip, a marshland harbors frogs and ducks as well as red-winged blackbirds. Bear right and walk south along the waterfront, past the buildings to the docks, tennis courts, and picnic areas. If you've come with kids, plan on a long pause at the playground. This one was created by someone with a fertile imagination: brick hills to climb, endless slides, and swings—all cushioned with tire chips for safe landings.

When you can lure the kids off the brick mountains, head south across the meadow to explore the earth sculpture with its furrows and hills. What a great landscape for make-believe forts or wild games of tag. In summer, the grassy bumps and the nearby beach ring out with the calls of children. Complete the loop

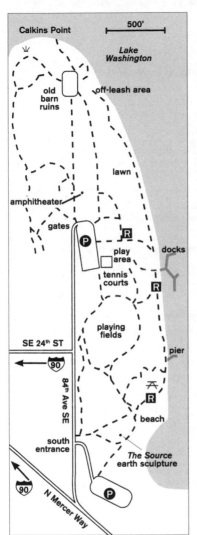

old barn ruins

off-leash area

Calkins Point

Lake Washington

500'

lawn

amphitheater

gates

play area

tennis courts

docks

playing fields

SE 24ᵗʰ ST

84ᵗʰ Ave SE

pier

beach

south entrance

The Source earth sculpture

N Mercer Way

90

90

with a stroll north again along the water's edge, past secret hideouts for the lake's feathered inhabitants, ending at the docks.

ADDRESS: 2040 84th Avenue SE, Mercer Island

GETTING THERE: From I-90 eastbound, take exit 7A (77th Avenue SE). Turn left at the stop sign, go across the freeway, then turn right onto N Mercer Way. Go 0.2 miles and turn left onto 81st Avenue SE. Go to the stop sign and turn right on SE 24th Street. When the road curves right, go left onto 84th Avenue SE into the park.

From I-90 westbound, take exit 7 (Island Crest Way). At the top of the ramp, turn right onto SE 26th Street. In 0.1 miles turn left on 84th Avenue SE to enter the park. The park is open from 6:00 a.m. until 10:00 p.m. daily.

CONTACT: Mercer Island Parks and Recreation Department, (206) 275-7609, www.mercergov.org. To volunteer, call the volunteer coordinator at (206) 275-7841.

SEATTLE

39 PIONEER PARK

Mercer Island, 8 miles southeast of Seattle

Explore 113 acres of forest on a labyrinth of trails in the island's center.

TRAIL	5 miles total; natural surface, paved
STEEPNESS	Gentle to moderate
OTHER USES	Bicycles; horses in southeast section and on Fire Station Trail in northwest section
DOGS	On leash
CONNECTING TRAILS	None
PARK AMENITIES	None; guidebook available at Mercer Island Parks office
DISABLED ACCESS	Much of perimeter trail of northwest section

Wander a labyrinth of trails through second-growth forest in this touch of wildness in the center of Mercer Island. Raccoons leave footprints on the dirt trails, and squirrels chatter from the branches.

Logged about 75 years ago, the forest now supports a variety of trees, including alder, maple, madrona, western hemlock, and Douglas fir. Many have English

ivy (an unwanted volunteer from nearby homes) clinging to their trunks like shaggy blankets or display a fine coating of blue-green lichen on their northern sides.

Park on Island Crest Way near SE 68th Street and dive in. Trails meander through each of the three sections of the park, which intersect at SE 68th Street and Island Crest Way. You can choose the company of horses (in the northwest and southeast sections) or not and choose level (northeast section) or sloping (southeast section) land. With many kid-created side trails, you could possibly get lost, or at least end up in someone's backyard. To maintain your bearings, listen for the traffic on Island Crest Way, and in the southeast section remember that uphill leads to the west and Island Crest Way.

Try a winter walk here, when the cold has hardened the dirt trails. With the leaves gone, you can look out through the sinewy forms of naked branches to Lake Washington. Oregon grape, sword ferns, cedars, and hemlocks all shimmer in vibrant green against the browns and grays of winter bark.

ADDRESS: SE 68th Street and Island Crest Way, Mercer Island

GETTING THERE: From I-90 eastbound, take exit 7B (Island Crest Way). The ramp leads directly onto Island Crest Way southbound. Go about 3 miles, and park at the ball fields on the west side of Island Crest Way at about SE 63rd Street. Limited on-road parking only.

From I-90 westbound, take exit 7 (Island Crest Way). Turn left at the top of the ramp and cross the freeway. Go straight onto Island Crest Way southbound, and proceed as above.

CONTACT: Mercer Island Parks and Recreation Department, (206) 275-7609, www .mercergov.org. To volunteer, call the volunteer coordinator at (206) 275-7841.

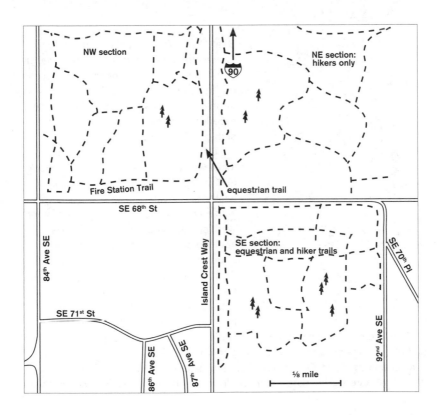

40 SEWARD PARK

6 miles southeast of downtown Seattle

Old-growth forest abounding with birds and beaches along Lake Washington's shoreline offers views of the Cascades from this 299-acre park.

TRAIL	5.7 miles; natural surface, paved
STEEPNESS	Level to gentle
OTHER USES	Bicycles on paved loop only
DOGS	On leash
CONNECTING TRAILS	Lake Washington Boulevard
PARK AMENITIES	Restrooms, amphitheater, art studio, playground, fishing pier, interpretive center, picnic shelters
DISABLED ACCESS	Paved trail, restrooms, picnic shelters

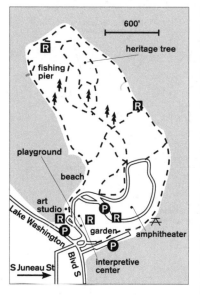

Seattle's largest tract of old-growth forest crowns thumb-shaped Bailey Peninsula, jutting into Lake Washington. Acquired by the city in 1911 as an island, Seward Park was transformed into a peninsula when the lake receded as a result of the building of the ship canal in 1916.

Deep in this forest of immense precolonial western red cedar, western hemlock, and Douglas fir, varied thrushes call in winter, and in spring the forest comes alive with mating songs and calls of the migrant warblers and kinglets. No city sounds impinge on this woodland with its varied undergrowth of sword fern, Oregon grape, thimbleberry, salal, and twinberry. The main trail follows the spine of the gentle ridge, with numerous side trails leading out of the forest to the lakeshore loop walk.

The forest trail and the shore are so different that it's hard to believe they're part of the same park. From the quiet tranquility of the old forest, you emerge to a faster-moving world. On the paved 2.6-mile shore loop, bicycles zoom by, and the in-line skaters skate-dance to music from their headphones. But with grassy

stretches on either side of the trail, there is plenty of room for everyone. In summer the beaches ring with the calls of children, and colorful kayaks can be seen on the calm water.

In fall, the southern part of the shore trail is lined in orange and red feathery sumac, salal, and hedges of snowberries, and the maples flash warm orange and yellow colors against the blue of the lake. Poison oak lurks among the shrubbery; look for its distinctive leaves in sets of three, shiny green in summer and turning red in fall. Tall madrona trees with their beautiful peeling bark accent the trail edges. Standing on the lakeshore in winter, you may see a variety of wintering waterfowl such as mergansers, grebes, and wigeons.

ADDRESS: 5900 Lake Washington Boulevard S, Seattle

GETTING THERE: From I-5 southbound, take exit 163A (Columbian Way) and stay left to cross the freeway onto Columbian Way. If northbound, take exit 163 and stay right to get on Columbian Way. Go southeast 1.4 miles and turn right on Beacon Avenue S. Go about 0.5 miles and turn left on S Orcas Street. Head east and at the T-junction at Lake Washington Boulevard S, turn right, then immediately left into the park.

CONTACT: Seattle Parks and Recreation Department, (206) 684-4396, www.seattle.gov/parks. For information on volunteering, visit the Friends of Seward Park website: www.sewardpark.org.

41 KUBOTA GARDEN

7 miles southeast of downtown Seattle

This 34-acre Japanese garden features a stream, ponds, native and ornamental plants, and art.

TRAIL	1.5 miles total; gravel, natural surface
STEEPNESS	Level to steep
OTHER USES	Pedestrians only
DOGS	Not allowed
CONNECTING TRAILS	None
PARK AMENITIES	Restrooms, gardens, benches, free guided tours on weekends (except in winter), map, picnic tables
DISABLED ACCESS	Some paths

This public garden, featuring exotic plants, walkways wide and narrow, waterfalls, and ponds is a place for meditation and quiet strolls. Pleasure comes not only from the visual but from the almost tactile sense of shape and design.

Originally a nursery of 20 acres surrounding an ambitious system of streams and waterfalls, and later passed on to Seattle by the Kubota family, the garden continues to provide a place of beauty through form and color, texture and fragrance. Labeling plants was not a priority of the Kubotas, nor is it now. Mature rhododendrons—some 15 feet high and of unknown lineage—bloom in spring, livening the garden with robust color. Migrating songbirds find refuge here, filling the air with their calls. Japanese red and black pines and both yellow and black bamboo grace the paths.

This is a garden for meandering, for viewing from all directions. You may have passed the arched Moon Bridge before, but now you tilt your head another way, the sun has dropped lower, and the garden reveals yet another aspect of color, texture, or shape. Climb the "Mountainside" to enjoy territorial views and perhaps to watch the golden carp in the Necklace of Ponds, 65 feet below. Experience the garden in all seasons and watch the colors and textures change.

ADDRESS: 9817 55th Avenue S, Seattle

GETTING THERE: From I-5 southbound, take exit 158 (Boeing Access Road). Turn left to cross the freeway and head straight up S Ryan Way. At the T-junction, turn left on 51st Avenue S. Turn right on Renton Avenue S, then right on 55th Avenue S. The parking entrance is on the right.

From I-5 northbound, take exit 157 (Martin Luther King Jr. Way). Follow Martin Luther King Jr. Way to S Ryan Way, turn right, and proceed as above.

CONTACT: Kubota Garden Foundation, (206) 725-5060, www.kubotagarden.org; Seattle Parks and Recreation Department, (206) 684-4584, www.seattle.gov /parks. Volunteering is welcome.

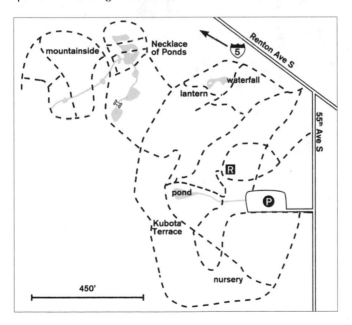

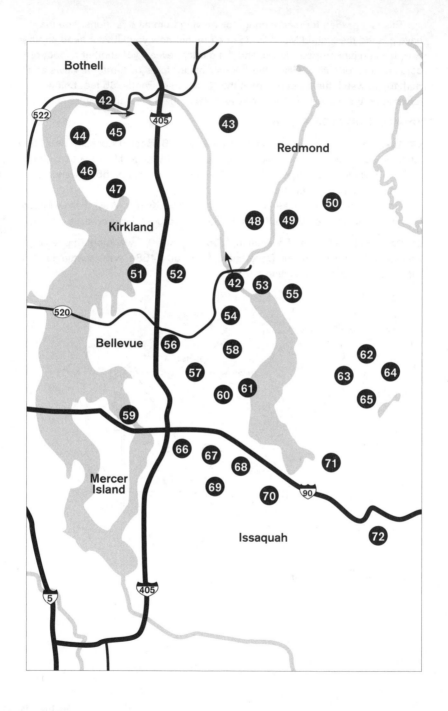

EASTSIDE
Bellevue, Redmond, and Issaquah

EASTSIDE

<u>42</u> SAMMAMISH RIVER TRAIL

Bothell, 13 miles northwest of Bellevue, to Redmond, 6 miles
northeast of Bellevue

*Walk or jog the Sammamish Slough's meadows and wetlands, with
their wood sculptures and Cascade views.*

TRAIL	9.4 miles one way; paved
STEEPNESS	Level
OTHER USES	Bicycles, horses
DOGS	Off-leash area in Marymoor Park, otherwise leash and scoop
CONNECTING TRAILS	Burke-Gilman Trail (Walk #25), Puget Power Trail (Walk #48), Marymoor Park (Walk #53)
PARK AMENITIES	Restrooms, picnic shelters, playing fields at various parks
DISABLED ACCESS	Trail, restrooms

Along this ribbon of still-rural Washington just minutes off I-405 and WA 520, you'll find miles and miles of walking opportunity. Listen to the soft murmur of water, and inhale the clean air of the countryside. In Redmond the trail borders Haida House, the studio of Dudley Carter, late artist in residence for King County, whose huge wood sculptures can be seen both there and at nearby Marymoor Park. Farther north, near 124th Street, you pass close to the Chateau Ste. Michelle winery, where a free tour may lure you in from the walk.

The trail follows the grassy banks of the gently flowing Sammamish River, which connects Lake Sammamish to Lake Washington. Although surrounded to the east and west by the creeping

Nasty Nettle or Yummy Veggie?

Nettles make a tasty vegetable, rich in vitamins, if cut young and steamed up for supper. But most of us meet them on the trail—on a tender bit of leg or arm. When brushed, the plant's little hairs break off, injecting formic acid—the same stuff we hate to get from biting ants. Baking soda will help neutralize the sting. But natural antidotes? Some say rubbing the brown spores of the sword fern on the spot helps. Others say the juice from the stem of wild impatiens (jewelweed) does the trick. If you don't normally have any baking soda with you, try rubbing with one of these plants. It might work. Native Americans used to flail themselves with stinging nettle to stay awake while out fishing all night on the Sound. Ouch!

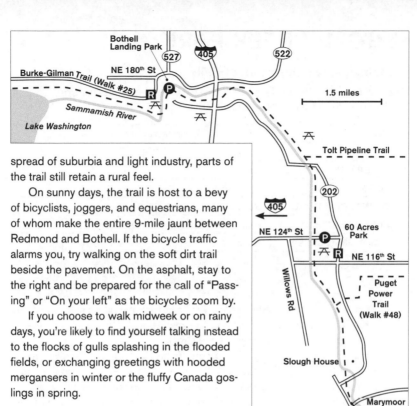

spread of suburbia and light industry, parts of the trail still retain a rural feel.

On sunny days, the trail is host to a bevy of bicyclists, joggers, and equestrians, many of whom make the entire 9-mile jaunt between Redmond and Bothell. If the bicycle traffic alarms you, try walking on the soft dirt trail beside the pavement. On the asphalt, stay to the right and be prepared for the call of "Passing" or "On your left" as the bicycles zoom by.

If you choose to walk midweek or on rainy days, you're likely to find yourself talking instead to the flocks of gulls splashing in the flooded fields, or exchanging greetings with hooded mergansers in winter or the fluffy Canada goslings in spring.

ADDRESS: *Park at Bothell Landing:* 9919 NE 180th Street, Bothell; *Marymoor Park:* 6046 W Lake Sammamish Parkway NE, Redmond

GETTING THERE: *Park at Bothell Landing:* From I-5 northbound, take exit 171 (WA 522/ Bothell/Lake City Way) and drive north 9.3 miles. In Bothell turn right on NE 180th Street into the Park at Bothell Landing.

From I-405 northbound take exit 23, or 23B from southbound (WA 522 W/ Bothell). Head west on WA 522 for 6.5 miles toward Bothell/Kenmore, and turn left on NE 180th Street into the Park at Bothell Landing.

Marymoor Park: See Walk #53 for directions. As you enter the park on the western side you will see the paved trail to your left, before crossing the river. A small parking fee applies.

CONTACT: King County Parks, (206) 477-4527, www.kingcounty.gov/recreation/parks

43 GOLD CREEK PARK

Woodinville, 12 miles north of Bellevue

Shaded forest trails make a good dry-weather workout through 35 acres above a peaceful creek.

TRAIL	2.8 miles total; natural surface
STEEPNESS	Steep
OTHER USES	Horses
DOGS	On leash
CONNECTING TRAILS	None
PARK AMENITIES	Picnic area, restrooms, lodge, map sign
DISABLED ACCESS	None

At first glance, this secluded county park with its stream and picnic area appears to offer nothing for a walker. But hidden behind a mantle of blackberries, a well-used trail climbs a forested ravine alongside Gold Creek.

The trail-map sign, drawn by a Boy Scout for his Eagle project, shows two loops, one north and the other south. Both begin with a steep climb up the edge of Gold Creek in quiet woods. The year-round creek gives moisture to the air, increasing the rich scent of humus and greenery. The trails in this park are used equally by walkers and horses, so they tend to be narrow, rough, and in places

worn into ruts by hooves. Always be aware that you might be sharing the trail with riders; step aside and let them pass.

For the south loop, take the first trail to the right, as it switches back higher on the hillside. Rising to a ridge, you leave the forest cover for a moment to touch the edge of suburbia, and then dive back into the green shelter like that which used to cover most of the Eastside 40 or 50 years ago before the housing developments came. Now on the north loop trail, you descend past Douglas firs and western red cedars up to 2 feet in diameter. Here downed logs and open glens invite a rest or picnic.

Throughout, the trail is steep, rising and falling on the contours of the west-sloping hill. This is a great training walk, or one to challenge your children. A mossy fence marks the northern park boundary. Descend finally to the Gold Creek streambed and return to the trailhead.

In this swatch of wildness there are few landmarks, except your memory of going along the edge of a ravine or a particularly steep hillside. Heading down, on any trail, should eventually return you to the trailhead.

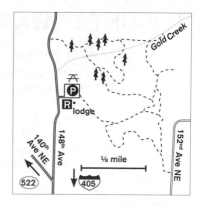

ADDRESS: 16020 148th Avenue NE, Woodinville

GETTING THERE: From I-405 northbound, take exit 20B (NE 124th Street). Turn right on NE 124th Street. Go 2.5 miles and turn left on Highway 202 (Woodinville/Redmond Road NE). Go straight for 1.5 miles. At a four-way stop go straight onto 148th Avenue NE. After 0.5 miles continue straight to stay on 148th Avenue NE. The park is 0.25 miles ahead on the right.

From I-405 southbound, take exit 23A (WA 522 E to WA 202, Woodinville, Monroe), staying left to merge onto WA 522. Take the Woodinville/Redmond exit. At the end of the ramp, turn right. Go straight and turn left on NE 175th Street. Turn right on 140th Avenue NE, go about 1.5 miles, and look for 148th Avenue NE merging on the left. Take a sharp left (almost a U-turn) onto 148th Avenue NE and go 0.25 miles uphill to the park on the right.

CONTACT: King County Parks, (206) 477-4527, www.kingcounty.gov/recreation/parks

<u>44</u> SAINT EDWARD STATE PARK

Kenmore, 12 miles northwest of Bellevue

Wander 316 acres of forested ravines and follow a stream flowing down to 3,000 feet of shoreline on Lake Washington.

TRAIL	7.5 miles total; natural surface, paved
STEEPNESS	Moderate to steep
OTHER USES	Bicycles prohibited (except on one trail); horses in southeast corner
DOGS	On leash
CONNECTING TRAILS	Big Finn Hill Park (Walk #45)
PARK AMENITIES	Restrooms, picnic areas, playing fields, swimming pool, tennis and racquetball courts, trail-map sign, gardens
DISABLED ACCESS	Paved trail around buildings, restrooms, buildings

Deep ravines cutting through a forest of mixed conifer, madrona, and big-leaf maple characterize this 316-acre park, the largest piece of undeveloped property on Lake Washington. Coyotes roam the grounds in early evening, and bald eagles often nest along the shoreline. The woodlands provide shelter for many foraging and upper-canopy birds, and red-tailed hawks cruise the open edges of the meadow. Waterfowl on the lakefront include grebes, geese, and all the native ducks.

With the parking lot on a rise high above the lake, the trails in Saint Edward are among the steepest found in the region. If the narrow leaf-strewn trails on hillsides daunt you, use the wide, gently graded Seminary Trail to reach the grassy "beach" on the waterfront. For more of a challenge, try the North Trail, which traverses a densely wooded hillside above a stream. Look here for white three-petaled trillium blooming in the spring. If you want to increase your aerobic exercise, return via the Grotto Trail: it's a strenuous but beautiful climb overlooking the graceful curve of a fern-draped grotto where weddings are often held.

Scattered among the hemlock, cedar, and Oregon ash, you'll see massive stumps with springboard notches cut more than 75 years ago. Look along the shoreline for rusted chains entangling many fallen trees. These are all that remain of the log boom once moored offshore.

ADDRESS: 14445 Juanita Drive NE, Kenmore

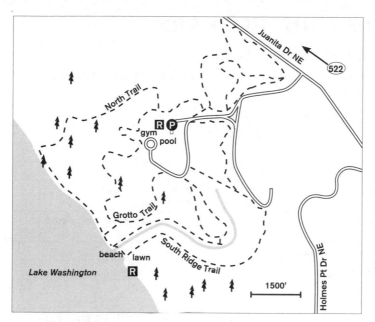

GETTING THERE: From I-405 northbound, take exit 20A (NE 116th Street). Turn left on NE 116th Street and go 1.5 miles to the light at 100th Avenue NW. Go straight through the light onto Juanita Drive NE. Go about 4 miles and, at the top of the hill, turn left into the park. At the fork, bear right and go up the hill to the parking lot. A Discover Pass is required for parking.

From I-5, take exit 171 (WA 522) and continue north over the top of Lake Washington. Turn south on 68th Avenue NE, which becomes Juanita Drive NE. Go 1.75 miles to the park entrance on your right and proceed as above.

CONTACT: Washington State Parks, (425) 823-2992, www.parks.wa.gov

45 BIG FINN HILL PARK

Kirkland, 8 miles north of Bellevue

Wander past wetlands and ball fields into forested ravines in this 220-acre park.

TRAIL	9.5 miles; natural surface
STEEPNESS	Level to moderate
OTHER USES	Bicycles
DOGS	On leash
CONNECTING TRAILS	Saint Edward State Park (Walk #44) and O. O. Denny Park (Walk #46)
PARK AMENITIES	Restrooms, picnic tables, playground, interpretive signs, ball fields
DISABLED ACCESS	None

Stroll along the low banks of the headwaters of Denny Creek. Listen to the sound of Pacific tree frogs near the pond. If the ground is saturated, you may choose to walk the gated service road that cuts the park from east to west, or on drier days, hike the natural trail cushioned with needles from the Douglas fir and western hemlock. Nurse stumps throughout the forest provide nutrients for huckleberry and salal. Like other second-growth forests in Western Washington, the trees of Big Finn Hill hide many mysteries of the past. Walking along the edge of the headwaters of Denny Creek, you'll see large stumps with rectangular slashes cut in their sides. These springboard notches are evidence of logging here about a century ago. Many of the stumps are burned from a long-ago fire. An orchard and remnants of a residence give further clues to the past use of this forested hillside. Nonnative birch trees might have flanked the entrance to the homestead entrance. Whether the homesteaders logged then burned the forest or their residence burned we may never know.

In spring this park buzzes with the cheers and calls of dozens of softball and baseball teams, and parking can be problematic. But most of the year the park provides open lawns for picnics, a bright playground area, and the richly scented western red cedar and Douglas fir forest. Wooden footbridges and an interpretive brochure have been created by Lake Washington School District's Environmental and Adventure School in conjunction with King County.

To get to the western half of the park, you have to cross Juanita Drive without a crosswalk, but here you'll find older forest, huge madrona trees, and more miles

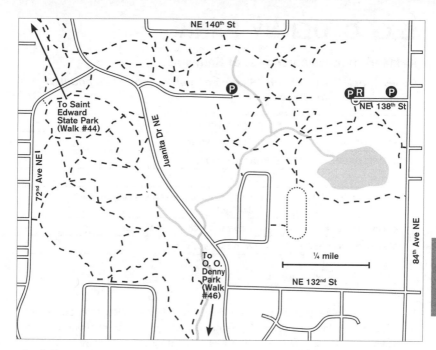

To Saint Edward State Park (Walk #44)

NE 140th St

72nd Ave NE

Juanita Dr NE

NE 138th St

84th Ave NE

To O. O. Denny Park (Walk #46)

¼ mile

NE 132nd St

of trail. To the north, you can connect to the extensive trail system of Saint Edward State Park, and to the south and west, smaller trails lead down Denny Creek to O. O. Denny Park and Lake Washington. On weekends and after school hours bike riders hit the trails, so choose another walking time or keep dogs and children close at hand, and be alert to the silent wheels.

ADDRESS: NE 138th Street and Juanita Drive, Kirkland

GETTING THERE: From I-405 northbound, take exit 20A (NE 116th Street). Turn left on NE 116th Street and go 1.5 miles to the light at 100th Avenue NW. Go straight through the light onto Juanita Drive NE. Go about 3 miles and turn right into the park.

From I-5, take exit 171 (WA 522) and continue north over the top of Lake Washington. Turn south on 68th Avenue NE, which becomes Juanita Drive NE. Go 2.4 miles to the park entrance on your left.

CONTACT: King County Parks, (206) 477-4527, www.kingcounty.gov/recreation/parks

<u>46</u> O. O. DENNY PARK

Kirkland, 11 miles northwest of Bellevue

Denny Creek flows through 46 acres of mature forest to a popular Lake Washington beach.

TRAIL	1-mile loop; natural surface
STEEPNESS	Moderate to steep
OTHER USES	Pedestrians only
DOGS	On leash
CONNECTING TRAILS	Via neighborhood streets: Big Finn Hill Park (Walk #45)
PARK AMENITIES	Restrooms, beach, picnic shelter
DISABLED ACCESS	Restrooms, beach area

Follow the contours of a ridge above Denny Creek in dense western red cedar and western hemlock stands. Sword ferns create a tufted carpet of undergrowth to hide mice, voles, and shrews. This forest of century-old trees is much as it might have been when Seattle developer O. O. Denny stepped ashore to survey the land for a homesite in the early 1900s.

To reach the forest trailhead, cross the road and start up the forest path to the right of the parking lot. The trail climbs steeply high above the ravine formed by the creek. At the top of the ridge, a graveled road intersects the trail. Turn around here or go left, through a small clearing past a pump house.

In summer you may see berry-rich scat lying on the ground at frequent intervals. Not cat, bear, dog, or deer. Coyote. These carnivores turn into berry eaters when other food is scarce or when berries are easy to forage. In the sunny patches on this western sloping hill, the salal and blackberries are abundant.

To complete the loop, cross the wooden bridge with interpretive signs, and descend into the Denny Creek ravine. Marvelous cedar and Douglas fir stumps hint at the past majesty of this forest. Members of the Finn Hill Alliance help maintain and improve this precious enclave of old forest.

On the beach side of the park, the creek has gouged an impressive ravine in its last push to the Sound. Stroll the grassy lawns, enjoy views of Mount Rainier, and watch for bald eagles overhead.

ADDRESS: 12032 Holmes Point Drive NE, Kirkland

GETTING THERE: From I-405 northbound, take exit 20A (NE 116th Street) and turn left on NE 116th Street. Go 1.4 miles to the light at 100th Avenue NW. Go straight through the light onto Juanita Drive NE. Go another 2 miles and turn left on 76th Place NE, which becomes Holmes Point Drive NE. Look for the park after 1 mile.

From I-405 southbound, take exit 20 (NE 124th Street). Turn right at the end of the ramp, and get in the left lane. Turn left at the first light onto 120th Avenue NE. Turn right on NE 116th Street and proceed as above.

CONTACT: Kirkland Parks and Community Services Department, (425) 587-3300, www.kirklandwa.gov/depart/parks.htm. To volunteer, contact www.finnhillalliance.org

47 JUANITA BAY PARK

Kirkland, 8 miles north of Bellevue

Boardwalks traverse 110 acres of wetlands along Lake Washington amid waterfowl and beaver ponds.

TRAIL	1.3 miles; boardwalk, paved
STEEPNESS	Level to gentle
OTHER USES	Bicycles
DOGS	On leash
CONNECTING TRAILS	None
PARK AMENITIES	Restrooms, interpretive signs, nature tours, picnic tables
DISABLED ACCESS	All trails, restrooms

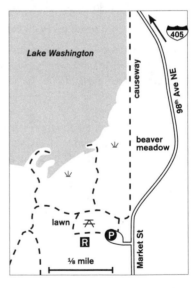

An apron of green lawn spreads out from the streets of suburbia, creating an elegant separation between the man-made and the natural. Below the lawns, hidden from casual view, are boardwalks that meander into natural marshes where blackbirds nest, turtles sun, frogs leap, and cattails sway in lakeside breezes.

This corner of Lake Washington has had a long and active past. Native Americans gathered food here on the shores of the once-higher lake. Later came the frog farmers and the truck gardeners, both working with the land and lake as it was. In 1932 a Kirkland real estate agent began an onslaught against nature by dumping thousands of truckloads of cedar bark, sawdust, and dirt to fill in the marshes and build a golf course. But the inexorable water won out, and despite berms and pumps, the course was finally closed in 1975.

Slowly, now, the lake reclaims its shaggy marsh shoreline. You can observe this wetland either from the broad paved causeway on the eastern edge of the lake or from the boardwalks that wend their way into the thickets of cattails and reeds.

Here you may see mallards and teals dabbling, mergansers diving, or beavers gliding across their carefully crafted ponds.

ADDRESS: 2201 Market Street, Kirkland

GETTING THERE: From I-405 northbound, take exit 20A (NE 116th Street). Turn left on NE 116th Street and go about 1.5 miles. Turn left (south) on 98th Avenue NE (which becomes Market Street), bordering the park. Turn right into the parking lot.

From I-405 southbound, take exit 20 (NE 124th Street). Turn right at the end of the ramp, and get in the left lane. Turn left onto 100th Avenue NE, which becomes 98th Avenue NE, which becomes Market Street. The park and parking lot are on the right.

CONTACT: Kirkland Parks and Community Services Department, (425) 587-3300, www.kirklandwa.gov/depart/parks.htm

48 PUGET POWER TRAIL

Redmond, 10 miles northeast of Bellevue

Meadows, rolling hills, and Cascade views merge into forest along Bear Creek.

TRAIL	3 miles one way; gravel, natural surface
STEEPNESS	Gentle to steep
OTHER USES	Bicycles, horses
DOGS	On leash
CONNECTING TRAILS	Sammamish River Trail (Walk #42), Farrel-McWhirter Farm Park (Walk #49), Watershed Preserve (Walk #50)
PARK AMENITIES	None
DISABLED ACCESS	None

Just north of downtown Redmond, this rugged stretch of green space is appealing for its ups and downs, bushes alive with birds, and striking views of the Cascades.

If walking under power lines is not your idea of fun, forget this trail. But perhaps you can play mental games to imagine these towering structures as some sort of 1950s *War of the Worlds* creatures or go into engineering bliss imagining the equations necessary to erect them. Or maybe, like the wildlife that frequents these corridors of steel and wire, you can ignore them. As you walk along the trail, look for scat and telltale footprints in mud. As for larger mammals, this corridor that stretches from the Sammamish River to Farrel-McWhirter Farm Park (Walk #49) boasts coyotes, raccoons, possums, deer, and lynx.

At the western end, the trail is accessible only from the Sammamish River Trail (Walk #42), between 60 Acres Park (off NE 116th Street) and downtown Redmond (off NE 85th Street near the city offices). As it heads east, the trail varies in its surroundings, sometimes following country roads, at other times bordering neighborhoods and backyards. There are several street crossings; be cautious at Redmond-Woodinville Road, which has a crossing light. For much of the trail, you walk in a narrow greenbelt of Scotch broom, blackberry, salmonberry, and horsetail. (Sometimes real horse tails, too, as you pass the fence of a friendly equine.)

After crossing Avondale Road (use the stoplight), the trail enters quiet second-growth forest, where evidence of long-ago logging shows in springboard slots on the moss-covered stumps. This is the more peaceful, magical end of the trail, with a soft, fir-needled path underfoot, a bridge over Bear Creek, and in spring, the pinkish floral bells of salal. The trail's east end is easily accessed at Farrel-McWhirter Farm Park (Walk #49).

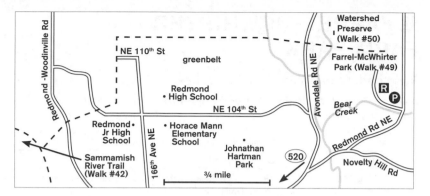

From Farrell-McWhirter east, the trail passes through more forest and wetland until it passes Redmond's Watershed Preserve (walk #50). From there the trail is a wetland for much of the year. Where you turn around depends on your time and mood. The trail is great for power walks and training but also for quiet contemplation. You might decide to set your sights on a certain street crossing. But be warned: there's always the lure of another Cascades view to draw you onward.

ADDRESS: 10403 Woodinville-Redmond Road NE. Trail crossing only. See connecting trails.

GETTING THERE: *60 Acres Park:* From I-405 northbound, take exit 20 (NE 124th Street). From I-405 southbound, take exit 20B (NE 124th Street). Go east on NE 124th Street about 1.5 miles and turn right on Willow Road NE. Go 1.5 miles and turn left on NE 116th Street. Once you cross the Sammamish Slough, park at 60 Acres Park. Walk south on the Sammamish River Trail about 0.5 miles, looking for the power lines and the sign for the Puget Power Trail on your left.

Farrell-McWhirter Farm Park: See Walk #49 for directions.

CONTACT: Redmond Parks and Recreation Department, (425) 556-2300, www.ci.redmond.wa.us/parksrecreation

49 FARREL-MCWHIRTER FARM PARK

Redmond, 10 miles northeast of Bellevue

Mackey Creek bisects 68 acres of mature forest and fields full of farm animals.

TRAIL	2 miles total; natural surface, paved
STEEPNESS	Level to gentle
OTHER USES	Bicycles on paved surfaces, horses on the Perimeter Loop Trail
DOGS	On leash
CONNECTING TRAILS	Puget Power Trail (Walk #48)
PARK AMENITIES	Restrooms, classes, horse arena, orienteering course, picnic shelters, playground
DISABLED ACCESS	Paved trail, restrooms (via gravel area), buildings

Beyond the seductive green lawn, the picnic area, and the farm animals lies an inviting swath of mature (nearly 100-year-old) forest. Wide natural trails form a loop inside the park for walkers, while horseback riders are confined to the outer trail and arena area.

Cool, shallow Mackey Creek bisects the park—open spaces to the south, forest to the north. In summer, day campers study the flora and fauna of the forest and stream habitat and learn to care for the rabbits, goats, pigs, ponies, ducks, and chickens.

To explore the forest, bid adieu to the animals and head north on paved Charlotte's Trail, then turn right into the forest on the wide soft-surfaced Upland Loop Trail. Wander under stately Douglas fir and inhale the spicy scent of western red cedar. In spring, orange and yellow salmonberries and white trillium punctuate the lush greenery, and white blackberry flowers promise sweet fruits for summer. Look for evidence of deer, and listen for the shriek of the red-tailed hawk high overhead.

> ### Tree of Life
> Native Americans had so many uses for the western red cedar that they called it the "tree of life." The wood made logs for houses, canoes, and household items. From the bark, they wove baskets and clothing. The needles made a natural insect repellent. The shredded bark served as diapers. Many Native Americans believed that leaning your back against the trunk infused strength.

ADDRESS: 19483 Redmond Road, Redmond

GETTING THERE: From I-405, take exit 14 (WA 520/Redmond) east, and merge onto Avondale Road. Go about 1 mile, and turn right on Novelty Hill Road. Go 0.25 miles and turn left on Redmond Road. Go 0.5 miles and turn left into the park.

From I-5, take exit 168B (WA 520, Bellevue) across Lake Washington. Continue east on WA 520, and proceed as above.

CONTACT: Redmond Parks and Recreation Department, (425) 556-2300, www.ci.redmond.wa.us/parksrecreation

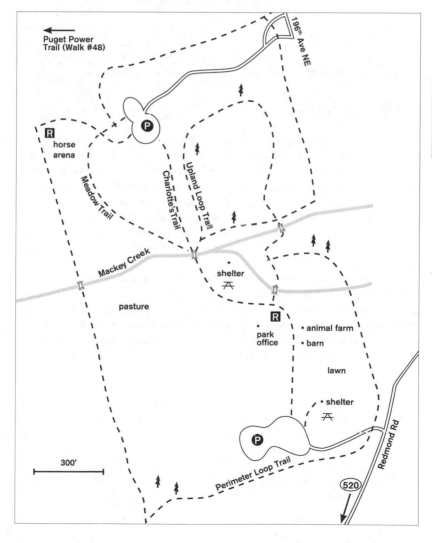

50 WATERSHED PRESERVE

Redmond, 11 miles northeast of Bellevue

800 acres of forest, wetlands, and Seidel Creek create habitat for many animals and birds.

TRAIL	7.5 miles total; natural surface, paved
STEEPNESS	Level to moderate
OTHER USES	Bicycles on multiuse trail, horses
DOGS	Not permitted
CONNECTING TRAILS	Puget Power Trail (Walk #48), Tolt Pipeline Trail
PARK AMENITIES	Restrooms, interpretive trail, maps
DISABLED ACCESS	Treefrog Loop interpretive trail, restrooms

Stroll the wetlands and ridges of richly scented forest in one of the Eastside's premier natural preserves. Crossed by streams and highlighted by fir- and maple-covered ridges and fern-filled ravines, this preserve is home to black-tailed deer, beavers, wood ducks, and playful, chattering Douglas squirrels. Close observers may see signs of black bears, and possibly coyotes and cougars.

Just minutes from WA 520, you can choose the short (0.3-mile) paved Treefrog Loop Trail with interpretive signs and benches by a beaver pond, or a heartier walk along the Siler's Mill Trail or Trillium Trail above the Seidel Creek ravine for a total of more than 5 miles.

There are two entrances to the park, and two regional trails cross the preserve: the Puget Power Trail (Walk #48), running east and west, is accessed at the preserve's southern entrance, and the Tolt Pipeline Trail, running north and south, is accessed at either the southern or northern entrance. These two multiuse trails add more than 4 miles of access for cyclists, hikers, and equestrians alike. Trails are clearly signposted for usage: multiuse, equestrian (which also allow hikers), or hikers only.

These sloping forests and wetlands were purchased from the Weyerhaeuser corporation in the 1920s and 1940s with the goal of creating a new water supply for the city of Redmond. But water quality never met state standards, and the land came up for use proposals ranging from an airport to a golf course to commercial development. In 1989 the City of Redmond began restoring habitat and establishing a systematic network of trails; in 1997 the preserve was dedicated.

Because of the sensitive nature of the wetlands and almost 100-year-old forest, pets of all kinds are prohibited within the preserve.

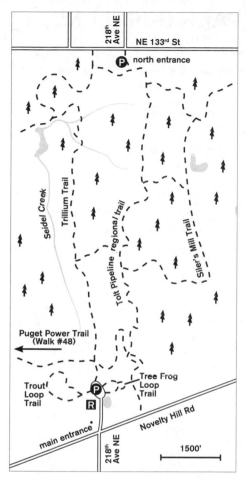

ADDRESS: 21760 Novelty Hill Road, Redmond

GETTING THERE: From I-405, take exit 14 (WA 520/Redmond) east to its end at Avondale Road. Continue straight on Avondale Road, and after 1.25 miles turn right on Novelty Hill Road. Drive 2.4 miles to 218th Avenue NE. The Watershed Preserve parking area is on the left.

From I-5, take exit 168B (WA 520/Bellevue) across Lake Washington. Continue east on WA 520 to its end at Avondale Road, and proceed as above.

CONTACT: Redmond Parks and Recreation Department, (425) 556-2300, www.ci.redmond .wa.us/parksrecreation

EASTSIDE

51 WATERSHED PARK (KIRKLAND)

Kirkland, 3.5 miles north of Bellevue

A meadow has Mount Rainier views, and the forested ravine hides a stream in this 73-acre park.

TRAIL	2.8 miles total; natural surface
STEEPNESS	Gentle to steep
OTHER USES	Bicycles allowed but pedestrians only preferred
DOGS	On leash
CONNECTING TRAILS	None
PARK AMENITIES	Interpretive tours
DISABLED ACCESS	None

Sunlight traces dancing pictures on the path. Bird calls and songs lilt from one tree to another. Mount Rainier stands tall above a valley of yellow Scotch broom. A clear pool quenches the thirst of a family of coyotes. And all of this is just minutes from both Kirkland and Bellevue.

From the 1930s to the late 1960s, a small reservoir in the watershed was built to supply Kirkland's water needs, but the system had too many leaks, and in 1967 Kirkland hooked up with Seattle for water. Today all that remain of this human effort are an empty reservoir and a few pipes partially buried beneath bracken and sword ferns.

For easy walking, follow the chip-lined paths from the 114th Avenue entrance in a long loop at the eastern edge of the for-

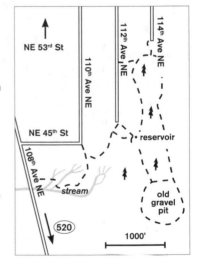

est, where rufous-sided towhees and Bewick's wrens hop about on the forest floor and in the branches of the madrona and maple trees. At the southern end, you come to a ridge above a Scotch broom–filled valley, carved out 35 years ago for gravel to build I-405. A sandy footpath that dips down into the valley makes another appealing walking loop.

From the 112th Avenue entrance, a steep but well-maintained trail heads west, sloping down and around old stumps and seedling-covered nurse logs. Follow the path into the ravine. Here, less freeway noise intrudes on the forest sounds, and soon the sound of the stream dominates. In the quiet, clear pool, shadows of minnows pattern the sandy bottom.

ADDRESS: 4500 110th Avenue NE, Kirkland

GETTING THERE: From I-405, take exit 14 (WA 520/Seattle) west, and exit immediately onto 108th Avenue NE. Go about 1 mile north, turn right on NE 45th Street, and continue until you reach 110th Avenue NE where you can park on the street. Alternatively, continue farther north on 108th Avenue NE and turn right onto NE 53rd Street, then turn right on either 112th Avenue NE or 114th Avenue NE and park at the end of the street; it's on-street parking in any case.

From I-5, take exit 168B (WA 520/Bellevue) across Lake Washington. Take the Kirkland (Lake Washington Boulevard NE) exit. Turn left at the end of the ramp, cross the freeway, and turn right on Northup Way. At the next light, turn left on 108th Avenue NE and proceed as above.

CONTACT: Kirkland Parks and Community Services Department, (425) 587-3300, www.kirklandwa.gov/depart/parks.htm

52 BRIDLE TRAILS STATE PARK

Kirkland, 5.5 miles north of Bellevue

Hikers and horseback riders can wander miles of trails through
482 acres of mature forest.

TRAIL	About 28 miles total; natural surface
STEEPNESS	Gentle to moderate
OTHER USES	Horses (which do have right of way)
DOGS	On leash
CONNECTING TRAILS	Bridle Crest Trail (many road crossings)
PARK AMENITIES	Restrooms, interpretive trail, picnic area, posted map, show ring, arena
DISABLED ACCESS	Restrooms, picnic area

You may not see the Douglas squirrels chomp on fir cones as though they were corn on the cob, but walking through this almost 100-year-old forest, you are likely to see many piles of discarded scales. Though only a mile from the freeway and the urban centers of Kirkland and Bellevue, this enclave of mature forest is a habitat for coyotes, raccoons, possums, native squirrels, and dozens of species of forest-dwelling birds.

It is like home, too, to many horseback riders, who regularly exercise their steeds on the more than 28 miles of natural-surface trails. When the state acquired the land in the 1930s, it soon became overrun by locals who thought of it as their private drag strip for cars and motorcycles. A neighborhood group formed, later becoming the Lake Washington Saddle Club, and took on the role of forest guardian. In the 1940s, members cleared the trails and built the show ring. Today Washington State and the club cooperate in maintaining the park, which is welcoming to both hikers and horses.

Entering by the big arena on 116th Avenue NE, take the 1.7-mile interpretive Trillium Trail heading up the gentle hill to the east, which quickly puts you under canopies of fir and hemlock that soon muffle the freeway noise. After a good rain, you'll find a few deep mudholes, so wear appropriate shoes. If the weather has been dry, you can probably negotiate the edges of the mire without mishap.

Bridle Trails is a great walk for those who know or want to get to know indigenous plants. Here you'll find several varieties of ferns, Oregon grape, huckleberry, salal, and many species of wild mushrooms, some edible and others poisonous.

To negotiate the miles of interweaving trails, study the trail map at the entrance and maybe stick to one of the marked trails such as the Trillium, Raven, or Coyote

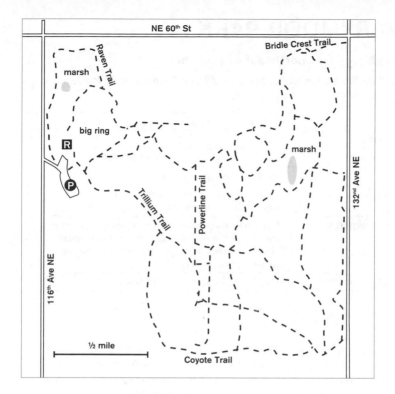

Trails. If you feel lost, just ask for directions. All the riders know their way around and are receptive to friendly hikers.

ADDRESS: 5300 116th Avenue NE, Kirkland

GETTING THERE: From I-405, take exit 17 (NE 70th Place). From northbound, turn right at the end of the ramp onto 116th Avenue NE, and go south about 1 mile to the park entrance on the left. Park at the northeast corner of the parking lot to access trails. From southbound, turn right at the end of the ramp onto NE 72nd Place, cross the freeway, then turn right again onto 116th Avenue NE and proceed as above. A Discover Pass is required for parking.

CONTACT: Washington State Parks, (425) 649-4275, www.parks.wa.gov. To volunteer, contact Bridle Trails Park Foundation, (425) 307-3578, www.bridletrails.org.

<u>53</u> MARYMOOR PARK

Redmond, 7.5 miles northeast of Bellevue

Bordered by the Sammamish River and Lake Sammamish, these 640 acres offer a bit of everything.

TRAIL	5 miles total; natural surface, paved
STEEPNESS	Level
OTHER USES	Bicycles, horses on equestrian trail only
DOGS	Off-leash area, otherwise on leash
CONNECTING TRAILS	Sammamish River Trail (Walk #42), East Lake Sammamish Trail (via Marymoor Connector)
PARK AMENITIES	Restrooms, bicycle velodrome, climbing rock, interpretive signs, model airplane field, museum, picnic shelters, playing fields, playgrounds, community garden, tennis courts
DISABLED ACCESS	Paved trails, restrooms, picnic areas

Marymoor's vast open spaces give this park a true year-round appeal. Walkers can choose to watch the bicyclists careen around the sloped velodrome, or gape at the nonacrophobic attacking tiny handholds on the climbing rock. An undulating whine and hum comes from the eastern edge of the park, where earthbound pilots put their model airplanes through their tricks.

For a more serene walk, take the nature trail south into the alder and oak forest. Interpretive signs guide you along a boardwalk over a peat bog, then out to

the northern shore of Lake Sammamish. Completing the loop, the boardwalk leads back along the Sammamish River through a thicket of blackberries and salal and the gentle shade of alders. Here songbirds chatter and flit, and on the river you can see the iridescent flash of the mallard drakes or the elegant suits of the Canada geese.

Where the boardwalk ends, be prepared to greet dogs. Hundreds of them. Marymoor's off-leash area is a mecca for dogs, where they can romp and dig on the water's edge and in the fragrant fields adjoining.

Year-round, keep the binoculars handy for a look at the red-tailed hawks circling

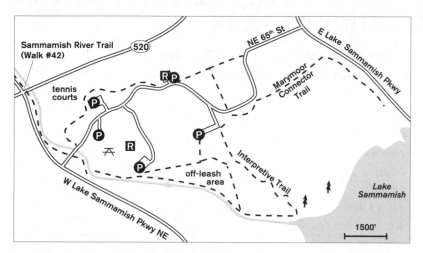

Sammamish River Trail (Walk #42)

520

tennis courts

NE 65th St

E Lake Sammamish Pkwy

Marymoor Connector Trail

Interpretive Trail

off-leash area

W Lake Sammamish Pkwy NE

Lake Sammamish

1500'

overhead. On hot summer days, expect a sky alive with hot-air balloons as they glide to rest on Marymoor's fields. Bring a camera, and flex your muscles if you want to help deflate the billowing nylon.

What is now the park was developed in the early 1900s as a family cattle farm. The original Willowmoor farmers used to boat across Lake Washington and then drive buckboards to the stately entrance of the farm. The old farmhouse remains, now a museum, as do the remnants of the drive and the bridge across the river. Inside, the museum takes you back to a time when the Eastside was a wild and rugged place.

ADDRESS: 6046 West Lake Sammamish Parkway NE, Redmond

GETTING THERE: From I-405, take exit 14 (WA 520/Redmond) east. Continue east on WA 520 for 4.8 miles to the West Lake Sammamish Parkway exit (signposted for Marymoor Park). At the end of the ramp, go right on West Lake Sammamish Parkway, then immediately left at the next light into the park.

From I-5, take exit 168B (WA 520/Bellevue) across Lake Washington, continue east on WA 520, and proceed as above.

CONTACT: King County Parks, (206) 296-4232, www.kingcounty.gov/recreation /parks. To volunteer, contact Friends of Marymoor Park: www.marymoor.org.

<u>54</u> ARDMORE PARK

5.5 miles northeast of downtown Bellevue

A 30-acre forest nestled in suburbia hides a small stream and wetland.

TRAIL	1.5 miles total; natural surface
STEEPNESS	Gentle to moderate
OTHER USES	Pedestrians only
DOGS	On leash
CONNECTING TRAILS	None
PARK AMENITIES	Playground, picnic tables
DISABLED ACCESS	None

This compact neighborhood park is a walker's dream, with wide wood-chip trails through a spacious forest of hemlock, cedar, and Douglas fir. Although it's nestled in the heart of suburbia, its sounds are sylvan, not motorized. In summer, robins hop along the trail, and chickadees and wrens call from the branches.

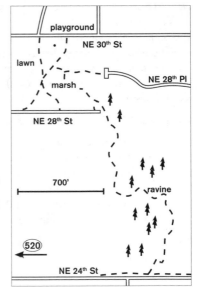

The trail, known to runners in the neighborhood as "The Warm-Up Trail," meanders up and down gentle terrain and along the sides of a ravine cut by a tiny stream, where bare earth on its sides tells of winter flooding. So open is the forest floor, the path gives the impression of even greater length than its true 1.5 miles. The spacious forest and the silence are so compelling that you could wish the trail went on and on through these sword-fern valleys and hills.

Summer visitors are rewarded with a feast of blackberries, red huckleberries, and thimbleberries. Traversing from south to north, you cross a bridge and angle up a short, steep hill some local walkers call "Cardiac Hill." An untrustworthy-looking rope swing dangles above a ravine, and moss-covered steps are remnants of once-loved tree houses built long ago by neighborhood kids.

The trail leads to a marshy patch of skunk cabbage in a cedar glen, but a sturdy puncheon bridge keeps your feet dry in this dell of old tree stumps. Here signposts point to several different park exits, each only a tenth of a mile away.

On the northwest corner lies the tiny lawn, perfect for picnics either before or after this charming walk.

ADDRESS:16833 NE 30th Street, Bellevue

GETTING THERE: From WA 520, take the 148th Avenue NE exit south. Go south on 148th Avenue NE, then left on NE 24th Street. Go east about 1.5 miles, and look on the left for the "Nature Trail" sign and entrance. Other entrances are located on suburban streets at NE 28th Street, NE 30th Street, and NE 28th Place. The picnic lawn lies along NE 30th Street. Parking is on-street and limited.

CONTACT: Bellevue Parks and Community Services Department, (425) 452-6885, www.ci.bellevue.wa.us/parks_intro.htm

EASTSIDE

55 EVANS CREEK PRESERVE

Sammamish and Redmond, 12 miles east of
downtown Bellevue

*Stroll or hike 2.6 miles of meadow, wetland, and forest trails that
crisscross these 179 acres of Northwest nature at its best.*

TRAIL	2.6 miles; natural surface
STEEPNESS	Gentle to steep
OTHER USES	Bicycles
DOGS	On leash
CONNECTING TRAILS	None
PARK AMENITIES	Picnic tables, restrooms, viewing platforms, interpretive signs
DISABLED ACCESS	Lower parking, picnic areas

Enter a sylvan wonderland of moss-covered firs, graceful alders, and ancient time-softened stumps as you begin the descent into the Evans Creek watershed. Well-contoured trails switchback and traverse this classic Northwest forest, leading east and downward to more open woodland and bright meadows. Vistas of the Cascades appear, and beaver-gnawed trees line the creeks.

With both an upper and a lower parking lot, Evans Creek Preserve offers a choice of steep forest walking or gentle strolling in the meadows. In summer the forest trails remain cool under alder and Douglas fir, and the open meadows are bright with pathways leading to many picnic spots. In winter, the meadows may be

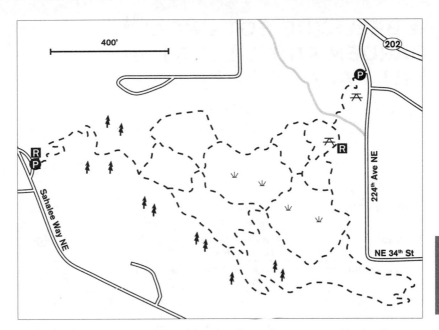

EASTSIDE

white with frost, while the sculpted forest trails are frost protected by the dense forest canopy.

With several miles of trails to wander, it's comforting to have well sign-posted intersections showing the trail choices. An interpretive brochure, available for download from the City of Sammamish website, entices young hikers to discover some of the wonders of the forest and meadow habitat.

ADDRESS: *Lower Parking Lot:* 4001 224th Avenue NE, Redmond; *Upper Parking Lot:* 3600 Sahalee Way NE, Sammamish

GETTING THERE: *Lower Parking Lot:* From Bellevue take WA 520 east and exit toward WA 202 E/Redmond Way. Continue east on Redmond Way, which becomes Redmond–Fall City Road, for about 3 miles. Turn right onto 224th Avenue NE to reach the lower parking lot within 0.5 miles.

Upper Parking Lot: As above, continue east on Redmond Way (Redmond–Fall City Road) for about 1.6 miles, and turn right onto Sahalee Way NE. Look for the parking lot on the left in about 1.2 miles.

CONTACT: Redmond Parks and Recreation Department, (425) 556-2300, www.ci.redmond.wa.us/parksrecreation; Sammamish Parks and Recreation Department, (425) 295-0585, www.sammamish.us/departments/parksandrec

56 BELLEVUE BOTANICAL GARDEN AND WILBURTON HILL PARK

2.5 miles east of downtown Bellevue

Wander 158 acres of native forest, wetlands, meadows, and landscaping.

TRAIL	3.5 miles; gravel, natural surface, paved
STEEPNESS	Gentle
OTHER USES	Pedestrians only in Bellevue Botanical Garden; bicycles in Wilburton Hill Park
DOGS	Not allowed in Bellevue Botanical Garden; leash and scoop in Wilburton Hill Park
CONNECTING TRAILS	Kelsey Creek Park (Walk #57), via streets on Lake-to-Lake Trail
PARK AMENITIES	Restrooms, concerts, docent-led garden tours, gift shop, horticultural classes, picnic tables, playground, playing fields, tennis courts
DISABLED ACCESS	Tateuchi Loop Trail, restrooms

Although Bellevue Botanical Garden is technically within the borders of Wilburton Hill Park, the two are very different places. In Wilburton, beyond the playing fields, you walk through a forest green with salal and Douglas fir; in the garden, you are led along established paths showcasing native and hybrid plants and vibrant floral displays.

For a good warm-up walk, head east from the Wilburton parking lot to the loop trail that borders the playing fields. As you enter the forest, it becomes a richly scented wood-chip trail zigzagging to the eastern boundary. Here, turn left along the quiet residential street for part of a block, then head back into the forest on a smaller, woodsy spur trail. Near the playing fields, you pass an innovative

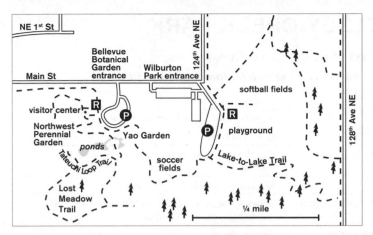

playground, where kids can scramble up and down the spiderweb and frolic in and out of the "town hall."

When you're ready for a quieter, slower stroll, step into the manicured year-round symphony of color in the botanical garden. The original owners, Cal and Harriet Shorts, toiled for many years to transform the heavy clay soil into the rich loam of the garden, and the work continues. Two years after the City of Bellevue received the land as a donation, the garden opened with 36 acres of woodlands, gardens, bogs, and meadows. Today it is a showplace for the Northwest Perennial Alliance, the Eastside Fuchsia Society, the King County Herb Society, and the North American Rock Garden Society.

Follow the graveled Tateuchi Loop Trail into a glory of huge rhododendrons set in a forest of hemlock and fir. The Yao Garden is a contemporary garden that combines both Japanese and Northwest influences. Along the western slope of the garden, the Perennial Border, already world famous, is reminiscent of an abstract painting created with plants, each carefully chosen for the hue and shape of both flower and foliage. The new Lost Meadow Trail to the south meanders through woodlands, meadows, and wetlands.

ADDRESS: *Bellevue Botanical Garden:* 12001 Main Street, Bellevue; *Wilburton Hill Park:* 100 124th Avenue NE

GETTING THERE: From I-405, take exit 13B (NE 8th Street). From northbound, turn right onto NE 8th Street. From southbound, turn left onto NE 8th Street. Go about 0.6 miles. Turn right on 124th Avenue NE, and follow it until it ends at a sharp right onto Main Street. Wilburton Hill Park is straight ahead. Turn right onto Main Street and find the Bellevue Botanical Garden entrance on the left.

CONTACT: Bellevue Botanical Garden Society, (425) 452-2750, www .bellevuebotanical.org/society.html; Bellevue Parks and Community Services Department, (425) 452-6885, www.ci.bellevue.wa.us/parks_intro.htm

57 KELSEY CREEK PARK

3 miles east of downtown Bellevue

Enjoy farm animals and search for forest wildlife in this 150-acre park.

TRAIL	2.5 miles total; gravel, natural surface
STEEPNESS	Gentle to steep
OTHER USES	Bicycles on gravel; pedestrians only on forest trail; horses
DOGS	On leash; not allowed in barn area
CONNECTING TRAILS	Bellevue Botanical Garden and Wilburton Hill Park (walk #56), via streets on Lake-to-Lake Trail
PARK AMENITIES	Restrooms, playground, classes, farm animals, historic cabin, picnic tables
DISABLED ACCESS	Restrooms, farm

Tucked neatly into a nook of suburban Bellevue, this well-loved park surprises newcomers with open meadows and fenced pastures, the baaing of sheep and the clucking of chickens. This early 1900s-style farm with its white fences, red barns, pens of pigs, and peacocks has long been a favorite with families wanting to show their children how farm animals were raised before the advent of chicken factories.

Where You Run Out of Breadcrumbs

If a park isn't too big, you can explore it in the same way as a maze, by "keeping one hand on the wall." If a trail map shows there are loops, you can continue taking right turns, thereby making your way back to where you started. In larger parks, such as Bridle Trails State Park, or on Cougar, Tiger, or Squak Mountains, it's best to develop a good sense of direction and walk with a friend, a cell phone, and a map. Look for map brochures at trailheads.

From the parking lot, cross a tributary of Kelsey Creek south to lawns, picnic areas, and a small marsh with wild ducks. Then climb the hill east to the barnyard. A graveled loop road takes you past the ducks and ponies, then to the south by the old pioneer log cabin, moved here for renovation and preservation.

Most visitors end their tour here, returning to picnic by the stream. But east of the barns and pony fields, another trail follows the pasture edge and then dives into the wooded hillside at the footbridge over Kelsey Creek.

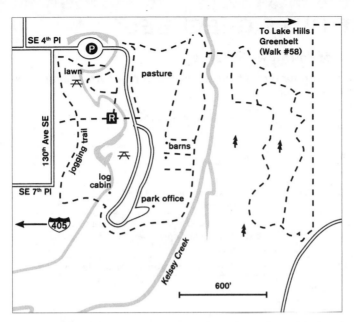

Here several adjoining loops take you up soft needle-padded paths and over footbridges above marshes. Wooden steps take you higher into the deciduous forest, where in fall the red and yellow leaves of the maples frame the farm buildings below, and in winter the vista opens to show a broad expanse of this farmland park. In spring look for the white hanging flowers, and in summer the red berries, of the Indian plum.

ADDRESS: 13010 SE 4th Place, Bellevue

GETTING THERE: From I-405, take exit 12 (SE 8th Street). Go east on SE 8th Street. Go under the railroad trestle to the light at Lake Hills Connector. Continue straight onto SE 7th Place. Go a few blocks, turn left on 130th Avenue SE, and then turn right onto SE 4th Place into the park.

CONTACT: Bellevue Parks and Community Services Department, (425) 452-6885, www.ci.bellevue.wa.us /parks_intro.htm

<u>58</u> LAKE HILLS GREENBELT

3.5 miles east of downtown Bellevue

Walk a 150-acre corridor through meadows and forest surrounding Larsen and Phantom Lakes.

TRAIL	3 miles total; gravel, paved
STEEPNESS	Level
OTHER USES	Bicycles
DOGS	On leash
CONNECTING TRAILS	Lake-to-Lake Trail, Phantom Lake Loop (both via streets)
PARK AMENITIES	Restrooms, classes, display garden, free nature walks late spring through September, community garden, ranger station
DISABLED ACCESS	Some trail sections, restrooms, ranger station

If you begin your walk at the Larsen Lake Blueberry Farm, you may see a single great blue heron standing motionless in a graceful posture among the lakeshore reeds, watching for fish, frogs, salamanders, and other aquatic prey. Ripples on the water tell of diving ducks, and between the water-lily pads, iridescent male mallards and their quacking brown mates glide. Both Larsen and Phantom Lakes, at the two ends of the Lake Hills Greenbelt, are important stopovers for waterfowl along the Pacific Flyway. As many as twenty-four species have been identified, including green-winged teals, northern shovelers, and ruddy ducks. In the twigs of the 40-year-old blueberry bushes, wrens and sparrows flit and twitter. In late summer look for flocks of cedar waxwings feeding on the berries.

Continuing around Larsen Lake, the trail turns east then south along the reed-lined irrigation channel, crosses Lake Hills Boulevard (there's a crosswalk with a flashing light), and then enters an open meadow rimmed by conifers—good hunting grounds for red-tailed, Cooper's, and sharp-shinned hawks. In the forest of Douglas fir and Sitka spruce, watch for signs of squirrels and the more secretive coyotes that travel the game trails through the undergrowth. River otters have been spotted in the lakes and the stream, as well as moles and muskrats along their banks.

At the corner of SE 16th Street and 156th Avenue SE, a small fruit stand operates through fall, selling fresh produce harvested from the rich peat-bog soils of the neighboring farms. If you turn west here, along SE 16th Street, you come immediately to the display garden, where you can pore over informative signs about a variety of herbs, flowers, and produce, and investigate a hands-on display of composting techniques. At the Lake Hills Greenbelt Ranger Station adjoining the garden, you'll find dioramas of the wildlife of the greenbelt and a three-dimensional display of the Larsen and Phantom Lakes drainage. Members of the Eastside chapter of the National Audubon Society often staff a booth to answer questions about the area's birds. Cross 156th Avenue SE diagonally to continue another quarter mile to the dock and boat launch on Phantom Lake.

ADDRESS: *Larsen Lake Blueberry Farm:* 14812 SE 8th Street, Bellevue; *Ranger Station:* 15416 SE 16th Street, Bellevue

GETTING THERE: *Larsen Lake:* From I-405, take exit 13 (NE 8th Street) and go east on NE 8th Street. Turn right on 148th Avenue NE. At the light at SE 8th Street, make a U-turn and go north 1 block to the blueberry farm parking lot.

Ranger Station: From I-90, take exit 11B (148th Ave SE/BCC) and go north to SE 16th Street. Turn right on SE 16th Street to the Community Farms parking lot.

CONTACT: Lake Hills Greenbelt Ranger Station, (425) 452-7225, www.ci.bellevue.wa.us/parks_intro.htm

---

But They're Such Fun to Feed!

Most park authorities prohibit the feeding of waterfowl. Here's why: Human food is junk food to waterfowl, with none of the nutrients they need. Undernourished birds are more susceptible to disease. Feeding entices waterfowl to overwinter, which means more breeding pairs and an ever-increasing number of ducks and geese in our lakes. Waterfowl waste contains parasites that cause swimmer's itch, an allergic rash you wouldn't wish on anyone. Clean water means more swimming beaches. Waterfowl waste not only pollutes, it also fertilizes aquatic weeds that choke out other plants and animals. You can't swim or fish in a choked lake.

59 MERCER SLOUGH NATURE PARK

2.5 miles south of downtown Bellevue

Boardwalks and interpretive trails wander through 320 acres of historic and environmentally important wetlands.

TRAIL	6.5 miles; boardwalk, natural surface, paved
STEEPNESS	Level to gentle
OTHER USES	Bicycles on paved trails (discouraged on soft-surface trails)
DOGS	On leash
CONNECTING TRAILS	Lake-to-Lake Trail (via streets), Mountains-to-Sound Greenway
PARK AMENITIES	Restrooms, classes, Environmental Education Center, interpretive trail, museum
DISABLED ACCESS	Paved trail along Bellevue Way, I-90, and 118th Avenue SE; restrooms

Just minutes from downtown Bellevue, you can stroll miles of secluded trails that surround the Mercer Slough and wetlands, a paradise for birds and bird-watchers alike. Here, in fall and spring, thousands of migrating waterfowl on the Pacific Fly-

way en route to and from the Arctic find vital haven. Many stay over for the winter, making their nests in the cattails and reeds along the edges of the slough. Not only a haven for waterfowl, the surrounding iris and cattail marsh, blackberry thickets, and cottonwood trees provide habitat for more than a hundred other species of birds, including eagles, pheasant, owls, swifts, thrushes, and more.

Long ago the Mercer Slough area was part of the vast marshlands that surrounded Lake Washington. Native peoples lived here, hunting muskrat and small mammals, fishing for salmon, and gathering edible roots and berries. In 1916, when the ship canal project lowered Lake Washington by 9 feet, the area could no longer support people whose livelihood depended on the bounty of the marshlands.

Today, 6.5 miles of trails, both paved (including some sidewalk) and wood chipped, twist through and around these preserved 320 acres. Overlake Blueberry Farm (open when berries are in season) and the historic Winters House add variety to a walk along Mercer Slough. From May to September you can rent a canoe and see the wetlands from the water trail through the park.

ADDRESS: *Winter's House:* 2102 Bellevue Way SE, Bellevue; *Environmental Education Center:* 1625 118th Avenue SE, Bellevue

GETTING THERE: *Overlake Blueberry Farm or Winters House:* From I-90, take exit 9 (Bellevue Way SE). Go about 0.25 miles north on Bellevue Way SE. The park is on your right.

Environmental Education Center: From I-90, take exit 10A or 10 (I-405/Bellevue) and go north. From I-405 take exit 12 (SE 8th Street/116th Avenue SE). Turn left onto SE 8th Street and then immediately turn left onto 118th Avenue SE. The Environmental Education Center will be on your left.

CONTACT: Bellevue Parks and Community Services Department, (425) 452-6885, www.ci.bellevue.wa.us/parks_intro.htm; Mercer Slough Environmental Education Center, (425) 452-2565

60 ROBINSWOOD PARK

4 miles southeast of downtown Bellevue

Bird-watch in an open forest, and stroll past lawns, a pond, and an off-leash area in this 60-acre park.

TRAIL	1 mile; gravel, natural surface, paved
STEEPNESS	Level to gentle
OTHER USES	Bicycles on paved trails
DOGS	Off-leash area, otherwise on leash
CONNECTING TRAILS	Lake-to-Lake Trail (via streets)
PARK AMENITIES	Restrooms, hospitality/retreat center, picnic shelter, playground, tennis center
DISABLED ACCESS	Restrooms, buildings, picnic areas, playground

As though they know the park is named for them, the red-breasted robins whinny and call *tut tut tut* as they hop slowly from the needle-lined path to the salal bushes. This rectangle of green neighborhood park so close to I-90 provides lawns for lazing on, a pond to explore, and a mile of trails through open forest.

If you sometimes feel closed in by the dense Northwest forest, this is a good park to explore, with its more open glades. Begin near Robinswood House on 148th Avenue SE, and if there are no wedding guests milling about, explore the secluded garden behind the house. Then head into the forest of Douglas fir and madrona.

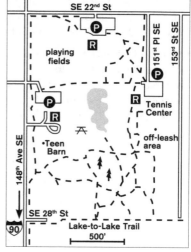

The trail makes weblike loops, leading finally to steps and the paved Lake to Lake Trail along the southern boundary. Turn east toward 153rd Avenue SE and reenter the forest heading north, where it seems light, even on overcast days. As is characteristic of young Douglas firs, the lower branches have fallen off as the upper ones seek light. The result: a forest of poles under an umbrella of green. The undergrowth of salal and Oregon grape is clearly visible, as are the robins and wrens that perch in the low shrubs. On this

gently padded natural trail, your feet make no sound, so the birds are less quick to take flight.

Soon you emerge at a green manicured lawn, where a small pond attracts kids with model boats and ducks seeking food. In spring you'll likely see a female mallard with her brood of peeping ducklings. To the east are the tennis center and off-leash area, but heading north returns you to forest and more quiet walking before you emerge at the playing fields.

ADDRESS: 2430 148th Avenue SE, Bellevue

GETTING THERE: *West Entrance:* From I-90 eastbound, take exit 11B (148th Avenue SE) and head north. The park is on the right just after SE 28th Street. From I-90 westbound, take exit 11 (161st Avenue SE, 156th Avenue SE, 150th Avenue SE). Turn right on 161st Avenue SE, left on Eastgate Way, right onto 148th Avenue SE, and proceed as above.

North and east entrances: They are off SE 22nd Street and 151st Place SE, respectively.

CONTACT: Bellevue Parks and Community Services Department, (425) 452-6885, www.ci.bellevue.wa.us/parks_intro.htm

---

Be a VIP

Many city and county parks departments have opportunities for volunteers. In King County, for example, they need people to help with administrative work, data entry, docent programs, fundraisers, trail restoration, and more. Call your local park authority, and ask if they have a VIP (Volunteers-in-Parks) program. Then get out and help the parks you love.

<u>61</u> WEOWNA PARK

Bellevue, 6 miles east of downtown Bellevue

This 80-acre swath of old forest is vibrantly alive with birdsong and big trees that line deep ravines sloping down to Lake Sammamish.

TRAIL	2.5 miles; natural surface
STEEPNESS	Gentle to steep
OTHER USES	Pedestrians only
DOGS	On leash
CONNECTING TRAILS	Lake-to-Lake Trail
PARK AMENITIES	Interpretive signs, picnic tables, viewing platforms
DISABLED ACCESS	None

Step from the manicured neighborhoods of Bellevue's suburbs into a forest left wild and free for many decades. Here, in this north-south greenbelt above Lake Sammamish, century-old Douglas firs rise above fern-bedecked ravines, and the beautifully maintained trails lead you on a walk in one of the city's finest forests. Huge stumps, softened by years of moss and rain, stand as reminders of the past. Rectangular holes in the tall snags tell of the pileated woodpeckers that call this forest their home. Under the canopy of western red cedar and big-leaf maples, an understory of sword fern, young alders, mahonia, and stinging nettle flourish. Even at the height of summer, the undergrowth is low enough to allow peekaboo views

of the glistening waters of Lake Sammamish far below to the east.

Weowna Park has long been on the map as a stretch of green between Lake Sammamish and the homes on the plateau above, but not until a few years ago were the random footpaths mapped, signposted, and transformed into graceful wood-chip trails. Long ago, Phantom Creek, which originally ran north from Phantom Lake, was reengineered by an innovative pioneer, who dug a ditch to allow the creek to drain to the east, into Lake Sammamish. Over the years, the creek wore away at the easily eroded glacial till, and the result today is a deep ravine marked by small waterfalls and pools during the wet months of the year. In summer, all that remains of this creek is a trickle of water-

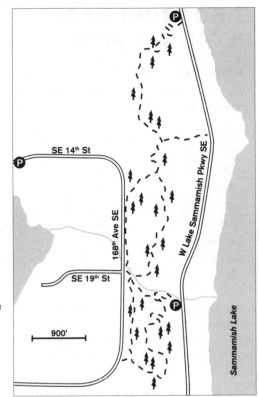

fall visible from a wooden viewing platform about 50 feet above the creek bed. The steep contours of this park offer double bounty: a good workout for those seeking it, and sumptuous views of fern-filled dales studded with the hefty trunks of fir and cedar.

ADDRESS: 1420 168th Avenue SE, Bellevue; also, 2010 and 335 West Lake Sammamish Parkway SE, Bellevue, with limited parking.

GETTING THERE: From I-90, eastbound, take exit 11B (148th Avenue SE). Take a slight right onto 148th Avenue SE. Go 0.8 miles and turn right onto SE 16th Street. Take a slight left onto SE Phantom Way. SE Phantom Way becomes SE 14th Street. Stay on SE 14th Street as it curves south to become 168th Avenue SE. Go 5 blocks to the trailhead on the left. Street parking only. Alternatively, park at Lake Hills Park, 1200 164th Avenue SE.

CONTACT: Bellevue Parks and Community Services Department, (425) 452-6885, www.ci.bellevue.wa.us/parks_intro.htm

<u>62</u> SOARING EAGLE REGIONAL PARK

Sammamish, 12 miles east of Bellevue

This 600-acre forest is home to a variety of mammals, including bear and cougar, and more than forty bird species.

TRAIL	13 miles; natural surface
STEEPNESS	Gentle to moderate
OTHER USES	Bicycles, horses
DOGS	On leash
CONNECTING TRAILS	Connector trail to Beaver Lake Preserve (Walk #64)
PARK AMENITIES	Restrooms, maps, trail junction markers
DISABLED ACCESS	None

In this airy, open forest, ferns bob and nod in the breeze and wren and robin calls surround you. Soft, narrow trails lead you from the main Pipeline Trail into older forest where moss-covered logs play nursery to young ferns and elderberry bushes. Other trails wind and twist through the green understory to a pond and wetlands. Although you are never more than half a mile from development, little to no traffic noise penetrates the woods here, high on the Sammamish Plateau. This is a wild park with relatively young trees. Along the Pipeline Trail, maples and alders dominate, while deeper to the north and south, where the land has not been so recently disturbed, hemlocks, western red cedar, and young Douglas firs are coming to dominate. The forest provides habitat for more than forty bird species, and black bears and cougars have been sighted.

Once a mountain biker's paradise (the trails were created and named by bikers), Soaring Eagle Regional Park has been somewhat gentrified now, and the well-signposted trails are shared equally by equestrians, bike riders, and walkers. In summer the salmonberries and thimbleberries grow lush and wild by the trail, and in winter, if the muddy trails don't deter you, there are peekaboo views of the Cascade foothills to the east. The best time to enjoy Soaring Eagle Regional Park is in the summer and early fall before the rains. Although the main Pipeline Trail has no intersection maps, all the smaller trail junctions have numbered posts with maps, so you always know where you are. Pipeline Trail is wide and level enough for strollers.

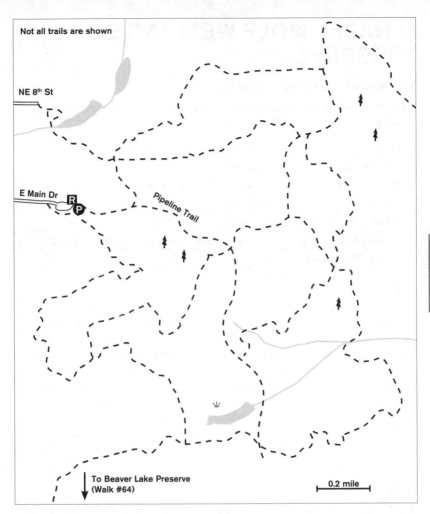

Not all trails are shown

NE 8th St

E Main Dr

Pipeline Trail

To Beaver Lake Preserve
(Walk #64)

0.2 mile

ADDRESS: 26015 East Main Drive, Sammamish

GETTING THERE: From I-405, take exit 14 (WA 520 Redmond/Seattle) and head east toward Redmond. Take the WA 202 exit and turn right onto WA 202/Redmond Way. Go 2.4 miles and turn right at Sahalee Way NE. This becomes 228th Avenue NE. Go 2.2 miles and turn left at SE 8th Street. Follow this street as it turns north and becomes 244th Avenue SE. Turn right on E Main Drive. Go 1.1 miles to the parking lot at the end.

CONTACT: King County Parks, (206) 477-4527, www.kingcounty.gov/recreation/parks

<u>63</u> HAZEL WOLF WETLANDS PRESERVE

Sammamish, 12 miles east of Bellevue

More than 100 acres of untouched forest and wetlands provide habitat for native plants and animals.

TRAIL	1.5 miles total; boardwalk, natural surface
STEEPNESS	Level to gentle
OTHER USES	Pedestrians only; horses on western perimeter trail
DOGS	Not allowed
CONNECTING TRAILS	Beaver Lake Preserve (Walk #64)
PARK AMENITIES	Interpretive signs, maps, viewpoint over wetlands
DISABLED ACCESS	None

Walk quietly through one of King County's most diverse and pristine wetland habitats, where osprey and bald eagles rest from a day of fishing on nearby Beaver Lake. In summer, salal plants are bedecked with white bellflowers, and yellow, orange, and red salmonberries glisten from their bushes. Slender blue dragonflies with alternating navy- and light-blue stripes alight on shrubs by the trail, and Douglas squirrels chatter on the trunks of the moss-covered western red cedars. In winter look for wood ducks and hooded mergansers on the pond.

The 116-acre wetlands preserve was named for one of Seattle's most active environmentalists, the late Hazel Wolf, on her one hundredth birthday. Access to

the preserve passes behind a new housing development, but within a quarter mile you have descended into a forest of big-leaf maples and sword ferns, where the heavy scent of wet earth and greenery surrounds you. Boardwalks and bridges lead over wetlands water so clear that it is surprising to hear it in motion. Look for footprints in the mud to see who has been feeding nearby—a muskrat, perhaps, or a family of beaver.

A loop trail leads to the viewing platform and interpretive signs over the marshes. Look for coots dabbling in the water, and listen for the deep *thrump* of bullfrogs and the call of red-winged blackbirds. By early summer the native water lilies should be in full bloom, with red-rimmed yellow flowers above heart-shaped leaves. In the rainy season the loop trail may not be passable due to high water. If so, you can still enjoy the edge of the wetlands by walking out and back on the one-way trails.

ADDRESS: 24735 248th Avenue SE, Sammamish (approximate)

GETTING THERE: From I-405, take exit 14 (WA 520 Redmond/Seattle). Go east (toward Redmond). Go about 5.5 miles and take the WA 202 E exit. Turn right at WA 202/Redmond Way. Go 4.4 miles and turn right at 244th Avenue NE. At the traffic circle continue south on 244th Avenue SE. Turn left onto SE Windsor Boulevard and continue onto 248th Avenue SE to the small parking lot under the power lines, on your left.

CONTACT: Sammamish Parks and Recreation Department, (425) 295-0585, www.sammamish.us/departments/parksandrec. For information on volunteering, visit www.forterra.org.

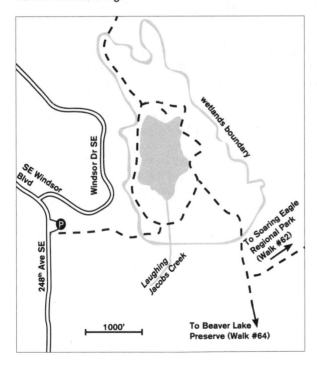

<u>64</u> BEAVER LAKE PRESERVE

Sammamish, 12 miles east of Bellevue

This mature 57-acre forest, with trees approaching old-growth status, is home to several endangered bird and amphibian species.

TRAIL	1.2 miles total; gravel, natural surface
STEEPNESS	Level to gentle
OTHER USES	Bicycles and horses on connector trail to Soaring Eagle Regional Park only
DOGS	On leash; dogs prohibited in adjoining Hazel Wolf Wetlands Preserve
CONNECTING TRAILS	Hazel Wolf Wetlands Preserve (Walk #63) and Soaring Eagle Regional Park (Walk #62)
PARK AMENITIES	Restrooms, interpretive signs, map, picnic area, viewing platforms
DISABLED ACCESS	Graveled trail, restrooms, parking lot

Walk a protected forest with sword ferns the height of an adult, and towering Douglas firs and western red cedar more than 200 years old. Imagine these trails before the pioneers arrived, when people of the Sammamish tribe would traverse the forest paths en route to the shores of today's Beaver Lake or stalk black-tailed deer through the understory. This forest and the adjoining Hazel Wolf Wetlands Preserve (Walk #63) are some of the least touched wild land in the Puget Sound region.

Trails loop to the north and south of the parking area (crossing West Beaver Lake Drive, so be wary of traffic). An interpretive trail with nature quiz questions provides entertainment and learning on the northern loop. Bridges cross Laughing Jacobs Creek and other sensitive wetlands. Spur trails on the south side of Beaver Lake Drive lead to a meadow and a shady stand of western red cedars. The city plans to extend the trails all the way to the edge of Beaver Lake, where you may see

osprey or bald eagles perched above the water, or flocks of colorful wood ducks or white-headed buffleheads.

If bringing a dog, be vigilant for the boundary signs demarcating Hazel Wolf Wetlands on the northwestern side of the preserve. Dogs are not allowed on the wetland trails, but luckily there are plenty of sights and smells to entertain a canine friend on the Beaver Lake Preserve trails.

ADDRESS: 1400 W Beaver Lake Drive SE, Sammamish

GETTING THERE: From I-405, take exit 14 (WA 520 Redmond/Seattle) and head east toward Redmond. Take the WA 202/Redmond Way exit and go east on WA 202. Go 2.4 miles and turn right at Sahalee Way NE. This becomes 228th Avenue NE. Go 5.4 miles and turn left at SE 24th Street. Go 1.3 miles and turn right to stay on SE 24th Street. Just after the Lodge at Beaver Lake, the road curves left to become W Beaver Lake Drive SE. Go about 0.9 miles and look for the parking area on the left.

CONTACT: Sammamish Parks and Recreation Department, (425) 295-0585, www.sammamish.us/departments/parksandrec

65 BEAVER LAKE PARK

Sammamish Plateau, 15 miles southeast of Bellevue

Lakeshore totem poles lead to 82 acres of forest and meadow trails near Laughing Jacobs Creek.

TRAIL	2 miles; natural surface and paved
STEEPNESS	Level to gentle
OTHER USES	Pedestrians only
DOGS	Off-leash areas, otherwise on leash
CONNECTING TRAILS	None
PARK AMENITIES	Restrooms, conference lodge, fishing area, picnic shelter, playground, playing fields
DISABLED ACCESS	Restrooms, lodge, picnic shelter, paved trails

In this sanctuary from suburbia on the Sammamish Plateau, silence is broken only by the call of birds and the trickle of Laughing Jacobs Creek. Beaver Lake Park is an interesting 400-acre mix of amenities, art, and nature. Two totem poles, carved by David Boxley under the King County 1 Percent for Art Program, illustrate salmon and beaver legends of the British Columbian Tsimshian people.

In recent years, toads have been the memorable wildlife attraction of the park, during a few weeks twice a year. Each spring, in April or May, hundreds of adult western toads migrate en masse back to their breeding grounds at Beaver Lake. By midsummer, the metamorphosed young toadlets journey through the park and across the road to drier forest, where they mature.

From the main parking area near the lake, the 1.5-mile loop trail begins south of the picnic shelter, in which are displayed three Native American house posts from Upper Skagit tribes carved by David Horsley—again, with King County arts funds. Pass the beaver pole and enter the forest. The trail loosely follows the lake edge south and then turns west to cross the creek. Huge snags tell of giant trees felled by wind or fire.

Wetland Inhabitants

Amphibians like the Pacific tree frog and the long-toed salamander inhabit the wetlands around Puget Sound. You may see the salamander tadpoles in the water or hear the song of the tree frogs. Blackbirds and marsh wrens nest in the cattails and reeds. The presence of these creatures indicates the health of the wetland ecosystem. Be sure to stay on boardwalks, and never allow pollutants to reach streams or ponds.

The west end of the park is where the action is: ball fields ringing with shouts and calls of children, and two off-leash areas for large and small dogs. Off-leash trails lead into the forest, so there is shade for the dogs and dog owners alike. Newly improved paved trails at the west end allow strollers and wheelchairs more access than in previous years. Several loop trails offer almost 2 miles of meandering walks.

ADDRESS: *North parking lot and lodge:* 25201 SE 24th Street; *West end and dog park:* 2526 244th Avenue SE, Sammamish

GETTING THERE: From I-405, take exit 14 (WA 520/Redmond) east to Redmond. Turn right onto WA 202 (Redmond–Fall City Road). Go 2.5 miles and turn right on Sahalee Way NE, which becomes 228th Avenue SE. Go 5.4 miles and turn left on SE 24th Street. Continue 1.5 miles to the park, which is on the right.

From I-90, take exit 17 (Front Street/E Lake Sammamish Parkway). Turn north on Front Street N/E Lake Sammamish Parkway. Go 2 miles and turn right on SE 43rd Way, which becomes 228th Avenue SE. Go 2.5 miles north and turn right on SE 24th Street. The park is on the right in 1.5 miles.

CONTACT: Sammamish Parks and Recreation Department, (425) 295-0585, www.sammamish.us/departments/parksandrec

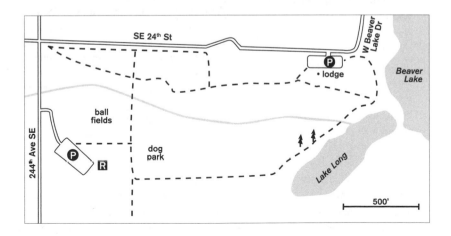

66 COAL CREEK NATURAL AREA

5.5 miles south of downtown Bellevue

Sylvan wilderness offers creekside forest wandering, old mines, and a waterfall in this 450-acre natural area.

TRAIL	6 miles round-trip; natural surface
STEEPNESS	Gentle to moderate
OTHER USES	Pedestrians only
DOGS	On leash
CONNECTING TRAILS	Cougar Mountain Regional Wildland Park (Walk #69)
PARK AMENITIES	Interpretive signs
DISABLED ACCESS	None

Like a green finger beckoning from the summit of Cougar Mountain toward Lake Washington, Coal Creek Natural Area entices those looking for a low-elevation wildlands walk. Leave your car and let the forest surround you with tangled masses of ferns, blackberries, maples, and cedars. From the western (lower) end, the trail closely parallels Coal Creek. Old fallen trees lie across the natural surface trail, their mossy coats worn away by countless feet passing over them. In some, notches scar the trunks where volunteers have cut steps for fellow hikers.

From the Coal Creek Parkway parking lot, the trail climbs steadily for 3 miles to the Red Town trailhead of Cougar Mountain Regional Wildland Park (Walk #69). Although there are a few tangent trails leading up to housing developments on the ridge or to streamside viewpoints, the main trail is well maintained with numerous new bridges.

Carved wooden signposts give directions and trail mileages. To make a loop of the walk, after crossing the creek on a footbridge, follow the Primrose Trail off to the left, which passes Sandstone Falls 1.4 miles from the trailhead. Farther along, you pass a side trail to Shazo Mine. This, like other abandoned mines, must be viewed from afar; signs at the Cougar Mountain trailhead just above here warn of odorless, colorless gases

Natural or Man-Made?

When you see small logs and branches blocking a fork in the trail, they may have been put there on purpose. Trail maintenance crews often close off old trails that are washed out, dangerous, or being replanted or moved. Steep, eroded trails may just be "social trails" that are not part of the trails system plan. Stay off anything that looks as if it would be a waterfall in the rainy season, and you'll do your part to help prevent erosion.

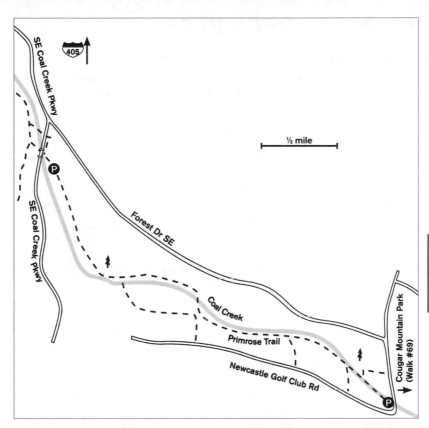

that may be present in any mine shaft. The Primrose Trail continues up a steep hillside, then joins the larger, better-maintained Coal Creek Trail. Turn right to complete the loop or left to meet up with other Cougar Mountain trails at the Red Town Trailhead (Walk #69).

In the past few years, many volunteers and Bellevue parks people worked to improve the trail and build footbridges, which have made this trail more family friendly, although it can still be a challenge with its 550-foot elevation gain. If you're equal to it, all of this adds up to the pleasure of a few hours spent in sylvan wilderness.

ADDRESS: 5600 Coal Creek Parkway SE, Bellevue

GETTING THERE: From I-405, take exit 10 (Coal Creek Parkway/Factoria). Turn east onto Coal Creek Parkway SE. Go about 1.25 miles (past the light at Forest Drive SE), and look on the left for a gravel parking lot before crossing the creek. Small trailheads lead from neighborhoods nearby.

CONTACT: Bellevue Parks and Community Services Department, (425) 452-6885, www.bellevuewa.gov/parks-community-services.htm

67 LEWIS CREEK PARK

Bellevue, 9 miles southeast of downtown

This 55-acre park combines the best of a suburban activities park with natural areas, including trails through forest, creek, wetlands, and meadow.

TRAIL	3 miles total; natural surface, paved
STEEPNESS	Level to moderate
OTHER USES	Bicycles
DOGS	On leash
CONNECTING TRAILS	Lakemont Park Trails to Lakemont Community Park (Walk #68)
PARK AMENITIES	Interpretive center, restrooms, playground, sports fields, picnic area
DISABLED ACCESS	Interpretive center, restrooms, wetlands trail

A gentle path, alternating between paved, gravel, and boardwalk, encircles lush wetlands where red-winged blackbirds grace the cattails and secretive Virginia rails call out with their repetitive high chirping. If you're lucky, you may see one scurrying to shelter as you approach its hiding place under the boardwalk. Several sturdy plank bridges cross the sensitive wetlands, which act as sponges to absorb and filter pollution, thereby protecting the water quality of Lewis Creek.

Beyond the sports fields, playground, and wetlands you can enter the quiet alder forest, where the only sounds are the shooshing of the water over rocks and logs in Evans Creek. This forest, in the fast-encroaching suburbs, has the important role of decreasing erosion and runoff. For walkers, it allows a respite

from urban life and time for quiet contemplation. Common birds in the park include crows, northern flickers, woodpeckers, robins, and wrens. Since the park is close to Cougar Mountain, larger mammals such as coyotes and even bobcats have been spotted.

Named after Phillip Lewis, who surveyed this area in the 1860s, the land was logged for its fir and hemlock, then purchased by the Peltola family for farming in 1921. Today, park rangers lead guided nature walks, and birding books and binoculars are available for checkout in the interpretive center, which is open daily from 10:00 a.m. to 4:00 p.m. except Mondays, Tuesdays, and holidays.

ADDRESS: 5808 Lakemont Boulevard SE, Bellevue

GETTING THERE: From I-90, take exit 13 (SE Newport Way/Lakemont Boulevard SE). Turn right and merge onto Lakemont Boulevard SE. Continue 2 miles and turn left onto SE 58th Street to enter the park.

CONTACT: Bellevue Parks and Community Services Department, (425) 452-4195, www.bellevuewa.gov/parks-community-services.htm

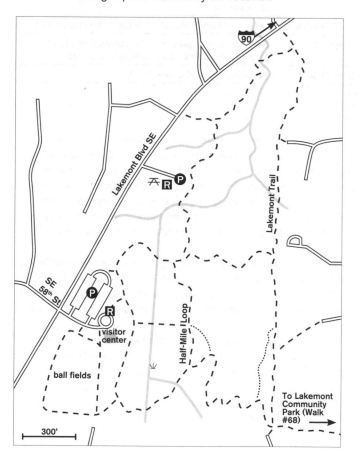

<u>68</u> LAKEMONT COMMUNITY PARK

Bellevue, 8 miles southeast of downtown Bellevue

Get the heart rate up as you descend and ascend the forested Lewis Creek ravine in 124 acres of forest where the only sounds are rushing water and birdsong.

TRAIL	3 miles; natural surface and stairs
STEEPNESS	Moderate to steep
OTHER USES	Pedestrians only
DOGS	On leash
CONNECTING TRAILS	Lakemont Park Trails to Lewis Creek Park (Walk #67)
PARK AMENITIES	Restrooms, interpretive signs, playground, picnic area, playing fields, skate park, tennis courts
DISABLED ACCESS	Restrooms, paved walkway only

Although Lakemont Community Park first appears as a rather strange city park (there's a large fenced sinkhole just beyond the restrooms and a fenced filtration pond, providing storm-water treatment), its true beauty reveals itself for those walking past the ball field. Here, the trail drops in a series of switchbacks through towering second-growth forest. Nurse logs lie tumbled across the creek, and maidenhair ferns grace the trunks of moss-covered trees. In the wet season, Lewis Creek bubbles and rushes far below, and the sounds of the city are drowned by water and birdsong.

By preserving vast stretches of green between Lake Sammamish and Cougar Mountain, the City of Bellevue has maintained a natural corridor for wildlife deep in the heart of suburbia. Deer are often spotted in this second-growth forest, and both black bears and cougars have also been seen. For the safety of all, please keep your dogs on leash.

This well-maintained forest trail drops 270 feet in a series of switchbacks and trestled staircases before crossing the creek. From here, you can climb up and wind through the neighborhoods a bit to find a kiosk leading back to the parking lot, or continue several more miles to Evans Creek Park. There is no easy in and out. Gauge your abilities (and those of your children) before descending too far down this path shaded by big-leaf maple and Douglas fir.

ADDRESS: 5170 Village Park Drive SE, Bellevue

GETTING THERE: From I-90, take exit 13 (SE Newport Way/Lakemont Boulevard SE). Turn right and merge onto Lakemont Boulevard SE. Continue 1.3 miles and turn left onto Village Park Drive SE. Go 0.2 miles to the park, on your left.

CONTACT: Bellevue Parks and Community Services Department, (425) 452-6885, www.bellevuewa.gov/parks-community-services.htm

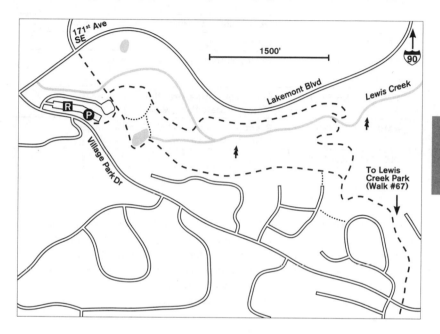

69 COUGAR MOUNTAIN REGIONAL WILDLAND PARK

Bellevue, 8.5 miles southeast of downtown

Groomed trails in more than 3,000 acres of untamed forest encourage exploration along streams and old mining areas.

TRAIL	From 1 mile to 50 miles; gravel, natural surface
STEEPNESS	Gentle to steep
OTHER USES	Horses on some trails; no bicycles allowed
DOGS	On leash
CONNECTING TRAILS	Coal Creek Natural Area (Walk #66), Squak Mountain State Park (Walk #70)
PARK AMENITIES	Restrooms, guided walks in summer, maps, historical sites
DISABLED ACCESS	None

Cougar Mountain Regional Wildland Park may be partially groomed, but it is not tamed. In its forest you'll find wildlife, streams, cliffs, ravines, and history. Deer, bobcats, porcupines, and black bears roam the 3,000-plus acres, and many species of forest-dwelling songbirds live in the canopy or in the lush undergrowth. Here, too, you'll see evidence of long-ago logging and mining.

To understand, and come to love, Cougar Mountain, with its almost 50 miles of trails, you need to start one step at a time. You may have read about its labyrinth of trails, which could foil a maze-trained laboratory rat and cause it to give up in despair. Thanks to massive efforts by King County Parks and the Issaquah Alps Trails Club (all volunteers), Cougar Mountain is becoming a walker-friendly place. And the Red Town Trailhead may be the best place from which to take an introductory walk.

At the parking lot, take a map from the information board; notice that south is at the map's top. Many loop walks are possible, ranging in length from 0.5 miles to many miles. Start small and

> ## How Long Will It Take?
> The average adult walks at about 2 to 3 miles per hour; children under age seven, about half that speed; bird-watchers—well, that depends. Variables include age and energy level, activities along the way, and trail conditions. Once you know your own pace and that of your friends or family, you'll know how long to allow for a 2-mile walk on level or hilly terrain.

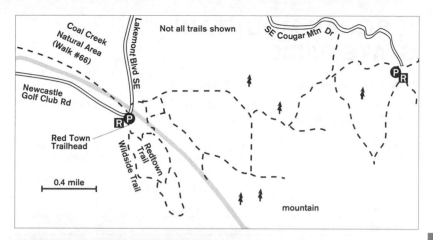

Coal Creek
Natural Area
(Walk #66)

Lakemont Blvd SE

Not all trails shown

SE Cougar Mtn Dr

Newcastle
Golf Club Rd

Red Town
Trailhead

Redtown Trail
Wildside Trail

0.4 mile

mountain

increase your distances as you become familiar with the trail markings and the map.

For a good introduction, try W1, the Wildside Trail. Angling due south from the parking lot, it passes a sign warning of danger from gases (mainly carbon dioxide) in mines. Believe it and heed it, but don't panic. You will be on well-traveled, open-air trails, not crawling through mine shafts. Wildside is a natural trail that crosses bridges over Coal Creek and threads through a vegetation-restoration project, an example of the dedicated care of the Trails Club volunteers. Make a loop back onto W2, Red Town Trail, for a sampler. On your next visit, branch out. Have fun.

ADDRESS: *Red Town Trailhead:* 7549 SE Newcastle–Coal Creek Road, Bellevue

GETTING THERE: *Red Town Trailhead:* From I-90, take exit 13 (SE Newport Way/Lakemont Boulevard SE). Merge onto Lakemont Boulevard SE. Continue south about 2.9 miles to the trailhead on the left at Coal Creek–Newcastle Road.

CONTACT: King County Parks, (206) 296-4232, www.kingcounty.gov/recreation /parks. For information on volunteering and year-round guided hikes and events, visit www.issaquahalps.org/home.

70 SQUAK MOUNTAIN STATE PARK

Issaquah, 11 miles southeast of Bellevue

Stroll a storybook interpretive trail, or walk high into more than 1,500 acres of forested Issaquah Alps.

TRAIL	About 13 miles total (including the 2-mile Equestrian Loop Trail and the 0.5-mile Pretzel Tree Trail); gravel, natural surface
STEEPNESS	Gentle (Pretzel Tree Trail) to steep
OTHER USES	Horses in southern part of park
DOGS	On leash
CONNECTING TRAILS	Cougar Mountain Regional Wildland Park (Walk #69)
PARK AMENITIES	Restrooms, interpretive trail, picnic area
DISABLED ACCESS	Restrooms

Preserved as a handful of second-growth forest amid the sprawl of suburbia, Squak Mountain State Park provides needed wildlife habitat and miles of walking trails. Like its neighboring Issaquah Alps parks—the Cougar and Tiger Mountain areas—Squak was pulled from the brink of random off-road destruction, and consequently hosts a spiderweb of paths. To ensure you don't get lost, stick to the signposted, well-maintained trails.

Only one official parking area serves the state park, on the southern boundary, off SE May Valley Road. From there, you can access a 0.5-mile interpretive trail named Pretzel Tree Trail. This level and easy walk caters to the young hiker, with many color-illustrated signs telling the story of the fictitious Mr. Mouse and his journey into the forest. Along the way he (and the young hikers) learn about the plants

and animals and are encouraged to find the "pretzel tree" (not a species, but a tree twisted like a pretzel).

Climbing the gravel access road (used only by park vehicles) about 0.4 miles leads you to the cutoff for the Equestrian Loop Trail (S4). Step from the gravel to the quiet, soft duff under large Douglas firs and big-leaf maples. This narrow, well-worn path twists its way

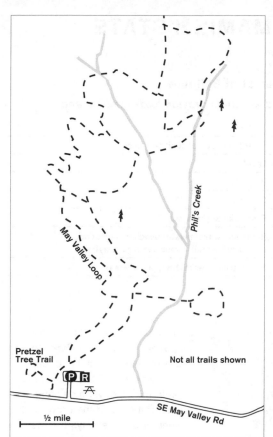

Phil's Creek

May Valley Loop

Pretzel Tree Trail

Not all trails shown

P R

½ mile

SE May Valley Rd

around old snags that stand like apartment buildings for bugs and birds alike. Sword ferns grace the slopes of the ravines above Phil's Creek, and the light plays on the leaves of the elderberry and salal.

Forks in the path are clearly marked with directions and distances, so you can choose to extend your walk, take a more strenuous cutoff, or, later, head up Phil's Creek Trail (S3) to the Central Peak. On this densely forested mountain, views are limited to the immediately surrounding hillsides, and even at the highest point the trees prohibit distance viewing. But the forest itself delights with its fragrance and terrain—and the chance of seeing the spoor of raccoons, mountain beavers, or even cougars or bears.

ADDRESS: 21430 SE May Valley Road, Issaquah

GETTING THERE: From I-90, take exit 15 (WA 900/Renton). Go south on WA 900 (Renton-Issaquah Road SE) through the stoplight on SE Newport Way. Drive south 3.5 miles to SE May Valley Road and turn left. Go 4.75 miles on SE May Valley Road, to the parking lot on your left. A Discover Pass is required for parking.

CONTACT: Washington State Parks, (425) 455-7010, www.parks.wa.gov

71 LAKE SAMMAMISH STATE PARK

Issaquah, 8 miles southeast of Bellevue

512 acres of meadows and wetlands provide bird-watching and other lakeside pursuits.

TRAIL	5.2 miles; natural surface, paved
STEEPNESS	Level
OTHER USES	Bicycles
DOGS	On leash
CONNECTING TRAILS	East Lake Sammamish Trail
PARK AMENITIES	Restrooms, freshwater beach, playground, interpretive trail, picnic shelters, playfields
DISABLED ACCESS	Paved trails, restrooms, picnic areas

An immense 512-acre lakeside park, Lake Sammamish State Park attracts hordes of beachgoers, sunbathers, and picnickers enjoying the mile of lakefront in the warm summer months. But beyond the crowds of summer, or on most days the rest of the year, you'll have miles of walking in relative solitude. On a wet day, power walkers can try the paved trails around the parking areas that lead through lawns and fields, past picnic shelters and restrooms.

The best walking, though, lies farther north at the end of the parking area. Here a small footbridge spans quiet Issaquah Creek, and interpretive signs tell about the watershed. Once across the creek, follow the wood-chip trail left under the shade of cottonwoods and firs to a point of land by the mouth of the creek. In summer this is a favorite spot for more remote picnics, sunbathing, and swimming.

If you want summer solitude, once you cross the creek turn right and follow hedgerows of blackberry brambles, which have fragrant blooms in July and succulent fruit in late summer. This natural trail winds its way along the creek and north through meadows (great for bird-watching) and scrub forest to the boat-launch

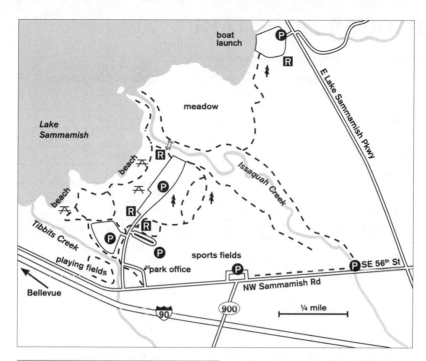

Map labels: boat launch, meadow, Lake Sammamish, beach, beach, beach, Tibbits Creek, playing fields, Bellevue, park office, sports fields, Issaquah Creek, E Lake Sammamish Pkwy, SE 56th St, NW Sammamish Rd, 90, 900, ¼ mile

Art along the Trails

Public artworks along these trails range in sophistication and variety from Native American carvings to children's mosaics, from the towering *A Sound Garden* to wrought-iron bench backs. These projects add variety and interest to the walks. Have you found the park with totem poles? Cast figures? An eagle? A sound garden? How about an earth sculpture?

parking area accessible off E Lake Sammamish Parkway.

ADDRESS: 2000 NW Sammamish Road, Issaquah

GETTING THERE: *Southern entrance:* From I-90 eastbound, take exit 15 (Renton/WA 900/Lake Sammamish State Park) and turn left on 17th Avenue NW, crossing over the freeway. At the T-junction, turn left onto NW Sammamish Road, and in 0.4 miles turn right into the park. Brown state park signs help guide you from the freeway. *Eastern entrance:* From the T-junction at NW Sammamish Road, turn right (east) and then left onto E Lake Sammamish Parkway; the boat launch and trailhead are across from 4460 E Lake Sammamish Parkway. A Discover Pass is required for parking.

CONTACT: Washington State Parks, (425) 455-7010, www.parks.wa.gov

72 TIGER MOUNTAIN

Issaquah, 14 miles southeast of Bellevue

Explore Tradition Lake and its wetlands, then branch out into more than 4,400 acres for more adventure.

TRAIL	20 miles; gravel, natural surface
STEEPNESS	Gentle to steep
OTHER USES	Horses, bicycles on designated trails
DOGS	On leash
CONNECTING TRAILS	Many Tiger Mountain trails
PARK AMENITIES	Restrooms, picnic shelters, interpretive trail
DISABLED ACCESS	Sections of Around the Lake Trail, restrooms

To have to choose one walk on Tiger Mountain is like being led to a smorgasbord and then being told to taste only one dish. Tiger Mountain, like its neighbor Cougar Mountain, must be sampled on many repeat trips. Both areas, because they are wildlands, challenge the timid walker with their numerous side trails and their sometimes-unmarked intersections. Start with one well-trodden, well-signposted trail. Learn the trailhead area, become familiar with the names of other trails, and then add them, one by one, to your hiking menu.

Tradition Lake Plateau is only a few minutes from downtown Issaquah and has thirteen trails to choose from. Many are level or nearly level. Most are signed. From the parking area, pass through the gate and follow the road as it gradually climbs to the power lines. Turn left to find the restrooms, interpretive signs, and map. If you don't have a map in hand (available at the Chamber of Commerce in Issaquah

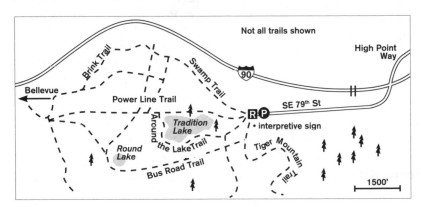

We're in Their Home

Cougars and bears still roam the forests bordering our eastern suburbs, but they usually stay far from people. To be safe, always keep children close. Never run from these large animals. For a bear, make noise and back away. If you happen upon a cougar, pick up children. Act tall and big. In either case, report the sighting to a park authority as soon as possible.

for $2.50), choose either the Around the Lake Trail or the Bus Road Trail for starters; both are clearly signed.

The Around the Lake Trail is graded for wheelchair accessibility. Follow its level wanderings on a hillside in lush forest. In spring, wildflowers such as western trillium and vanilla leaf brighten the shadows under the Douglas fir and western red cedar. Pale-green new growth on the lady ferns uncurls like sleeping caterpillars. Down to your right, you'll see glimpses of Tradition Lake—in winter a full body of water, in summer half mint fields and marsh and half water. There are no trails close to the water's edge, in order to protect the fragile habitat of the many woodland animals that live there, but the distance only adds to the lake's charm: a tantalizing glimpse of gentle reflections on pristine water.

After the second interpretive sign along the trail, wheelchairs must turn back. At this point, the crunching gravel gives way to a soft trail crossed by many roots. From here, you can continue on around Tradition Lake to a junction with the Power Line Trail, turning right to return to the trailhead on it; or from the point where gravel turns to natural surface, you can take a small trail to the left to emerge on the wide, smooth Bus Road Trail. To the right, this trail takes you deeper onto the plateau to other trails and Around the Lake; to the left, it returns you, past the old Scenicruiser bus wreck, to the trailhead. And there's still so much more to see! Next, consider branching out!

ADDRESS: 26999 SE 79th Street, Issaquah

GETTING THERE: From I-90, take exit 20 (High Point Way). At the end of the exit ramp, turn right and then right again onto SE 79th Street (the frontage road). Park along the roadside. A Discover Pass is required for parking.

CONTACT: Washington State Department of Natural Resources, (360) 825-1631, www.dnr .wa.gov. To volunteer, contact the DNR or the Washington Trails Association.

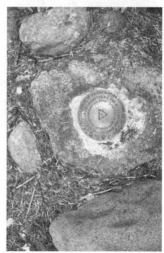

EASTSIDE

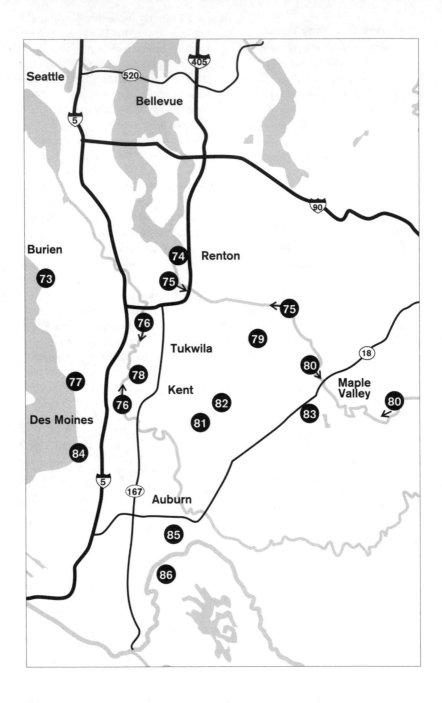

SOUTH KING COUNTY
Renton, Kent, and Des Moines

73 SEAHURST PARK

Burien, 4 miles north of Des Moines

182 acres of forest trails and Puget Sound beach provide saltwater exploration and views of the Olympic Mountains.

TRAIL	2 miles; natural surface, paved
STEEPNESS	Level to steep
OTHER USES	Pedestrians only
DOGS	On leash
CONNECTING TRAILS	None
PARK AMENITIES	Restrooms, playground, Environmental Science Center (ESC), picnic shelters
DISABLED ACCESS	Paved trail, restrooms, picnic shelters, ESC

A rugged ravine and a mature forest of big-leaf maples and conifers welcome you to this park by the Sound. Forest trails lace the steep fern-strewn hillsides under moss-draped trees. The beach, at high or low tide, feels wild and open. Views extend west to Vashon Island and the Olympics. Bald eagles may soar above the water, where loons and grebes dive for fish.

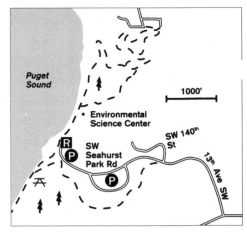

Just minutes west of Seattle-Tacoma International Airport, this park is a microcosm of Puget Sound forest and tidal habitat. At low tide, the gently sloping beach invites exploration. Although the Seahurst beach has no rock-lined tide pools, small puddles preserve gallons of the last high tide, and in them often lounge colorful kelp crabs and red rock crabs. Also common are the smaller beach crabs (about 1.5 inches across the body), and the greenish hairy beach crab and its purplish companion. Drift logs make a natural playground for children.

If the tide is high, or if you prefer dry feet, you can stroll the gravel trail above the beach for almost a mile each way. The old seawall was removed in 2013 and 2014 to allow a natural beach to re-form. The beach and steep forest trails in the

north of the park are well maintained. To the south of the parking lot, the forest trails are primitive and not maintained, but according to park rangers, it's a challenge to get lost: all trails lead to the park boundaries, to the parking lot, or back down to the beach.

ADDRESS: 1600 SW Seahurst Park Road, Burien

GETTING THERE: From I-5 northbound, take exit 154 (WA 518 W/Burien). From southbound, take exit 154B. Go west on WA 518 for 3 miles, where it changes names in Burien to SW 148th Street. Continue 0.7 miles, turn right on Ambaum Boulevard SW, go a few blocks, and turn left onto SW 144th Street. Go 3 blocks and turn right on 13th Avenue SW (signposted for the park), which becomes SW 140th Street and winds down to the park on Seahurst Park Road.

CONTACT: Burien Parks, (206) 988-3700, www.burienwa.gov. For volunteer information, visit www.seahurstpark.org.

74 GENE COULON MEMORIAL BEACH PARK

Renton, 7 miles north of Kent

The trail and facilities on this cozy 57-acre corner of Lake Washington attract bird-watchers, beachgoers, and boaters.

TRAIL	1.5 miles one way; paved
STEEPNESS	Level
OTHER USES	Pedestrians only
DOGS	Not allowed
CONNECTING TRAILS	None
PARK AMENITIES	Restrooms, playground, picnic shelters, interpretive trail, swimming beach, cafés, tennis courts
DISABLED ACCESS	Trail, restrooms, buildings

Hundreds of coots, their white bills poking the grass for food, waddle awkwardly over the lawn. On the water, dozens of mallards, Canada geese, and gulls cavort and swim. Lining the log booms like sentries, the gulls declare their territory with raucous calls.

Gene Coulon is a long sliver of a park—in places, less than 100 feet wide—sandwiched between Lake Washington and the Burlington Northern Santa Fe Railway. Yet it's so carefully designed that its broad, level shore walk, equipped with interpretive signs and landscaped with native plants, attracts walkers year-round. In summer you share it with boisterous children and quiet sun worshippers; in fall, winter, and spring you share it with waterfowl and fellow walkers.

Though the park is most heavily used in summer for its beach and boat launch, the lakeside walk has unexpected beauty in winter. Grasses are tawny yellow against the dark blue of the lake, and among the bare-stemmed bushes hang winter's boldest ornaments: white snowberries and red rose hips. As the trail traces the contours of the lake, it crosses marshes and miniature gardens of native plantings. Before the restaurants arrived, the old pilings in Trestle Marsh marked the former railroad, cedar mill, and log-dumping site. In spring on Nature Island Bird Sanctuary, you may see nesting mallards and Canada geese. In any season, you can add distance to your stroll by exploring the boardwalks that surround the floating picnic area.

ADDRESS: 1201 Lake Washington Boulevard N, Renton

GETTING THERE: From I-405, take exit 5 (WA 900/Issaquah, Sunset Boulevard). Go west under the freeway on NE Park Drive. Cross the railroad tracks and take a hard right at the light onto Lake Washington Boulevard N. The southern park entrance is on the left in a few hundred yards. Other parking is available if you continue north on Lake Washington Boulevard N.

CONTACT: Renton Parks Division, (425) 430-6600, www.rentonwa.gov

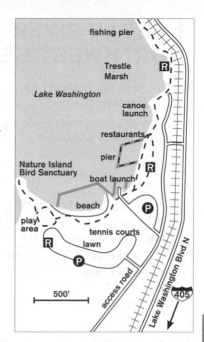

All Five Senses

Walking is a sensory experience. Teach kids to look, listen, touch, smell, and taste. Teach them the difference between edible and nonedible berries, and between touchable and untouchable plants. Be sure you know which is which.

75 CEDAR RIVER TRAIL (NORTHWEST SECTION)

Renton, 6 miles north of Kent, to Jones Road bridge, 5 miles east of Renton

A salmon-spawning river leads from Lake Washington alongside artwork, parks, and forest.

TRAIL	8 miles one way; paved
STEEPNESS	Level
OTHER USES	Bicycles
DOGS	Off-leash area, otherwise on leash
CONNECTING TRAILS	Cedar River Trail (Southeast Section) (Walk #80)
PARK AMENITIES	Restrooms, picnic areas at parks
DISABLED ACCESS	Paved trail, restrooms, picnic areas

To experience one of the best examples of urban greenery by a river's edge, begin at Lake Washington at the mouth of the Cedar River and walk south through a manicured park. After crossing under I-405, the trail changes to a more natural, forested setting.

So close is the clear, shallow Cedar River that when it rises only a foot at flood time, water covers the walkway. (Call the city for conditions after heavy rains.) At the Downtown Renton Library, which spans the river, continue south, past sculptures and through Liberty Park. Street crossings take you under the I-405 trestle to the Renton Community Center and another trailhead in Cedar River Park, where there is a fenced off-leash area.

Access to this section begins with a pedestrian bridge across the Cedar River. From here the trail, still well paved, traverses fields and enters a cool second-growth forest. Visible through a veil of cottonwoods and alder, the Cedar River parallels the path. In summer, swallows swoop for insects over the water, and year-round, birds forage and sing in the maple and hemlock hillside to the south. In fall you may see the spawning salmon making their way upstream. The trail closely parallels the highway, becoming more a bicycler's than a walker's trail. Those with a yen for a long walk can carry on the full 12 miles to Maple Valley.

ADDRESS: *Northern end:* 1060 N Nishiwaki Lane, Renton
Renton Community Center: 1715 SE Maple Valley Highway, Renton

GETTING THERE: *Northern end:* From I-405 northbound, take exit 2 (WA 167/ Rainier Avenue S). Stay left to get onto Rainier Avenue S. Continue 0.4 miles.

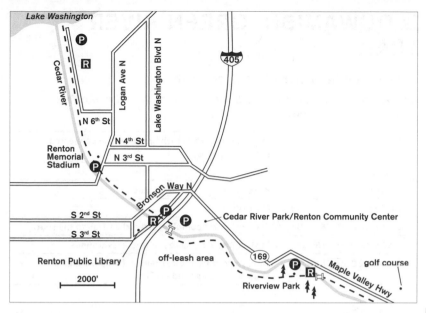

Turn right onto Airport Way, which becomes Logan Avenue N. Go 0.4 miles and turn left onto N 6th Street. In 0.2 miles turn right onto Nishiwaki Lane to reach the trailhead parking.

From I-405 southbound, take exit 5 (WA 900 E/Park Avenue N) and turn right onto Park Avenue, which becomes Logan Avenue. Go 0.6 miles. Turn right onto N 6th Street and proceed as above.

Renton Community Center: From I-405, take exit 4 (WA 169 S) and follow signs for Maple Valley Highway (WA 169). Take the first right into Cedar River Park. The trail is behind the community center.

CONTACT: Renton Parks Division, (206) 430-6600, www.rentonwa .gov. To volunteer, contact Friends of the Cedar River Watershed: fcrw.wordpress.com.

<u>76</u> DUWAMISH–GREEN RIVER TRAIL

Tukwila, 4 miles north of Kent, to Kent

An open riverside trail wanders through varied habitat and offers Cascade Range views.

TRAIL	13.5 miles one way (with breaks and unconnected sections); paved
STEEPNESS	Level
OTHER USES	Bicycles along some stretches
DOGS	On leash
CONNECTING TRAILS	Starfire Sports complex, Interurban Trail to the south
PARK AMENITIES	Restrooms, art, picnic shelters, playgrounds
DISABLED ACCESS	Trail, restrooms at Bicentennial Park, Briscoe Park, and Van Doren's Landing Park

A slice of peace between light industry, shopping malls, and freeways, the Duwamish–Green River Trail teases with reminders of a less industrialized time in the Tukwila and Kent region.

The best starting point is either toward the north end at Bicentennial Park in Tukwila or toward the south end at Van Doren's Landing Park in Kent.

> **Petering Out?**
>
> Keep energy up with water and snacks. Reward kids for reaching landmarks like hilltops or streams. Tell them how far they've walked (in miles!) and congratulate them.

From Bicentennial Park the trail goes 0.5 miles north along the river, crosses under I-405, and goes into the 54-acre Starfire Sports complex (which includes Fort Dent Park). For the next mile, it skirts the landscaped edge of the park and crosses an old-style trestle footbridge that marks the confluence of the (now mainly

dry) Black River and the Green River. The trail follows the Green River north another 3 miles.

Heading south from Bicentennial Park, the trail hugs the riverbank. Where the river makes a sharp U-curve at S 180th Street, a lovely footbridge spans it, offering walks on either side. (If you don't cross, the trail soon peters out into industry.) On the

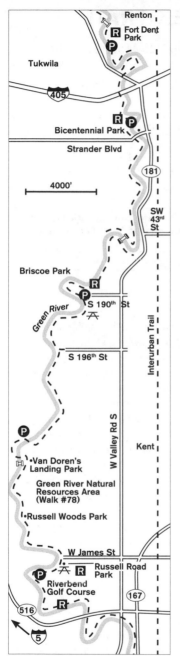

south side, a left turn takes you to a trailhead on West Valley Road S; a right turn takes you south into Kent and, in about a mile or so, to Briscoe Park at S 190th Street. Here you'll find park amenities, including disabled access and a launch for hand-carried boats.

If you start at Van Doren's Landing Park and walk south, you can make a side trip east on the Puget Power Trail into the Green River Natural Resources Area (Walk #78), 300 acres of wetland and bird-watching at its best. South from Van Doren's Landing Park, a short walk on Russell Road brings you to another peaceful stretch starting at Russell Woods Park, until you reach the junction with the Interurban Trail near S 259th Street.

Fall and early winter visitors can enjoy the thrill of watching hundreds of salmon swim the river to their spawning grounds. Contact the Washington Department of Fish & Wildlife for more information.

ADDRESS: *Bicentennial Park:* 6000 Christiansen Road, Tukwila; *Van Doren's Landing Park:* 21861 Russell Road, Kent

GETTING THERE: *Bicentennial Park:* From I-405, take exit 1 (WA 181 S/W Valley Highway). Go south on W Valley Highway for 0.4 miles. Turn right on Strander Boulevard. Cross the river and turn right into the park.

Van Doren's Landing Park: Follow the directions above to W Valley Highway. Continue south on W Valley Highway, which becomes 68th Avenue S. Turn right on S 212th Street. Go 1.25 miles. Turn left on Russell Road. Go 0.5 miles; the park is on the right.

CONTACT: Tukwila Parks and Recreation Department, (206) 433-1800, www.tukwilawa .gov/residents/parks-recreation; Kent Parks, Recreation, and Community Services Department, (253) 856-5100, www.kentwa.gov /parksandrecreation

77 DES MOINES CREEK TRAIL

SeaTac, 2 miles north of Des Moines, to Des Moines, 1 mile north of downtown

A gentle trail through 96 acres of woodland along Des Moines Creek joins with 60 acres of beach park.

TRAIL	2 miles one way; natural surface, paved
STEEPNESS	Gentle
OTHER USES	Bicycles
DOGS	On leash
CONNECTING TRAILS	None
PARK AMENITIES	Restrooms, fishing pier, historical information, picnic area, playground at Des Moines Beach Park; none in northern end
DISABLED ACCESS	Paved trail, restrooms at marina

In a deep green cleft in the suburbs south of Seattle-Tacoma International Airport, Des Moines Creek Trail follows the bubbling, salmon-spawning stream toward Puget Sound. Fully paved all the way to Des Moines Beach Park, this forested trail can be walked either downstream or upstream, the grade fairly gentle either way.

From SeaTac the trail leads south between buttresses of blackberries, appearing to be nothing more than a paved right-of-way for the city utility cars. But as it rounds a corner and begins to slope gently downward, the berries give way to ferns, and the alders disappear under the overhanging canopy of big-leaf maples and Douglas firs. After about 0.25 miles of walking, the sound of churning water can be heard along with calls of forest birds. And then the stream appears, deep in its own ravine, clear and inviting as it flows over native rocks. Nature is reclaiming the area cleared of houses years ago in anticipation of airport runway expansion.

The paved trail means good walking year-round, but for those venturing off the pavement, the many steep dirt paths on the high hillside to the west become impassable in wet weather. No problem, though, for the mountain bikers who careen along the dirt trails in all weather, keen on sliding, jumping, and climbing the convoluted maze of byways. Fortunately, the paved trail by the creek has a center line so that bicycle and foot traffic is fairly orderly. Side trails over the creek and up the hillside lead to bordering neighborhoods.

Closely hugging the creek near the fenced-off wastewater treatment facility, the trail dives back into the forest and descends gently, passing under Marine View Drive until it reaches the historical buildings and open lawn of Des Moines

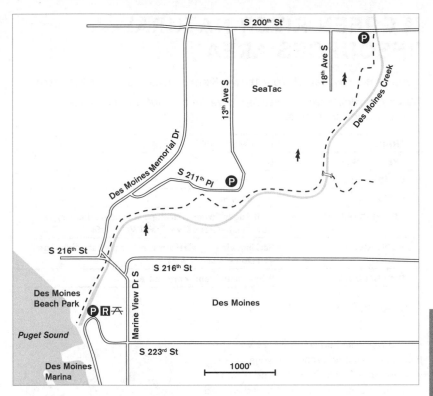

Beach Park. Here you leave the scent of wet forest and inhale the rich heady scent of seawater. If the tide is out, there are acres of beach to explore and wading birds to watch. Surf scoters, goldeneyes, and grebes dabble, paddle, and muck about in the food-rich estuarine soup. Gulls call, cheer, and squabble over clams as the creek makes its last burbling yards to the sea.

ADDRESS: *Northern end:* 2151 S 200th Street, SeaTac; *Beach end:* 22030 Cliff Avenue S, Des Moines

GETTING THERE: *Northern end:* From I-5, take exit 151 (S 200th Street/Military Road). Go west on 200th Street until the road dips sharply. Find trailhead parking on the left.

Beach end: From I-5, take exit 149 (WA 516 W/Kent). Go west on Kent–Des Moines Road for 2 miles, and merge right into Marine View Drive S. Go about 5 blocks and turn left on S 223rd Street. This drops down the hill and becomes Cliff Street, which enters the park.

CONTACT: SeaTac Parks and Recreation Department, (206) 973-4780, www.ci.seatac.wa.us; Des Moines Parks, Recreation, and Senior Services Department, (206) 870-6527, www.desmoineswa.gov

78 GREEN RIVER NATURAL RESOURCES AREA

4 miles northwest of downtown Kent; 7 miles south of Renton

Watch for wildlife from a viewing tower in this 300-acre restored refuge and open space.

TRAIL	1.3 miles; gravel
STEEPNESS	Level
OTHER USES	Pedestrians only
DOGS	Not allowed
CONNECTING TRAILS	Kent Puget Power Trail along southern boundary, Duwamish–Green River Trail (Walk #76)
PARK AMENITIES	Parking, viewing platforms; picnic area at adjoining Van Doren's Landing Park
DISABLED ACCESS	Wheelchair-friendly gravel trail

Let the welcome sun warm you as you stroll this open space and restored wetlands in western Kent. Listen for the sound of wind in the tall grasses and the call of red-winged blackbirds in the reeds, and keep an eye out for evidence of coyotes—fur-filled scat on the pathways. On clear days Mount Rainier forms a dramatic backdrop to the southeast.

Previously a wastewater lagoon system with storm-water detention ponds, the Green River Natural Resources Area (also known as Kent Ponds) has undergone a face-lift with the addition of thousands of young native shrubs, tree plantings, and wheelchair-friendly paths. The wetlands and surrounding meadows are a natural breeding, brooding, and feeding site for more than 160 bird species, and are home to more than fifty mammal species, including river otter, beaver, coyote, and deer. At 300 acres, this is one of the largest man-made wildlife refuges in the United States.

For the best bird-watching, fall and winter are good times to visit, when the grasses are low and the pond is more visible. Flocks of migrating birds use the

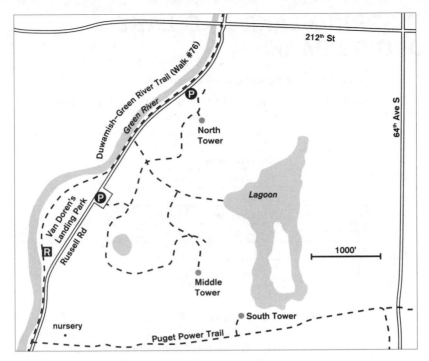

area as a rest and staging place on their way south. On the water you may see ruddy ducks, great blue herons, and American coots; look overhead or on the bare tree branches for merlins and bald eagles. Two tall viewing platforms accessible from the Green River Natural Resources Area paths and one accessed from Kent's paved Puget Power Trail on the southern boundary offer bird's-eye views over the meadows. Due to the sensitive nature of the Green River Natural Resources Area, dogs are not allowed in the reserve.

ADDRESS: *Van Doren's Landing Park:* 21861 Russell Road S, Kent

GETTING THERE: From I-405, take exit 2 (WA 167 Renton/Auburn) and head south on WA 167. Go 4 miles and take the S 212th Street exit. Turn right and go 2 miles. Turn left onto Russell Road. More parking is at Van Doren's Landing Park, 0.5 miles away.

From I-5, take exit 152 (Orillia Road). Turn east on Orillia Road, which becomes S 212th Street. Cross the Green River and turn right on Russell Road.

CONTACT: Kent Parks, Recreation, and Community Services Department; (253) 856-5100; www.kentwa.gov/parksandrecreation

<u>79</u> SPRING LAKE AND LAKE DESIRE PARK

8.5 miles southeast of downtown Renton

Get a workout climbing through 390 acres of lush forest to a rocky outcrop for a great view of snowy Mount Rainier.

TRAIL	4.5 miles; natural surface
STEEPNESS	Gentle to steep
OTHER USES	Bicycles and horses except on Peak Trail
DOGS	On leash
CONNECTING TRAILS	McGarvey Park to the north
PARK AMENITIES	None
DISABLED ACCESS	None

Rising a full 400 feet above the placid waters of Spring Lake and Lake Desire, smooth boulder–topped Mount Echo beckons walkers with a yen for a workout and a view. This forested King County park is home to bobcats, owls, bears, and foxes, yet lies quietly above the nearby recreational lakes and neighborhoods of Maple Valley.

This park is a walkers' destination, with nary a playground or sports field in sight. One comes here to traipse in the best of the Northwest nature and forest. Next to the small parking lot at the base of the trail, an informational sign helps you choose your walking trails. Head up the service road (wonderfully soft and more like a wide trail than a road), then cut off to the right into the forest on the signposted Peak Trail. So steep is this final 200-foot ascent to Mount Echo's viewpoint that neither horses nor bicycles are allowed. A well-maintained trail of log steps leads you up and around the hillside until you come to the broad,

rock-surfaced peak. On clear days look south into the face of glacier-covered Mount Rainier.

A winter walk promises glimpses of Lake Desire far below as you peer through the bare branches of the alders and maples. The lower forest is lush with sword ferns that line the gentle ravine, through which a small brook tumbles. In the green seasons you'll be

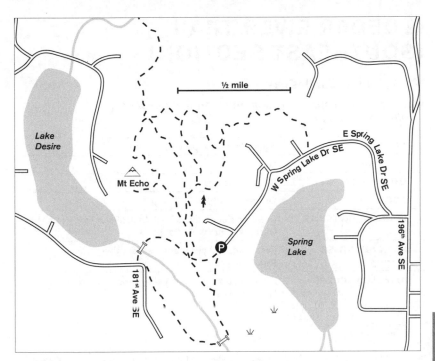

walking through a sylvan wonderland of tall canopied trees and huge old-growth stumps amid mahonia and sword ferns. Even then, the view from the peak is clear for great mountain scenery.

If you're not up for a hill climb, meander the trails to the north of the trailhead, or take the 1.3-mile loop through the bog and wetlands of Spring Lake to the south.

ADDRESS: 18800 West Spring Lake Drive, Renton (approximate)

GETTING THERE: From I-405, take exit 4 (WA 169/Maple Valley). Go 6.3 miles on the Maple Valley Highway and turn right onto 196th Avenue SE. Go 1.4 miles and turn right onto SE 183rd Street, then right again onto E Spring Lake Drive. Stay right, merge onto W Spring Lake Drive, and follow it around the lake to the end of the road. To park on the left by the boat launch a Discover Pass is required, but it is not required at the trailhead.

CONTACT: King County Parks, (206) 477-4527, www.kingcounty.gov/recreation /parks

<u>80</u> CEDAR RIVER TRAIL (SOUTHEAST SECTION)

Maple Valley, 8 miles east of Kent

Watch birds and spawning salmon along this forested rails-to-trails path.

TRAIL	6 miles one way; paved and natural
STEEPNESS	Level
OTHER USES	Bicycles, horses
DOGS	On leash
CONNECTING TRAILS	Green-to-Cedar Rivers Trail; Cedar River Trail (Northwest Section) (Walk #75)
PARK AMENITIES	Restrooms and picnic areas at Landsburg Park Trailhead
DISABLED ACCESS	Paved section at Maple Valley end; some access at Landsburg Park

Lined with cottonwoods, alders, and mixed conifers, this converted rails-to-trails path is wide and smooth, and, being raised above the surrounding wetland, offers year-round dry-footed walking. A wild cry might break the stillness as a bald eagle rises from the river, a salmon clutched in its talons. In summer, golden-crowned kinglets call from the trees, swallows dive for insects, and dippers bob along the riverbanks like tireless windup toys.

Running a course straighter than the Cedar River, the trail takes you alternately from forest to riverside to bridge. Beginning across from Foley's Produce, the trail is paved all the way north to Renton. If you walk or bicycle, you can go as long as your feet and time hold out. On this stretch, the trail closely borders the Maple Valley Highway. See Walk #75, Cedar River Trail (Northwest Section), for another lovely stretch of regional trail.

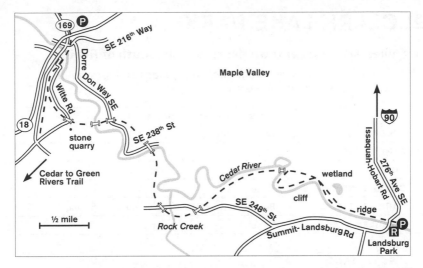

Heading southeast from Foley's, the pavement ends near the intersection with the Green-to-Cedar Rivers Trail (also known as the Lake Wilderness Trail). From here, the trail takes on its most natural surroundings. After passing a stone quarry and Rock Creek, the trail enters ever wilder landscape as you close with the river. About 1 mile from Landsburg Park (the easternmost trailhead), a reconstructed 1908 railroad bridge spans the river. High above the water, you have an eagle's-eye view both up- and downstream to cliffs, eddies, and rapids. From here you can continue on the raised railbed or, river height permitting, explore the sandy path that traces the river's edge to Landsburg Park.

ADDRESS: *Foley's Produce:* 21419 SE Renton Maple Valley Road, Maple Valley (public parking is across the street); *Landsburg Park:* SE 253rd Street and Landsburg Road SE, Ravensdale

GETTING THERE: *Foley's Produce:* From I-405, take exit 4 (WA 169/Maple Valley). Go south on WA 169 for 9.9 miles. The park is on the east side of the road, across from Foley's Produce.

From I-5 north, take exit 142A (WA 18 Auburn/North Bend) and go east 15.6 miles on WA 18. Take the SE 231st Street exit and follow signs to WA 169 (Maple Valley). Turn north on WA 169, cross under WA 18, and park on the right, across from Foley's Produce.

Landsburg Park: Follow the directions above to WA 169, but stay on WA 169 past WA 18 and turn left onto SE 216th Street. Go east for 3 miles and turn right onto 276th Avenue SE (Issaquah-Hobart Road). Go 2.4 miles to Landsburg Park. The trail begins on the west side of the road.

CONTACT: King County Parks, (206) 477-4527, www.kingcounty.gov/recreation /parks. To volunteer, contact Friends of the Cedar River Watershed: fcrw .wordpress.com.

<u>81</u> CLARK LAKE PARK

4.5 miles east of downtown Kent; 18 miles south of Renton

This 130-acre park provides wetlands, lakes, meadows, groves of forest, and great mountain views.

TRAIL	2 miles; boardwalk, natural surface
STEEPNESS	Level to gentle
OTHER USES	Bicycles
DOGS	On leash
CONNECTING TRAILS	None
PARK AMENITIES	Benches, interpretive trail, viewing and fishing dock
DISABLED ACCESS	None

Leave the edge of suburbia and walk through restored meadows where plump heads of lavender, clover, and bright-yellow buttercups brighten the summer greenery. The land is in transition, slowly being reclaimed from its long-ago use as farmland. A quiet dell of Douglas fir and hemlock resounds with birdsong, and bird boxes offer shelter to nesting flickers. Nestled in the center of this passive-use park, 7-acre Clark Lake is home to native bass and rainbow trout. The graveled paths lead you through meadows and shady stands of forest, while nearer

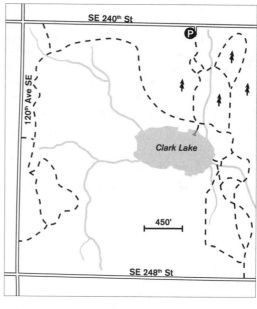

to the lake's edge you walk on securely built boardwalks over sensitive wetlands and out to the lake's edge on a viewing and fishing platform. The trail rises from the lake to the north and east, and even with summer's luxuriant growth, the lake is visible. In summer, the once-domestic cherry trees drape with ripe red fruit, which is plundered by resident raccoons. In fall, the leaves stand brilliant with color against a backdrop of blue sky and the white cone of Mount Rainier to the south, and coho salmon may be seen in the stream.

In years past, the stream was home to both coho and Chinook salmon; with the help of volunteers, the stream is being cleared of invasive plants and replanted to provide improved habitat for the fish and other native wildlife. The original 29 acres were first annexed by the city in the early 1990s, and since then Clark Lake Park has been growing bit by bit as more land is purchased. Eagle Scout troops have built information kiosks at the entrances, and scores of volunteers have created boardwalks, fencing, and loop trails. Although the tannin-brown waters of the lake are tempting on hot summer days, swimming is not allowed due to underwater natural hazards.

> **Pack It In, Pack It Out**
>
> Many parks and most natural-surface trails have no trash collection. Carry a plastic bag in your pocket or a day pack for trash. If you've got a dog on leash, you should be carrying plastic bags for scooping.

ADDRESS: 12540 SE 240th Street, Kent (approximate)

GETTING THERE: From I-405, take exit 2 (WA 167 S). Go south on WA 167 for 4.2 miles. Exit at 212th Street SE. Turn left and follow 212th Street SE as it

becomes 208th Street SE. In 1.8 miles turn right onto 116th Avenue SE. Go 2 miles and turn left onto SE 240th Street. The park is in 0.6 miles on the right.

Other trailheads with on-street parking are on 120th Avenue SE and SE 248th Street.

CONTACT: Kent Parks, Recreation, and Community Services Department; (253) 856-5100; www.kentwa.gov /parksandrecreation

82 SOOS CREEK TRAIL

4 miles east of downtown Kent

Walk miles of paved trail along a creek and through 775 acres of forested wetlands.

TRAIL	7.5 miles one way; paved
STEEPNESS	Level to gentle
OTHER USES	Bicycles, horses (horses may be on side trail)
DOGS	On leash
CONNECTING TRAILS	None
PARK AMENITIES	Restrooms, brochure, interpretive walks, picnic tables; playgrounds at trailheads
DISABLED ACCESS	Trail (though parts do not meet ADA standards), restrooms

Just inches above the marshes, this paved path cuts a straight dark line through one of the finest wetlands in South King County. Chickadees call *chicka dee dee dee* from the branches of alder and oak. A red-tailed hawk soars overhead. Soos Creek Trail is a walker's hidden paradise just minutes from downtown Kent.

Marshes like this one have an all-season appeal. In summer the trail is busy with skaters, cyclists, and walkers, and the marsh plants are tall and thick with green stalks and golden-brown cattails. The landscape feels enclosed and intimate. In winter the wet meadow areas predominate, with hardhack, alder, willow, and many bird species. In winter, too, you can see through the brush to the hillsides of fir and hemlock that rise from the creek.

The park's shape is defined by meandering Soos Creek. The northern end is near Gary Grant Park northeast of Kent; the southern end is near Lake Meridian Park on Kent-Kangley Road. Along the length of the trail, you pass through several

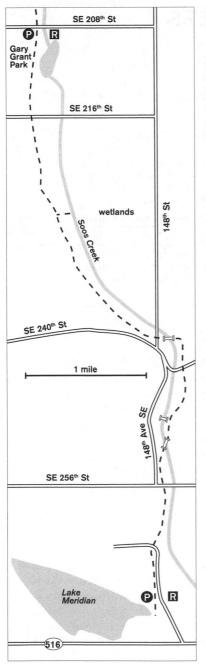

distinct types of wetlands. Ponds are home to great blue herons, ducks, geese, cattails, rushes, skunk cabbage, and wild roses. Scrub wetlands remain flooded year-round. In the forested wetland you'll walk beside vine maple, cedar, salmonberry, and elderberry; then you climb to the upland forest, with its second-growth cedars, maples, and ferns.

Originally owned by the Northern Pacific Railroad, the land was logged in the late 1800s by large timber companies. After that, Finnish pioneers arrived, clearing the land with oxen and horses to raise fruits and vegetables. Look for remnants of the old orchards along the trail.

ADDRESS: *Gary Grant Park:* SE 208th Street and 136th Avenue SE, Kent; *Trailhead near Lake Meridian Park:* SE 266th Street and 148th Avenue SE

GETTING THERE: *Gary Grant Park:* From I-405, take exit 2 (WA 167 S/Auburn). Go south 3.9 miles on WA 167. Turn left (east) on SE 212th Street, which becomes SE 208th Street, and find the park trailhead in 3 miles.

From I-5 northbound, take exit 149A (WA 516, Kent); from southbound, take exit 149 (WA 516, Kent). Head east on WA 516 and exit onto WA 167 N. Go north on WA 167 for 2 miles, turn right on SE 212th Street, and proceed as above.

CONTACT: King County Parks, (206) 477-4527, www.kingcounty.gov/recreation/parks. Check the website for information on interpretive walks.

<u>83</u> LAKE WILDERNESS ARBORETUM

Maple Valley, 8 miles east of Kent

Walk 42 acres of garden paths, an old railroad grade, and forest trails to the edge of Lake Wilderness.

TRAIL	3 miles total; gravel, natural surface
STEEPNESS	Level to gentle
OTHER USES	Pedestrians only on self-guided loop; horses and bicycles on Lake Wilderness Trail (also known as the Green-to-Cedar Rivers Trail)
DOGS	On leash; not allowed on nature loop trail
CONNECTING TRAILS	Green-to-Cedar Rivers Trail
PARK AMENITIES	Nature trail brochure and map, plant sales; Lake Wilderness Park offers restrooms, picnic area, beach, meeting rooms, playgrounds, tennis
DISABLED ACCESS	Garden trails

Located on the edge of Lake Wilderness Park, the Lake Wilderness Arboretum leases land from the county for a show garden with walking trails and interpretive information. In one walk, you can enjoy both an ornamental garden of native plants and a natural second-growth forest typical of the Cascade foothills.

The Lake Wilderness Arboretum Foundation, a nonprofit volunteer group, has created these gardens to provide examples of native plants and to teach why it's important, when choosing nonnative ornamental plants, to select those that will thrive here without extra water or fertilizer. On the garden trails, you can see a wide variety of rhododendrons, both species and hybrids, and showy trees such as the purple-leafed smoke tree and unusual maples. Spring is, of course, spectacular with color, but each season offers some new and colorful changes in the garden. Volunteers are needed—there are always more plantings and projects in the works.

North across the old railroad grade, you enter a mature second-growth forest. On the self-guided loop, you can read about and observe this transitional forest, in which the more shade-tolerant western hemlocks and western red cedars are slowly replacing the Douglas firs. From high in the canopy, secretive warblers sing and tiny brown creepers spiral their way up the trunks in search of bark-dwelling insects. Orange lichen paint intriguing patterns on the trunks of the big-leaf maples.

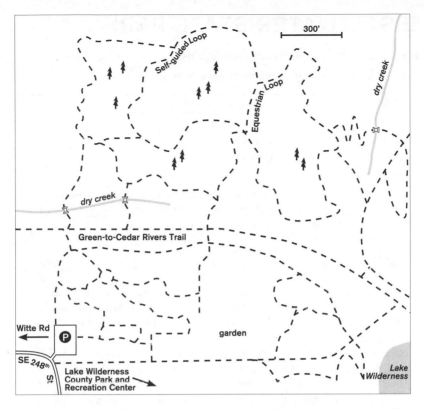

To extend your walk, head either east or west on the railroad grade, part of the Green-to-Cedar Rivers trail. This raised gravel walk is dry even in the wettest months and maintains a natural forest setting for more than a mile in each direction. To the northwest it joins the Cedar River Trail (Walk #80) in 1.6 miles.

ADDRESS: 22520 SE 248th Street, Maple Valley

GETTING THERE: From I-405, take exit 4 (WA 169/Maple Valley). Go east for 10 miles on WA 169 to Maple Valley. After crossing WA 18, turn right on Witte Road. Go 0.8 miles and turn left on SE 248th Street. Go 0.5 miles to the arboretum next to Lake Wilderness Park.

From I-5, take exit 142A (WA 18 Auburn/North Bend). Exit WA 18 at WA 169. Turn right on SE 231st Street, then right (south) on WA 169. Go 0.3 miles, turn right again (south) on Witte Road, and proceed as above.

CONTACT: Maple Valley Parks and Recreation Department, (425) 432-9953, www.maplevalleywa.gov/departments-services/parks-recreation. For volunteer information, visit www.lakewildernessarboretum.org.

<u>84</u> SALTWATER STATE PARK

2 miles south of downtown Des Moines

Explore 88 acres along McSorley Creek from forest to beach.

TRAIL	2 miles; natural surface
STEEPNESS	Level to steep
OTHER USES	Bicycles
DOGS	On leash
CONNECTING TRAILS	None
PARK AMENITIES	Restrooms, picnic areas, playground, underwater park; summer only: camping, concession stand
DISABLED ACCESS	Restrooms, camping, picnic areas

At low tide, 1,500 feet of rocky beach creates a multitude of tide pools. Here red and yellow starfish cling, crabs scuttle, and snails creep. Inland, cool, shaded forest lets you wander over a hillside to a bluff overlooking Puget Sound and seagoing vessels.

One of the most popular state parks on the sound, Saltwater sees upward of three-quarters of a million visitors a year. The nice thing is, they come mostly in summer and on warm weekends, and most of them visit the beach. With careful timing, you can be virtually alone on the beach, communing with clams and mussels or watching the antics of the seagulls and crows as they drop the mollusks from the air to the concrete for an instant breakfast. At high tide, walk the several hundred yards of paved walkway next to the seawall.

For a forest stroll, leave from the playground and follow the soft-surfaced path along the hillside under a mix of Douglas fir and big-leaf maple. This forest was last logged more than 75 years ago, and the second-growth trees are reaching a hefty size. The lush undergrowth helps to muffle the sounds of visitors and the hum of traffic on the bridge overhead. The trail loops back to the McSorley Creek ravine at the eastern end of the campground. Other trails lead from the valley, make loops, and return. On the north side of the camping area, a footbridge crosses the creek, which once again is seeing a salmon run.

What Is That?

Find out by joining a naturalist-led walk. Most are free. Call your city or county parks department for information. Parks also offer classes in outdoor-related topics such as gardening, birding, geology, animal care, naturalist studies, and science. Fees may apply.

ADDRESS: 25205 8th Place S, Des Moines

GETTING THERE: From I-5, take exit 149 (Kent-Des Moines/WA 516). Go west on WA 516 for 1.9 miles to Marine View Drive. Turn left, go 1.2 miles to S 252nd Street and 8th Place S, and turn right into the park. A Discover Pass is required for parking.

CONTACT: Washington State Parks, Saltwater State Park Office, (253) 661-4956, www.parks.wa.gov

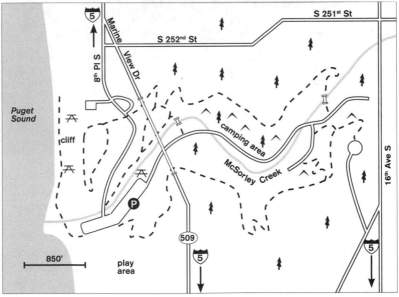

<u>85</u> GAME FARM AND GAME FARM WILDERNESS PARKS

Auburn, 9.5 miles southeast of Kent

Glacier-fed White River cuts through 120 acres of landscaped and wild parks.

TRAIL	4 miles; natural surface, paved
STEEPNESS	Level
OTHER USES	Bicycles
DOGS	On leash
CONNECTING TRAILS	White River Trail (Walk #86)
PARK AMENITIES	Restrooms, playgrounds, art, picnic shelters, playing fields, sports courts; disc golf and camping in Game Farm Wilderness Park
DISABLED ACCESS	Paved trail, restrooms, amphitheater, picnic shelters

Two nonidentical twin parks line the sides of the milky, glacier-fed White River (which becomes the Stuck River as it passes the parks). Here you can choose civilization, amenities, and landscaping at Game Farm Park in the north, or a wilder, less gentrified park in the south.

Game Farm Park (named for its past history as a site on which shooting stock was raised) throbs with activity. Colonnades of landscaping trees border playing fields that are interconnected with more than 2 miles of paved walkways. Come for people-watching on weekends and for solitude on damp winter days. Park near the amphitheater at the southern end and walk past the picnic shelters toward the river. The almost-century-old diversion dam divides park landscaping from river wilderness. Walk along it, or step over it to find an unmaintained but well-used path on the riverbank. Follow this path of sand and rounded river rocks east along the river. Side trails lead to possible wading and picnic areas on the shores. (See Don't Get Carried Away, page 179.) Beaver-toppled trees, with their

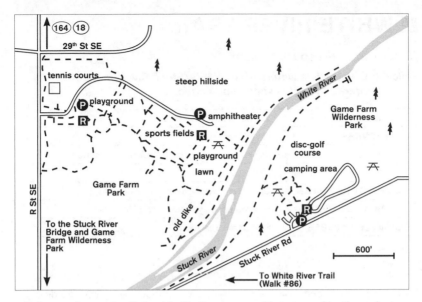

telltale gnawing marks, lie jumbled in the river, awaiting removal by the rodents or the next flood.

Across the river in Game Farm Wilderness Park (accessed via the R Street SE bridge), a campground, restrooms, and picnic shelters are the only amenities. An actively used disc-golf course parallels the sand-and-rock path that leads along the river. Across the water, 150-foot-high bluffs are a geological window to the past, while today's trees cling tenaciously to the sandy walls. West from the day-use area, a short paved trail invites walkers, baby strollers, and wheelchairs.

Watch for dippers—small brown birds that bob and hunt for food along the rocky rapids. Breathe deeply of this fresh river-scented air.

ADDRESS: *Game Farm Park:* 3030 R Street SE, Auburn; *Game Farm Wilderness Park:* 2401 Stuck River Drive, Auburn

GETTING THERE: From I-405, take exit 2 (WA 167 S/Auburn). Go about 10 miles south on WA 167 to WA 18. Go east on WA 18 to the WA 164 (Auburn Way) exit. Head south for 0.9 miles and stay left for Howard Road. Go 0.25 miles and turn right onto R Street SE. Go 0.7 miles to Game Farm Park on your left. For Game Farm Wilderness Park continue on R Street SE, cross the river, and turn left.

From I-5, take exit 142A (WA 18 E/Auburn). Go 4 miles east on WA 18, take the WA 164 (Auburn Way) exit, and proceed as above.

CONTACT: Auburn Parks, Arts, and Recreation Department; (206) 931-3043; www.auburnwa.gov/things_to_do/parks_trails.htm

<u>86</u> WHITE RIVER TRAIL

Auburn, 11 miles south of Kent

*Follow the blue-white waters of the White/Stuck River on a paved
trail bordered by cottonwoods and conifers.*

TRAIL	2.2 miles; paved, natural
STEEPNESS	Level to gentle
OTHER USES	Bicycles; horses on soft-surface parallel trail
DOGS	On leash
CONNECTING TRAILS	Game Farm Wilderness Park (Walk #85)
PARK AMENITIES	Restrooms, playground, art, picnic area
DISABLED ACCESS	Paved trail, restrooms

There is something both invigorating and peaceful about walking by the side of a
swiftly flowing river. The slow pace of foot travel contrasts with the swift motion of
the river, the energetic sound of moving water, and the sight of a lone rock fighting
the force of the river flowing over it. Above and surrounding it all is the freshwater-
scented breeze. The White River Trail has the added attraction of a smooth, paved
walkway so that you can watch the river as you walk, without being overly mindful
of your feet. Perhaps you'll spot a great blue heron wading in an eddy or a bright-
blue kingfisher perched on a maple branch, searching for its next meal. If you
begin in Roegner Park, you can follow a loop trail to the west, return to the park

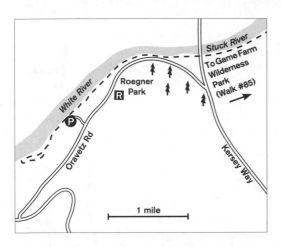

and its amenities, and then walk upstream as far as you like before retracing your steps.

Is it called the White River or the Stuck River? The answer is both. Until the end of the nineteenth century, the White River, together with the Green and Black Rivers, formed the Duwamish River, which emptied into Elliott Bay in Seattle. The Stuck River flowed toward Tacoma. Farmers in the Kent Valley, forever worried about flooding, used to dynamite the rivers, and in one mishap, they diverted much of the flow of the White River to the Stuck Valley. A huge flood in 1906 changed the landscape further, and the White River was diverted permanently. Today the White and the Stuck are the same river, and they flow into the Puyallup River en route to Tacoma's Commencement Bay. The milky color of the river is from the finely ground rock, the glacial till, that is carried by the water as it flows from the glaciers on Mount Rainier.

ADDRESS: *Roegner Park:* 601 Oravetz Road, Auburn

GETTING THERE: From I-5, take exit 2 (WA 167/Kent/Auburn). Go south on WA 167. After 14 miles, take the exit toward Algona Pacific. Go 0.3 miles and turn left onto Ellingson Road. Go 1.5 miles and turn right onto A Street SE. Go 0.7 miles and turn left onto Lakeland Hills Way. Turn left onto Oravetz Road SE. Go 0.4 miles. Roegner Park is on the left after the high school.

To begin at Game Farm Wilderness Park, 2401 Stuck River Drive, Auburn, follow directions for Walk #85.

CONTACT: Auburn Parks, Arts, and Recreation Department; (253) 931-3043; www.auburnwa.gov/things_to _do/parks_trails.htm

Don't Get Carried Away

Rivers can change character rapidly from shallow and placid to raging, murky torrents during and after local storms or Cascade storms that increase the snowmelt. Don't walk or play along riverbanks during heavy rain or when flood warnings are in effect. Both controlled rivers (such as the Cedar, Green, and White) and free-flowing rivers (such as the Snoqualmie, Carbon, and Snohomish) are potentially hazardous.

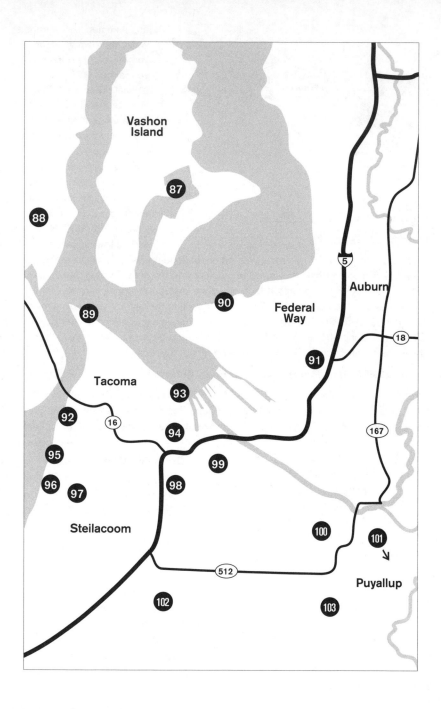

TACOMA

87 BURTON ACRES PARK

Vashon Island, 14 miles north of Tacoma (with ferry ride)

Leave the beach on Quartermaster Harbor to wander 68 acres of cathedral-forest trails.

TRAIL	1.1-mile loop, including center trails; natural surface
STEEPNESS	Gentle
OTHER USES	Bicycles
DOGS	On leash
CONNECTING TRAILS	None
PARK AMENITIES	Restrooms, boat launch, boat rentals, picnic tables
DISABLED ACCESS	Restrooms

Enter a forest cathedral almost a century old. The deeply furrowed bark of the old Douglas firs leads your eyes upward. Between the pillar-like trunks, neat clusters of sword fern and Oregon grape grow as if arranged like offerings. Walk silently on paths filled with fir needles. The big-leaf maples grow multiple trunks like candelabras.

Saved from the enthusiasm of nineteenth-century farmers for burning stumps and clearing acreage, these 68 acres belonged to Miles Hatch, a Tacoma businessman who started a college at Burton, where he pioneered in the late 1800s. Although the park has a small beach, picnic area, and boat launch, its allure lies in the forest. Enter it from either of two paths that lead from Burton Drive across from the boat launch. By turning right every time the trail splits, you can experiment with making a loop. If you find that your choice has led you to a house, retrace your steps to the junction and take the other path.

The northern section (the Enchanted Forest) has an open and spacious feel. The squat stumps with their rectangular springboard holes look like sylvan dwarves in a Disney cartoon. Fallen giant trees show the shallow root system of the Douglas firs and how easily they are uprooted in winter windstorms.

As you take the loop trail, you'll notice subtle changes. In the western

Seashells in the Forest?

Chances are, these shells were brought not by children but by birds. Northwest crows and gulls have learned that the easiest way to open their shellfish meals is to let gravity and impact do the work. They pick up a shell from the beach, fly high, and drop it—repeatedly—until lunch is laid out for them. Oysters on the half shell, anyone?

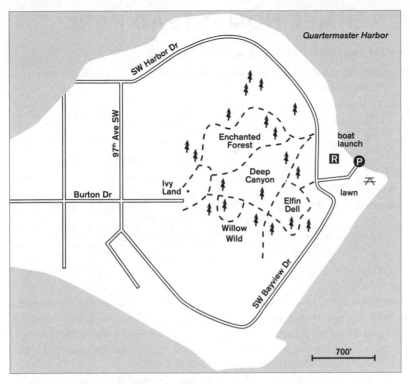

section (Ivy Land), English ivy has invaded from the bordering neighborhoods, threatening to engulf the shrubbery and stumps. The brush, too, is higher, composed of blackberry and nettle, and the trees trunks are smaller. A gentle decline in the trail takes you back into the past, back into the cathedral of older trees.

ADDRESS: 8900 SW Harbor Drive, Burton, Vashon Island

GETTING THERE: From the Tahlequah ferry terminal (southern Vashon Island), go north on Vashon Highway SW about 4.8 miles. Turn right on SW Burton Drive and go north for 0.4 miles. Turn left onto 97th Avenue SW and continue around the peninsula as it becomes SW Harbor Drive. At the boat launch and park sign, find the trail on the right.

From the northern Vashon Island ferry terminal, go south on Vashon Highway SW about 8.8 miles. Turn left on SW Burton Drive and proceed as above.

CONTACT: Vashon Park District, (206) 463-9602, www.vashonparks.org

<u>88</u> SEHMEL HOMESTEAD PARK

Gig Harbor, 10 miles northwest of Tacoma

Circumnavigate 98 acres of historic homestead on boardwalks and soft forest trails.

TRAIL	4.4 miles; paved, boardwalk, natural surface
STEEPNESS	Level to gentle
OTHER USES	Bicycles
DOGS	On leash
CONNECTING TRAILS	None
PARK AMENITIES	Restrooms, picnic areas, playground, ball fields, art, amphitheater, heritage garden
DISABLED ACCESS	Paved walkways, amphitheater, restrooms

Unlike many ball field–centric parks that offer a few walking paths in and around the fields, Sehmel Homestead has not forgotten its rural origins. Though most visitors to this 98-acre park outside Gig Harbor come for the sports fields or playground, those with a yen for some quiet walking will seek the well-signposted, broad, and well-maintained paths that encircle the park.

To visit the best of the park, begin in the northern parking lot near the grass-stepped amphitheater, and take the perimeter loop in a clockwise direction. A few boardwalks lead over marshy wetlands, then the trail enters a sparse forest behind the soccer fields. But carry on south and keep your left hand on the wall for the best wetlands and forest. On a quiet day you may see deer or catch the red and white flash and *rat-a-tat-tat* of the pileated woodpecker. Sparse forest gives way

to ancient stumps cut by decades of springboard notches, now draped in a carpet of moss and sporting large healthy trees atop the massive stumps. Cedar groves will beguile even reluctant walkers with their rich pungent scent and soft padding of needles underfoot.

The Sehmel Homestead is a legacy passed down through four generations. In 1891 Henry Sehmel, an immigrant from Germany, filed for homesteading papers on 160 acres of land. He and his wife, Dora, raised their children there, as did the next three generations. The Sehmels were active community citizens, involved in midwifery, logging, and produce farming. After 110 years of family ownership, Henry and Dora's great-grandson Bill Sehmel helped the county plan the layout and facilities of the park after its purchase in 2002.

ADDRESS: 10123 78th Avenue NW, Gig Harbor

GETTING THERE: From I-5, take exit 132 (WA 16/Gig Harbor/Bremerton). Go west on WA 16 for 12.2 miles and take the exit onto Burnham Drive NW. In 0.2 miles at the traffic circle, take the fourth exit to stay on Burnham Drive. At the next circle take the first exit to continue on Burnham. In 300 feet turn left onto Sehmel Drive NW and go 1.6 miles. Turn left onto 78th Avenue NW, where you will see the park on the left. Trail maps are available in the PenMet Parks office on-site.

CONTACT: PenMet Parks, (253) 858-3400, www.penmetparks.org

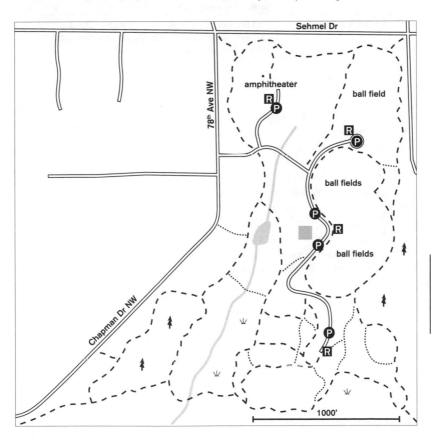

<u>89</u> POINT DEFIANCE PARK

5 miles northwest of downtown Tacoma

Stroll along 700 acres of forest trails and saltwater beach; visit gardens and the Fort Nisqually Living History Museum.

TRAIL	11 miles; gravel, natural surface, paved
STEEPNESS	Level to steep
OTHER USES	Pedestrians only in forest; bicycles on paved trails
DOGS	On leash
CONNECTING TRAILS	None
PARK AMENITIES	Restrooms, beach, gardens, picnic shelters, playgrounds, aquarium, children's entertainment, logging museum, zoo
DISABLED ACCESS	The Promenade (1 mile, Owen Beach to Point Defiance Marina boathouse), park facilities (sawdust-covered trails in Never Never Land)

It would be hard to choose one trail above all others in this 700-acre park on the northwest tip of Tacoma. Whatever your pleasure in walking trails, you'll find it here. Near the main entrance at N Park Avenue and Pearl Street, paved trails circulate throughout the formal park zone with its pond and gardens. Explore the world-class Rose Garden, the Japanese Garden, and, for a steeper walk, the Native Garden. Stroll the paved Promenade from the boathouse to Owen Beach on Commencement Bay. On Five Mile Drive, the Rhododendron Garden, ablaze with color in the early spring, leads to more wooded paths. High in the interior of the park, the Spine Trail, bisecting the park through its wild old forest, provides quiet on natural trails and an intimacy with nature not found near the beach and picnic areas.

For views of the water and the Olympics, try the walk north from the Vashon Island viewpoint on Five Mile Drive. This wooded trail passes wondrous old Douglas firs, cedars, and hemlocks. The earthen path muffles sounds, and as the trail curves farther from the road, the silence settles around you. Because of the age of this forest (more than 100 years), the undergrowth is sparse and a carpet of needles

Who Was Douglas?

David Douglas was a Scottish naturalist who explored the Pacific Northwest (then called the Columbia District) with the permission of the Hudson's Bay Company in the 1820s. His name is linked in scientific nomenclature to eighty plants and animals, including the Douglas fir and the Douglas squirrel.

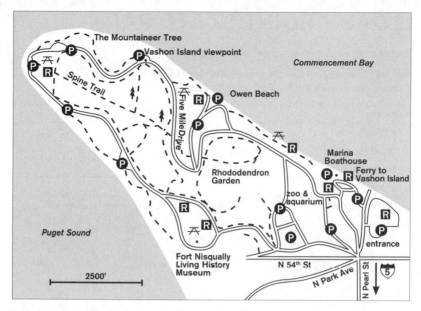

The Mountaineer Tree

Vashon Island viewpoint

Commencement Bay

Spine Trail

Five Mile Drive

Owen Beach

Marina Boathouse

Ferry to Vashon Island

Rhododendron Garden

zoo & aquarium

Puget Sound

entrance

Fort Nisqually Living History Museum

N 54th St

N Park Ave

N Pearl St

2500'

lies on the forest floor. Go past the footpath to the beach, continuing until you come to the immense Mountaineer Tree. This Douglas fir, the largest living tree in the park, measures 218 feet tall and is more than 400 years old. If it survives the forces of nature (and human vandalism), it could still be standing 500 years from now.

ADDRESS: 5400 N Pearl Street, Tacoma

GETTING THERE: From I-5, take exit 132 (WA 16 W/Gig Harbor/ Bremerton). Go 3.6 miles west on WA 16 to the 6th Avenue/Pearl Street exit. Turn left on 6th Avenue, then right on Pearl Street/WA 163. Go north 3 miles on N Pearl Street, which ends at the Point Defiance Park entrance. On Saturday and Sunday mornings, the Five Mile Drive outer loop is closed to motorized vehicles, but other access points are open.

CONTACT: Metro Parks Tacoma, (253) 305-1000, www.metroparks tacoma.org

TACOMA

<u>90</u> DASH POINT STATE PARK

Federal Way, 13 miles north of Tacoma

A Puget Sound beach and creekside forest feature interpretive and beach activities in this 398-acre park.

TRAIL	11 miles total; natural surface
STEEPNESS	Level to steep
OTHER USES	Bicycles on some trails
DOGS	On leash
CONNECTING TRAILS	None
PARK AMENITIES	Restrooms, playground, campgrounds, picnic shelters, interpretive trail
DISABLED ACCESS	Restrooms, campsites

The snow-covered peaks of the Olympics jut into the ice-blue sky to the west. Bald eagles glide or beat their wings against the winter wind, holding in place over the whitecaps of the water. Seagulls screech and harass the eagles for a share of the meal. Bold and dramatic, this is Puget Sound in winter, seen from the wind-whipped beach at Dash Point.

But whatever the season, the low-tide beach is always inviting with its long strolls (3,300 feet each way) along firm and rippled sand. Views are fine across the East Passage to Maury Island, Vashon Island, and the Olympics. On hot summer weekends, the beach area is crowded with families and children. Driftwood, adorned in black and silver mussel shells and rosettes of barnacles, accents the gently sloping beach. To the north, where the park hillsides pitch steeply to the beach, fir and madrona trees lie across the sand, their roots torn loose from the hill. But at low tide, you can skirt these and walk until your calves ache.

To escape the crowds or the rising tide, head inland for quiet forest walks. From the southwestern corner of the beach parking lot, a dirt-and-sand trail pursues the creek under high maples, firs, and red alders. These miles of trail are

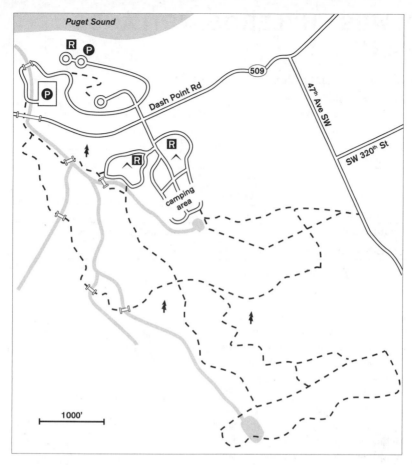

for worry-free wandering—some lead nowhere, some to east campground loops. Sturdy wooden bridges span the stream, and steps with railings ease the steep climb from beach to bluff.

ADDRESS: 5700 SW Dash Point Road, Federal Way

GETTING THERE: From I-5, take exit 143 (Federal Way/S 320th Street). Turn west on S 320th Street. Go about 4.7 miles and turn right on 47th Avenue SW. At the next T-junction, turn left onto Dash Point Road (WA 509). The park entrance is on the right in about 0.5 miles. A Discover Pass is required for parking.

CONTACT: Washington State Parks, (253) 661-4955, www.parks.wa.gov

91 WEST HYLEBOS WETLANDS PARK

Federal Way, 11.5 miles northeast of Tacoma

Walk on boardwalks over 12,000-year-old peat through this 120-acre urban oasis of wetland and wildlife.

TRAIL	1.7-mile loop; boardwalk
STEEPNESS	Level
OTHER USES	Pedestrians only
DOGS	Not allowed
CONNECTING TRAILS	None
PARK AMENITIES	Restrooms, interpretive trail, picnic tables
DISABLED ACCESS	Trail, restrooms

Nestled in the heart of Federal Way, this small enclave of native wetland is a schoolroom in the wild. Rich, earthy scents accompany you along the dry boardwalk trail. Interpretive markers call attention to wetland plants and common inhabitants of the peat bog and streambank. The walkways "float" on a cushioning of 36 feet of peat that dates back 12,000 to 15,000 years. Moss drapes heavily from the limbs of the big-leaf maples.

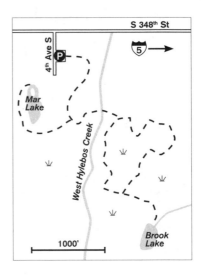

This park has caught the attention of environmental groups, researchers, and nature enthusiasts alike. But the main thrust of interest in the park came from the Marckx family, who donated 25 acres to the State in the late 1980s with the dream of creating a wetlands preserve. In 2004, Hylebos Wetlands was transferred to the City of Federal Way, and the current 120 acres support dozens of species of moss, lichen, and fungi. Coho salmon have returned to the stream, flashing ruby-red scales against the green of the forest.

Birds, although not easy to see because of the dense vegetation and the low light, raise their voices in a chorus of song in the early morning and serenade the

sunset. Hawks and other birds of prey frequent the park and its surroundings. Great blue herons feed at Mar Lake as though it were a breakfast buffet.

Don't plan to visit Hylebos immediately after a heavy winter storm; the stream floods several times each winter, prohibiting access to Brook Lake and leaving the boardwalks slippery.

ADDRESS: 411 S 348th Street, Federal Way

GETTING THERE: From I-5, take exit 142B (WA 18 W/Federal Way). Turn west on WA 18/S 348th Street toward Federal Way. Go 1.3 miles and turn left onto 4th Avenue S, where you will find the parking lot.

CONTACT: Federal Way Parks, Recreation, and Cultural Services Department; (253) 835-6960; www.cityoffederalway.com/page/parks-recreation-cultural -services. To volunteer, contact Friends of the Hylebos: www.hylebos.org.

TACOMA

92 TITLOW PARK

5 miles west of downtown Tacoma

Explore 75 acres of parkland with Olympic Mountain views by the Tacoma Narrows.

TRAIL	2.5 miles; gravel, natural surface, paved
STEEPNESS	Level to gentle
OTHER USES	Pedestrians only on forest trails; bicycles
DOGS	On leash
CONNECTING TRAILS	None
PARK AMENITIES	Restrooms, playground, community center, fitness course, picnic shelters, playing fields, swimming pools, tennis courts, spray park
DISABLED ACCESS	Restrooms, paved trail, buildings, pool

The beauty of Titlow Park hides behind the busy facade of a swimming pool, playing fields, buildings, and two lagoons: one fresh, one tidal. To leave the high concentration of people, dogs, and ducks, walk past the activities areas, heading north on the gravel trail that parallels the Burlington Northern Santa Fe Railway tracks. Suddenly the crowds dissipate, and you walk in the shade of alders and graceful madronas. A fitness course winds its way over stream and wetlands through the forest.

At the maintenance road, turn left toward the beach and take the overpass safely over the railroad tracks. Here, in a secluded strip of forest above the sand, you'll find picnic tables and viewpoints over the water. To explore the beach, follow the old boat-launch ramp down. At low tide you have 0.5 miles of sand and crabs, clams and seaweed to explore before reaching the southern end of Titlow.

Separated from the rest of the park by the railroad tracks, the southwestern corner features views, picnicking, and beachcombing. High on the old ferry dock pilings, wooden birdhouses await nesting martins. Interpretive signs tell

Kid Tip: Choose Walks with Variety

Avoid long, straight trails when walking with children unless they want to try out their tricycle while you walk. Playgrounds make good bribes for the end of a trail well walked. Streams are fun, but not if they're protected for salmon and can't be played in. You almost can't go wrong with beaches, but you may want the beach to be the destination, not the walk itself. It's hard to get kids to move when there is so much stuff to be picked up and played with.

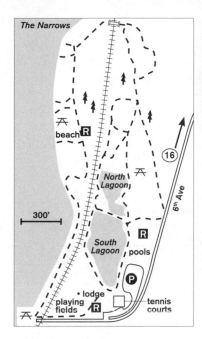

about the tidal zones and the creatures living there. This is a favorite point for scuba divers and kayakers, so there's always lots of activity to watch. At high tide, you can walk the 0.25-mile access road between the tracks and the beach for fine views of the water and the Tacoma Narrows Bridge.

ADDRESS: 8425 6th Avenue, Tacoma

GETTING THERE: From I-5, take exit 132 (WA 16 W/Gig Harbor). Go about 4.5 miles west on WA 16. Exit onto Jackson Avenue and turn left (south). Go one block and turn right on 6th Avenue to reach the park.

CONTACT: Metro Parks Tacoma, (253) 305-1000, www.metroparkstacoma.org

TACOMA

<u>93</u> WRIGHT PARK

Downtown Tacoma

This urban park of 27 acres offers a sanctuary of nature in downtown Tacoma.

TRAIL	1.5 miles total; gravel
STEEPNESS	Level to gentle
OTHER USES	Bicycles
DOGS	On leash; not allowed in conservatory
CONNECTING TRAILS	None
PARK AMENITIES	Restrooms, playground, picnic areas, classes, community center, horseshoe pits, lawn bowling, wading pool, conservatory
DISABLED ACCESS	Restrooms, community center, conservatory, paths

Moist, warm air awakens the sense of smell, and brilliant floral colors stimulate eyes weary of Washington's ever-present green. Birds of paradise, exotic orchids, tropical bromeliads, and poinsettias paint a wild palette of color inside the W. W. Seymour Botanical Conservatory (open daily from 10:00 a.m. to 4:30 p.m.; free admission). Outside, exotic trees from Asia and Europe add new and unfamiliar forms to the lawns etched by zigzagging paths.

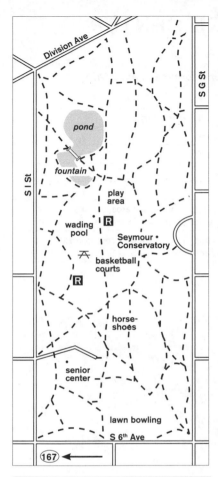

A patch of elegant greenery in historic Tacoma, this 100-year-old park is unique in its spacious landscaping. Follow the paths up and down gentle hillocks. Pause to watch the antics of the mallards on the pond or feel the emotion created by sculptor Larry Anderson's *The Leaf*, south of the community center. But people, more than plants, animals, and art, are the focus of this lively park. As you walk, watch the gyrations of intense young basketball players, the graceful moves of the lawn bowlers, and the directed concentration of the horseshoe players. Then carry on with your walk—there are lots of tree species to learn.

ADDRESS: S 6th Avenue and S I Street, Tacoma

GETTING THERE: From I-5, take exit 132 (WA 16 W/Gig Harbor). From WA 16, take the first exit, Sprague Avenue, and go north 1.5 miles to S 6th Avenue. Turn right (east) on S 6th Avenue to S I Street and the park. There is curbside parking around the park.

CONTACT: Metro Parks Tacoma, (253) 305-1000, www.metroparkstacoma.org

---

This Isn't New York!

Try saying "Hi." You may not talk to strangers on the street, but camaraderie develops among walkers. Some neighborhood trails have been responsible for creating whole new social groups.

94 TACOMA NATURE CENTER

3 miles west of downtown Tacoma

Snake Lake's 71 acres of wetlands and forest are alive with birds and wildlife.

TRAIL	2.5 miles; paved, natural surface
STEEPNESS	Level to moderate
OTHER USES	Pedestrians only
DOGS	Not allowed
CONNECTING TRAILS	None
PARK AMENITIES	Restrooms, playground, picnic area, classes, interpretive center, interpretive trail
DISABLED ACCESS	First Bridge Loop Trail (0.5 miles), restrooms, interpretive center

The forest here seems intimate, as though nature were wrapping you in earth and lake smells, vine and shrub textures, and the songs of birds. Ten feet from the trail and indifferent to human presence, the wood ducks continue pecking, grooming, and twittering on the muddy bank of Snake Lake. Each line of their vivid, poster-colored heads stands out in sharp contrast to the brown earth.

Winter is a rewarding time to visit this small, snake-shaped lake in the midst of commercial Tacoma. Where only a corner of water remains unfrozen, the ducks, geese, and grebes congregate in massive displays of color and motion. The snowberry and blackberry thickets stand crisp and naked without their greenery, letting you watch the wrens flit from twig to twig.

Warmer weather, though, invites you to explore all 71 acres. Walk the Bridge Loop Trails, pausing on the bridges or in the wildlife blinds along the trail, to see what creatures come to feed among the reeds. Year-round waterfowl include mallards, Canada geese, herons, and wood ducks. A climb up the Hillside Loop above the lake promises more exercise and the refreshing cool of shade. Early-morning visitors may see prints of the resident red foxes or raccoons.

The Tacoma Nature Center has displays, hands-on activities for adults and kids, interpretive information, and a gift shop. The preserve is open daily from 8:00 a.m. until dusk; the interpretive center is open Monday through Saturday from 9:00 a.m. to 4:00 p.m. (free admission).

ADDRESS: 1919 S Tyler Street, Tacoma

GETTING THERE: From I-5, take exit 132 (WA 16 W/Gig Harbor/Bremerton). Go 2.5 miles west on WA 16 and take the 19th Street E exit. Turn right on S 19th Street, then right again on S Tyler Street. Parking is on the left.

CONTACT: Metro Parks Tacoma, (253) 591-6439, www.metroparkstacoma.org

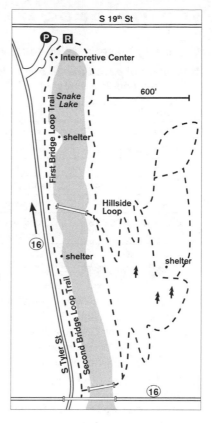

<u>95</u> CHAMBERS BAY LOOP

University Place, 9 miles southwest of Tacoma

Walk miles of paved trail in bright light or forest glen overlooking the sound on 900 acres.

TRAIL	3.5 miles; paved
STEEPNESS	Level to moderate
OTHER USES	Bicycles
DOGS	Off-leash area on beach, otherwise on leash
CONNECTING TRAILS	Central Meadow Loop Trails and 2 miles of beach
PARK AMENITIES	Restrooms, picnic areas, playground
DISABLED ACCESS	Grandview Trail, restrooms; Soundview Trail slopes exceed 10 percent

Sounds of the city diminish as you step from the hilltop parking lot on Grandview Drive onto the gently sloping Soundview Trail. Two paved trails encircle the Chambers Bay Golf Course and together offer a piece of magic just south of the Tacoma Narrows. Whether you walk from the northern corner past the colorful playground or from the southern corner near the club house, you'll be rewarded with ever-widening views of the sound and, on a clear day, the Olympic Mountains to the west.

The northern portion of the Soundview Trail winds back and forth through shady glens before emerging onto the open space at the edge of the golf course. From here the trail parallels the coastline and the Burlington Northern Santa Fe Railway line. Up to eighty passenger and freight trains chug past daily, and their plaintive horns may be the only man-made sounds you'll hear on this 2-mile walk. At the southern end, a graceful arching walkway takes you over the tracks onto

a 2-mile stretch of Puget Sound beach. Here, dogs can run as they will south of the bridge, and children will enjoy exploring all the drift logs piled like a giant's matchsticks on the beach.

The huge, almost artistic concrete structures are all that remain of the era when

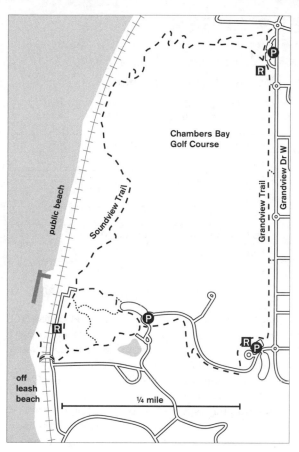

this land was used for a quarry and the sand and gravel were transported along conveyor belts to the shore. The walk up the southern end of the trail may be hot on a sunny day, but the full 200 feet that were lost in elevation have to be regained. To avoid the hills on Soundview Trail, you can park at the southwest lot, walk the coast trail until the incline is too much, then return.

For another level trail, more suitable to wheeled vehicles, a stroll along the Grandview Trail may be just what you seek. Here, you will have to ignore the sounds of mellow traffic on Grandview Drive, but you can turn your attention to the rolling, intricately contoured hills of the golf course, the movements of trains far below, or tugboats on the sound.

ADDRESS: *North end:* 5000 Grandview Drive W, University Place; *south end:* 6320 Grandview Drive W, University Place

GETTING THERE: From I-5, take exit 130 (S 56th Street/Tacoma Mall). Go west on 56th Street for 2.5 miles, where it becomes Cirque Avenue W. Go 2.7 miles to reach Grandview Drive W. For parking on the south end, turn left and go 0.7 miles to the lot on the right. For the north end, turn right, then left into the playground parking lot.

CONTACT: Pierce County Parks and Recreation Department, (253) 798-4176, www.piercecountywa.org/parks

96 CHAMBERS CREEK CANYON TRAIL

University Place, 12 miles southwest of Tacoma

Walk along a clear, salmon-spawning creek that flows through lush forest into Chambers Bay on Puget Sound.

TRAIL	1.5 miles one way; natural surface
STEEPNESS	Steep
OTHER USES	Pedestrians only
DOGS	On leash
CONNECTING TRAILS	None
PARK AMENITIES	Restrooms Memorial Day to Labor Day only
DISABLED ACCESS	None

Hike high on a wildland hillside of moss-covered big-leaf maples and Douglas firs you can hardly fit your arms around. Look out into the canopy of trees and down to the shimmering glimpse of Chambers Creek. Listen to the silence of the forest, broken by the song of a thrush or the rustling of a squirrel in the brush.

An unpretentious beginning leads to this well-traveled trail in a mature forest, just minutes from the I-5 corridor south of Tacoma. In summer, take a moment to walk to the bridge over Chambers Bay before starting up the trail; the forest is so dense with summer greenery that this may be your only chance to see the estuary, which resounds with the calls of the killdeer and the shrills of the gulls. In winter, the big-leaf maples drop their screening leaves and allow views from the trail to the stream and estuary below.

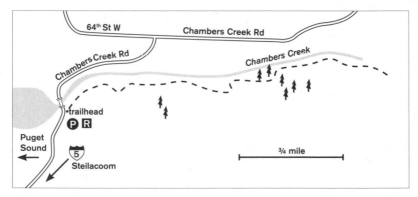

This trail is rough and steep. It's not advisable in wet weather, but when it's dry you can follow it to the top, where houses announce the end of parkland. Along this steep climb up the shoulder of the creek ravine, listen for the forest birds and the chattering squirrels. Pause at the spacious glen where the hillside is carved into an amphitheater of fern and salal.

Finding Your Way

Not all trails remain as they were originally built. Trees fall down. Trails get flooded out. Signs fall down or are faded. New neighborhoods crop up like dandelions, so driving directions can also change. Keep a sense of direction, and always walk with someone else.

Several side trails drop down toward the stream. The first leads to a clearing by the bay, the second to a high viewpoint over clear, rushing Chambers Creek. Old stumps make homes for owls and provide food for flickers and sapsuckers. Watch for trail improvements as Pierce County puts new trail plans into action.

ADDRESS: 10000 Chambers Creek Road W, University Place

GETTING THERE: From I-5, take exit 130 (S 56th Street). Go west on S 56th Street for 2.5 miles, where it becomes Cirque Drive W. Go 1.9 miles and turn left onto 67th Avenue W. In 0.8 miles 67th Avenue turns right to become Chambers Creek Road W. Go 2.5 miles and cross the Chambers Creek Bridge. Look immediately on the left for a small parking area and trail sign.

CONTACT: Pierce County Parks and Recreation Department, (253) 798-4176, www.piercecountywa.org/parks

TACOMA

<u>97</u> FORT STEILACOOM PARK

Steilacoom, 11 miles southwest of Tacoma

Meadows by Waughop Lake offer bird-watching, historical sites, and mountain views from this 340-acre park.

TRAIL	10 miles; natural surface, paved
STEEPNESS	Level to moderate
OTHER USES	Bicycles, horses
DOGS	Off-leash area, otherwise on leash
CONNECTING TRAILS	None
PARK AMENITIES	Restrooms, picnic areas, playground, playing fields
DISABLED ACCESS	Waughop Lake trail, picnic area, playground

From fort to farm to county park, these grounds represent a chronicle of Washington history. Parade grounds from the 1850s have given way to meadow grasses, and old buildings have succumbed to the weight of time. There was never a stockade at Fort Steilacoom, which protected the settlers at the bustling Steilacoom port from 1849 to 1868. When soldiers left, it was the farm that supplied the state mental hospital (which still lies to the north). Today, as you walk these spacious meadows, you can see the old hospital cemetery grounds, dating from 1876 to 1953, and the restored 1930s farm buildings and barns.

From the southwestern corner of the parking area near the barns, head west toward Waughop Lake. A wheelchair-accessible 1-mile trail circumnavigates the lake under the shade of elms and redwoods. Willows gracefully dip their branches to the water, and mallards paddle about.

Climb the knoll on well-worn footpaths, past several old orchards and lines of poplars. At the top, you'll find the imposing ruins of the 1940s patients' ward, now used as a site to train emergency personnel in earthquake or bombing preparedness. Views here expand west to the Olympics and to Fox, McNeil, and Anderson

Islands in the Tacoma Narrows. To the east Mount Rainier looms, and below you see Waughop Lake and the Pierce College campus.

Other trails weave like a spiderweb through the meadows up to the southern forest boundary. Though you have 340 acres to explore, you're not likely to get lost: there's plenty of long-distance visibility across the meadows and from the hillocks.

ADDRESS: 8714 87th Avenue SW, Lakewood

GETTING THERE: From I-5, take exit 127 (WA 512/S Tacoma Way). Stay left (if northbound) or right (if southbound) for WA 512 and S Tacoma Way/Lakewood. Go 0.9 miles on S Tacoma Way and turn left onto Steilacoom Boulevard SW. Go 3.3 miles and turn left onto 87th Avenue SW, then right into the park.

CONTACT: Lakewood Parks and Recreation Department, (253) 589-2489, www.cityoflakewood.us/parks-and-recreation/parks

<u>98</u> WAPATO PARK

6.5 miles south of downtown Tacoma

Stroll around Wapato Lake with its bird sanctuaries, wetlands, and mature forest in this 80-acre park.

TRAIL	1.4 miles; natural surface, paved
STEEPNESS	Level to gentle
OTHER USES	Bicycles
DOGS	Off-leash area, otherwise on leash
CONNECTING TRAILS	None
PARK AMENITIES	Restrooms, picnic area, playground, fishing pier, garden, ball fields; summer only: concessions, paddleboats
DISABLED ACCESS	Paved trail along lake, restrooms, picnic area

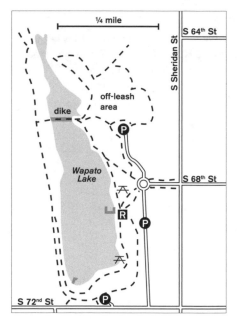

Formal gardens and a white-trellised pergola welcome you to 27-acre Wapato Lake, which takes its name from the previously abundant aquatic root the Native Americans harvested from the lake. Not much of this busy park recalls such quieter times, but away from the picnic areas and playing fields, you can find sanctuaries of marshland and mature forest.

North of the garden entrance, an off-leash area attracts dozens of dog lovers and their canine friends. Beyond that, you'll find a stone bridge from 1933 funded by the Works Progress Administration. In the forest, follow footpaths to the 0.67-mile fitness course or continue on the road, cutting left toward the marshland. A high footbridge lifts you over the cattails where red-winged blackbirds nest. Marsh wrens call *tsuck, tsuck* and flit from bush to bush. Kids can fish year-round, and you can pause in your meander to watch the bottoms-up antics of the coots and mallards feeding among the water lilies. On the western side of the lake, join the trail again to complete a loop around the lake.

Hundred-year-old fir and hemlock offer summer shade near the swimming area and summer concessions. Footpaths connect the open lawns, playing fields, southern picnic area, and parking lot. Look for the old wrought-iron lightpost slowly being absorbed by the dense bark of a Douglas fir.

ADDRESS: 1401 S 68th Street, Tacoma

GETTING THERE: From I-5, take exit 129 (S 72nd Street). Go east on S 72nd Street for 2 blocks and turn left (north) on S Sheridan Street. The entrance is on the left at S Sheridan Street and S 68th Street.

CONTACT: Metro Parks Tacoma, (253) 305-1000, www.metroparkstacoma.org

4 miles east of downtown Tacoma

Soft forest trails in a 290-acre park hug the side of a lush ravine above a clear stream, which teems with salmon in the fall.

TRAIL	2 miles one way; natural surface
STEEPNESS	Gentle to steep
OTHER USES	Pedestrians only except for bicycles on dedicated single-track trails
DOGS	On leash
CONNECTING TRAILS	None
PARK AMENITIES	Benches, restrooms, picnic area, mountain-bike park
DISABLED ACCESS	Picnic area near western entrance at E 42nd Street and E Roosevelt Avenue

Traverse a fern-covered and forested hillside above a salmon-spawning creek that has carved a pebbled gully for itself. Listen to the call of birds over the soft murmuring of the water. Tacoma's Swan Creek Park is most often visited by people wanting to cool off on a hot summer's day, let the kids play in the detention pond fed by Swan Creek, or watch the coho and Chinook salmon make their arduous way up the stream in the fall. But past the pond and the footbridge, a trail leads deep into a fine old forest of towering Douglas firs and moss-bedecked big-leaf maples leaning elegantly over the stream.

> **Love That Dog!**
>
> Other walkers would probably love your dog if they knew him or her. But dogs belong on a leash (where posted) to protect wildlife, minimize their impact on the habitat, and avoid disturbing other walkers and pets. Many parks now patrol and ticket leash offenders.

Saved from becoming a landfill back in the 1960s, Swan Creek is now a showcase of mature Northwest forest and an active salmon stream. Even in summer, when there are no salmon in the stream, the water runs clear and bright over a pebbled streambed, and the old logs and rocks guarantee good hiding places for the newly hatched fry in winter. The trail begins near the pond and climbs slowly, staying near the level of the stream. Numerous "social trails" lead to the water's edge, where you can rest on a downed log or picnic on a shady bank.

The wet season brings standing water to parts of the trail, so while the boardwalks are welcome, they can be slippery. This is a good place to practice "walk or look," because if you try to take in the beauty of the forest while walking, it is easy

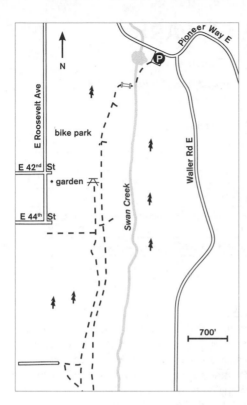

to fall on the narrow trail criss-crossed with tree roots.

In 2015 the county carved 50 acres out of the park's 290 for the city's first mountain-bike park. More than 3 miles of dedicated trails crisscross the hilly western corner of the park, where bikers jump and slide along the single-track one-way trails. These trails are well marked for bicycles, and as walkers it's best to leave them to it. There's still plenty of fine walking to be had along the traverse trails above the stream.

ADDRESS: Pioneer Way E and Waller Road E, Tacoma

GETTING THERE: From I-5 southbound, take exit 135 (Bay Street/River Road/WA 167 N). Take the first left onto Bay Street, crossing under I-5. Continue straight through the light where Bay Street becomes River Road. Stay right past the cemetery and merge onto Pioneer Way E. The parking lot is just past the Clay Art Center on the right.

From I-5 northbound, take exit 135 (River Road/WA 167 N/Puyallup). Stay on River Road and continue as above.

CONTACT: Metro Parks Tacoma, (253) 305-1000, www.metroparkstacoma.org

<u>100</u> CLARKS CREEK PARK

Puyallup, 10 miles southeast of Tacoma

Watch spawning salmon or hike a mixed forest hillside in this 55-acre park.

TRAIL	4.5 miles; natural surface
STEEPNESS	Gentle to steep
OTHER USES	Bicycles
DOGS	Off-leash area, otherwise on leash
CONNECTING TRAILS	DeCoursey Park
PARK AMENITIES	Restrooms, playground, picnic areas, ball fields, fitness course
DISABLED ACCESS	Paved trails from parking lots, restrooms

When the fall colors brighten the hillside above Clarks Creek in Puyallup, the clear-running creek itself comes to life with hundreds of spawning salmon. Known for its runs of Chinook, chum, and coho salmon, the creek is part of the Puyallup River Watershed, and fish, both from a hatchery and wild, make their way up the creek to the gravel beds to spawn. Volunteers have worked with city and county ecologists to improve the riparian ecology of the creek and its banks. The local trout hatchery, owned by the Puyallup Tribe, is highly acclaimed for its innovative

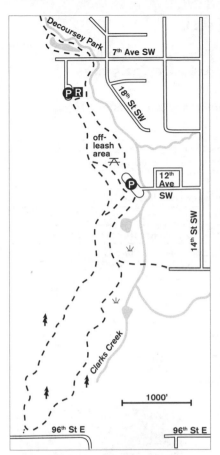

techniques of recreating a natural setting for the young fry within the hatchery and is open to the public.

Once the fall and winter fish runs are over, the creek returns to its placid burble down from the forested hillsides, through the natural wetlands, and northward toward the Puyallup River. Clarks Creek Park offers a variety of activity, from power walks along paved walkways near the tennis courts and ball fields in the north, to playing catch with your canine friend in the 0.67-acre off-leash area, to a hearty stroll along forest paths.

A wide crushed-gravel path leads upward from the off-leash area, but as you climb higher the path gets narrower and more meandering. High on the hillside to the west, the myriad trails are favorites of the local mountain bikers, so beware of fast-moving cyclists on weekends or during school holidays. If the cyclists are out, a better bet for quietude is to stick to the eastern paths, in the lower ravines, although these paths cross a sensitive wetland and are almost impassable in winter or after heavy rains. A gentle stroll can be extended by crossing 7th Avenue and enjoying the pondside trails through tiny DeCoursey Park to the north.

ADDRESS: 1900 7th Avenue SW, Puyallup

GETTING THERE: From I-5, take exit 135 (WA 167 N/Puyallup). Go 0.5 miles on WA 167 toward Puyallup, and make a slight right onto Pioneer Way S. Continue on Pioneer Way for 5.2 miles. Turn right onto S Fruitland, then left onto 7th Avenue SW to reach the parking lot, which will be on your right.

CONTACT: Puyallup Parks and Recreation Department, (253)-841-5457, www.cityofpuyallup.org/248/parks-recreation

<u>101</u> FOOTHILLS TRAIL

Puyallup, 8.5 miles southeast of Tacoma, to McMillin,
14 miles southeast of Tacoma, to Buckley, 22.5 miles
southeast of Tacoma

*Meander through Carbon River farmland and small historic towns
with views of Mount Rainier.*

TRAIL	26 miles; paved from Puyallup to South Prairie; natural and paved from South Prairie to Buckley
STEEPNESS	Level to gentle
OTHER USES	Bicycles; horses on soft shoulder
DOGS	On leash
CONNECTING TRAILS	Extension south to Carbonado, undeveloped
PARK AMENITIES	Restrooms, picnic areas at trailheads
DISABLED ACCESS	Paved trail

Imagine riding with the engineer in the locomotive of a Burlington Northern train along the floodplain of the glacial-silted Carbon River. Ahead looms Mount Rainier, mighty volcano of ice and snow. The river beside you is white and rushing, cutting its path through a millennium of rocky till. Tannin-brown streams swirl and join the opaque river.

Now, although the railroad runs no more, the route is open to those seeking a slower mode of transport. Thanks to the Foothills Rails-to-Trails Coalition and Pierce County, 26 miles of long-abandoned railbed are available for recreation from McMillin to Buckley, with a spur from lower Cascade Junction to Wilkeson and Carbonado. The coalition and the county are working to fulfill their vision of a 12-foot-wide nonmotorized asphalt trail and linear park system throughout Pierce County, eventually leading all the way from King County's Interurban Trail to Mount Rainier.

Riverside scenery and mountain views are just two of the pleasures of walking the Foothills Trail. Picnic areas dot the trail, as well as cow pastures, scenic footbridges over the river, and even a bison and pygmy goat farm. From McMillin,

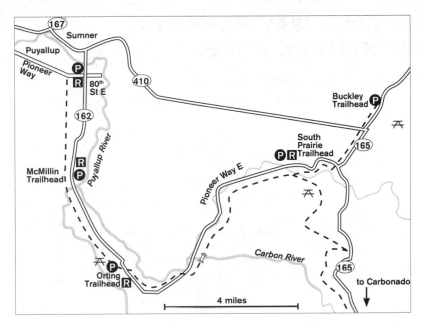

the paved trail heads south through Orting, then swings east to cross the Carbon River. Eagles grace tall trees, watching for small rodent meals in the meadows below. This stretch, beginning in Orting, along the Carbon River, is one of the best walking sections, with its mix of farmland, meadows, and river scenery. Walk out and back as far as your energy carries you.

To enjoy the full length of the trail, bicycles may be in order, but numerous access points (the trail runs parallel to WA 162 in many places) allow you to explore on foot a few miles at a time. Near the towns there are many street crossings; be sure to keep children and pets closely supervised.

ADDRESS: *Trailheads:* 13810 80th Street E, Puyallup; 14000 WA 162, McMillin; 646 N River Avenue, Buckley

GETTING THERE: *Puyallup Trailhead:* From I-5, take exit 135 (WA 167 S/Puyallup). Go 6.2 miles on WA 167 and turn right onto N Meridian. Go 0.5 miles and turn left onto E Pioneer. Go 2.1 miles and turn left onto 134th Avenue E. Turn right onto 80th Street E, and go 0.2 miles to the trailhead.

McMillin Trailhead: From I-5 north- or southbound, take exit 135 (WA 167 S/Puyallup). Go 1.2 miles on WA 167 and exit at WA 410 (Sumner/Yakima). Go 1.3 miles and take the WA 162 exit toward Orting. Go 4.5 miles to the trailhead.

Buckley Trailhead: From I-5 north- or southbound, take exit 135 (WA 167 S/Puyallup). Go 1.2 miles on WA 167 and exit at WA 410 (Sumner/Yakima). Stay on 410 east in Buckley; the trailhead is located at the armory.

CONTACT: Pierce County Parks and Recreation Department, (253) 798-4176, www.piercecountywa.org/parks

<u>102</u> SPANAWAY PARK AND BRESEMANN FOREST

Spanaway, 15 miles south of Tacoma

Wooded trails and sunny paths crisscross 300 acres of forest and wetland in these sister parks.

TRAIL	About 8 miles; gravel, natural surface, paved
STEEPNESS	Level to gentle
OTHER USES	Bicycles on designated trails
DOGS	On leash
CONNECTING TRAILS	None
PARK AMENITIES	Restrooms, picnic shelters, playground, ball fields, swimming beach, interpretive signs, boat rentals, Sprinker Recreation Center, climbing wall
DISABLED ACCESS	Restrooms, paved trails, picnic shelters, ball fields at Spanaway Park; none in Bresemann Forest

Follow a wide graveled trail along the edge of Spanaway Lake, or explore shaded trails through a wetland or forest—all just minutes from downtown Tacoma.

Like a mink changing color for the winter, this park, too, changes with the seasons. In summer the manicured lawns resound with families and children playing, motorboats, and Jet Skis on the lake. The snack bar attracts crowds, and the aromas of ketchup and grilling supper fill the air. You can walk here then, but sometimes it's an effort: it's easy to rely on the car to move from one end of the long park to the other.

Off-season, though, Spanaway Park regains a more natural feel. Fishermen cast their lines in hope of bass or trout. Migrant waterfowl glide on the still

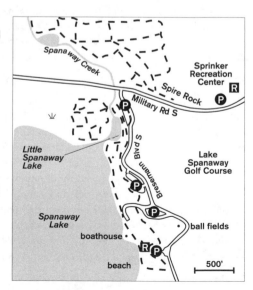

waters, and you can stroll the waterfront trail, then return by the upper playing fields, beneath majestic Douglas firs.

At the northern end, where the lake empties to a stream, two footbridges lead into a more sylvan setting of alders and willows, salal and ferns. The dirt trail is narrow, with exposed roots and rocks, climbing a gentle hill and then dropping to a wetland. Follow a stone-lined footpath along the edge of the wetland, onto the nearly 3 miles of new trails near Little Spanaway Lake, and then return over the footbridges.

Just north, across Military Road, Bresemann Forest invites walkers to explore the many miles of interpretive trail and informal forest paths. These natural surface, sometimes rough trails begin near the Spire Rock, a community climbing wall, and loop into the forest and along Morey Creek.

ADDRESS: 14905 Bresemann Boulevard S, Tacoma

GETTING THERE: From I-5, take exit 127 (WA 512 E/Puyallup). Go east for 2 miles on WA 512 and turn right (south) on WA 7 (Pacific Avenue S). Go 3 miles and turn right on Old Military Road S (152nd Street E). Go 0.5 miles to the park's main gate on the left. Sprinker Recreation Center and forest trails are on the right (north) side; the lake is on the left. Parking fee of $3 may apply.

CONTACT: Pierce County Parks and Recreation Department, (253) 798-4176, www.piercecountywa.org/parks

<u>103</u> NATHAN CHAPMAN MEMORIAL TRAIL

South Hill, 12 miles southeast of Tacoma

A smooth, paved trail leads you past wetlands and through mature second-growth forest.

TRAIL	1.6 miles one way; paved
STEEPNESS	Level
OTHER USES	Bicycles
DOGS	On leash
CONNECTING TRAILS	1-mile loop in South Hill Community Park; Heritage Recreation Center
PARK AMENITIES	None on trail; restrooms, picnic tables, and playgrounds at South Hill Community Park and Heritage Recreation Center trailheads
DISABLED ACCESS	Restrooms, trail

Join dozens of dog walkers, stroller pushers, and folks just out for a walk along this wide paved corridor through large fir and hemlock trees and past small wetland ponds. So well hidden is this 1.6-mile trail that you can forget the stress of city life just minutes away. On sunny days, bright patches of light filter down from the canopy, cheering a winter day, and in summer the trees offer enough shade to cool a warm-day outing.

Army Sergeant First Class Nathan Chapman, for whom the trail was named, was not only a resident of South Hill but was also the first American to die from enemy fire in Afghanistan. A memorial with an information plaque is erected at the South Hill Community Park end of the trail.

The trail was built as a connector from the South Hill Community Park, where you'll find a 1-mile loop trail through more open meadows with picnic tables to the ball fields and amenities of the Heritage Recreation Center to the north. These trails lie near the South Hill Heritage Corridor, and on plaques at the center you

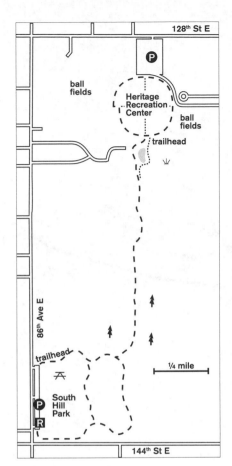

can read some of the history of the 1853 Longmire-Byles wagon train that crossed over the Naches Pass Trail through South Hill.

ADDRESS: 14201 86th Avenue E, South Hill

GETTING THERE: From I-5, take exit 127 (Mount Rainier/Puyallup) and follow signs for WA 512 E. Exit WA 512 at Canyon Road E and go south. Turn left immediately onto 112th Street E. Go 2 miles and turn right onto 86th Avenue E. South Hill Community Park is on the left in 0.5 miles. The Nathan Chapman Memorial Trail leaves from the northern end of the parking lot.

CONTACT: Pierce County Parks and Recreation Department, (253) 798-4176, www.piercecountywa.org /parks

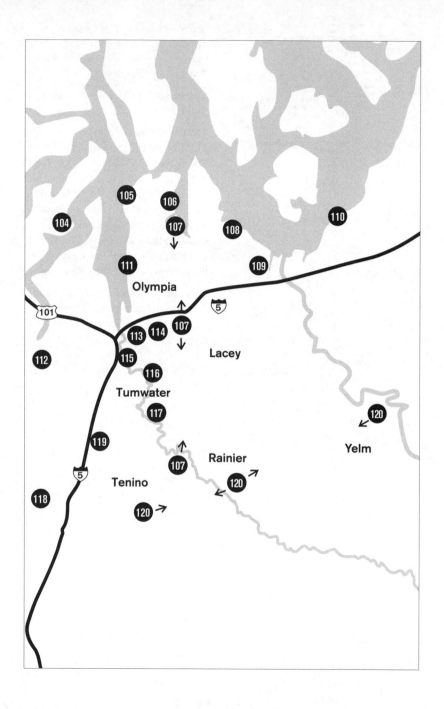

OLYMPIA

OLYMPIA

<u>104</u> FRYE COVE PARK

12 miles northwest of downtown Olympia

Forested trails through 86 acres lead to southern Puget Sound views at an Eld Inlet beach.

TRAIL	3 miles total; gravel, natural surfaces
STEEPNESS	Level to gentle
OTHER USES	Pedestrians only
DOGS	On leash
CONNECTING TRAILS	None
PARK AMENITIES	Restrooms, playground, picnic area, shelters, beach
DISABLED ACCESS	Gravel trail from parking lot to picnic area, restrooms

Tucked away on one of many finger inlets of southern Puget Sound, this forest and beach park entices with the twin luxuries of silence and seclusion.

When you enter the forest in summer, the big-leaf maples and alders shield you from the brilliance of the sun on the sound. Licorice ferns adorn the moss on the maples like miniature Dr. Seuss characters on parade around the tree trunks. Catkins from the red alders dangle above the trail and speckle the path.

Last logged a hundred years ago, the forest has a mature presence, and the air carries the heady scent of cedar and salt. Hemlocks, some more than 200 feet tall, drape their graceful branches above the trail. Benches and observation decks are placed for glimpses of the Sound and beach below, and a raised walkway carries you over a dense ravine of sword ferns.

After you complete a forest loop on Cove Trail and return to the parking lot, you can descend a gentle-to-steep trail to arrive at the southern end of the beach. Air holes of a million clams dapple the sand-and-mud beach at low tide,

and palm-sized clams and oysters provide feasts for crows and gulls. If the kids get tired of clams and sand, they can find lots of entertainment on the new playground near the shelters.

ADDRESS: 4000 61st Avenue NW, Olympia

GETTING THERE: From I-5, take exit 104 (US 101 N/Aberdeen). Stay on US 101 toward Shelton, and take the Steamboat Island Road exit. Go north on Steamboat Island Road NW for about 5.8 miles, and turn right on Young Road NW. Go about 2 miles, and turn left on 61st Avenue NW into the park.

CONTACT: Thurston County Parks and Recreation Department, (360) 786-5595, www.co.thurston.wa.us/parks

<u>105</u> BURFOOT PARK

6 miles north of downtown Olympia

Forest trails through 60 acres descend to 1,000 feet of Budd Inlet beach with State Capitol views.

TRAIL	3.8 miles; natural surface
STEEPNESS	Moderate to steep
OTHER USES	Pedestrians only
DOGS	On leash
CONNECTING TRAILS	None
PARK AMENITIES	Restrooms, picnic shelters, playground, interpretive trail
DISABLED ACCESS	Horizon Trail (a 0.25-mile braille trail), restrooms, shelters, picnic area

Most of the wonder of Burfoot Park is hidden from the casual first-time visitor. The central lawn and picnic area is so large and appealing that you might believe it's all there is to the park. But drive or walk the parking loop, and you'll discover the three trail entrances into the cool enchantment of the forest, which descends to the beach on Budd Inlet.

For an easy stroll, start on the Horizon Trail nature loop, which documents the changes in the forest since it was logged in the 1890s. Moisture encourages moss and old man's beard to grow prolifically, and they cover the trees with a thick green shawl.

To the north, from the Rhododendron Trail, the right-fork Beach Trail descends the ridge of a ravine carpeted with sword fern. Here, the wrens call and hop on downed logs, their short perky tails bobbing. A clear *rat-a-tat-tat* may sound from above. High on a snag, pileated woodpeckers with iridescent red crests may be circling the tree, probing the bark for grubs. Farther along the fern-bedecked ravine, more snags bear the characteristic rectangular holes made by these birds, the largest western woodpeckers.

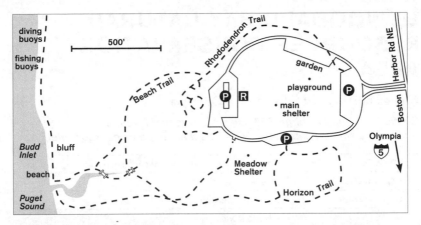

Though there are several trails, there is no need for signs; all trails lead to the beach. At low tide, crows stride the pebbled shore, and great blue herons may be feeding on small fish in the shallows. Massive drift logs make natural playgrounds for kids or a romantic resting place to sit and talk. To the south, the dome of the State Capitol rises between forested hills.

ADDRESS: 6927 Boston Harbor Road NE, Olympia

GETTING THERE: From I-5, take exit 105 if northbound, or exit 105B if southbound (City Center/Port of Olympia). Follow Port of Olympia signs and merge onto Plum Street. Go north on Plum Street (which becomes E Bay Drive, and then Boston Harbor Road NE). After 6 miles look for the park on the left.

CONTACT: Thurston County Parks and Recreation Department, (360) 786-5595, www.co.thurston.wa.us/parks

<u>106</u> WOODARD BAY NATURAL RESOURCES CONSERVATION AREA

5 miles northeast of downtown Olympia

Gentle trails wind through 870 acres of protected forest and shoreline where seals, bats, and birds flourish on Henderson Inlet.

TRAIL	3 miles; boardwalk, natural surface, paved
STEEPNESS	Level to gentle
OTHER USES	Pedestrians only
DOGS	Not allowed
CONNECTING TRAILS	Chehalis Western Trail (Walk #107) from the Overlook Trail parking lot
PARK AMENITIES	Restrooms, picnic areas, interpretive signs, nature classes, canoe launch (seasonal)
DISABLED ACCESS	Parking lot to picnic area on Henderson Inlet via Whitman Road

Beginning at the paved access road (gated for all vehicles except DNR and ADA), stroll 0.5 miles through moss-draped second-growth forest to Henderson Inlet. You may hear the sharp hammering of woodpeckers or the hoarse, barking sound of the green-backed heron. If the breeze is right, you'll smell the salt water before you see it. The state of the tide determines whether you see shimmering, wet mud or hear the lapping of wavelets on the shore. The clearing at the tip of land called Weyer Point was once a bustling log dump where timber was transferred from railroad cars to the water, to be floated to mills in Everett. Interpretive signs bring the history to life.

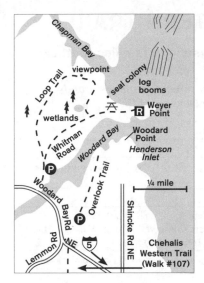

The logging sounds are gone now, giving way to the persistent chatter of belted kingfishers as they hover, searching for lunch below. Soon you may hear the yaps and groans of harbor seals, sometimes three hundred to four hundred of them. In this maternity colony, females and their pups rest on the log booms or sun themselves on the shores. They are easily stressed, so enjoy them from afar. With binoculars, you can watch the cormorants, Canada geese, and gulls standing like nursemaids on old pilings above sleeping seals. Scientists recently discovered a colony of small brown Myotis bats that hibernate under the offshore wharves.

For variety, take the loop trail through the forest back to the entrance. This natural path ranges up and down gentle hillocks and through forest wetlands over wooden boardwalks. Overhead stand massive maples with spreading branches that could hold swings for giants. Sturdy cedars and hemlocks embrace their nurse logs or form their own colonies of two or three trunks growing together. When the trail parallels the shore of Chapman Bay high on a ridge, you can look down on the flocks of shorebirds or solitary great blue herons feeding.

If you crave more exercise or forest immersion, Woodard Bay's Overlook Trail leaves from the Chehalis Western Trail parking lot (see Walk #107) just a minute south on Woodard Bay Road. This is a gravel and natural surface trail to the mouth of Henderson Inlet.

ADDRESS: 6998 Woodard Bay Road NE, Olympia

GETTING THERE: From I-5 southbound, take exit 108 (Martin Way/Sleater-Kinney Road NE). Go north on Sleater-Kinney Road NE for about 5 miles, until it takes a sharp turn to the left, becoming 56th Avenue NE. Go immediately right on Schinke Road NE, which becomes Woodard Bay Road NE. The Overlook Trail parking lot with restrooms is here.

To reach the primary trailhead, cross upper Woodard Bay on a bridge. Park immediately on the right by the gated entrance to Whitman Road. Bike racks are inside the gate, past the (summer only) kayak launching ramp. There may be seasonal trail closures to protect wildlife.

A Discover Pass is required for parking.

CONTACT: Washington State Department of Natural Resources, (360) 577-2025, www.dnr.wa.gov

<u>107</u> CHEHALIS WESTERN TRAIL

5 miles northeast of downtown Olympia to 14 miles southeast of Olympia via Lacey

This rail-to-trail pathway cuts through farmland, wetlands, ponds, and forests from Woodard Bay to the Deschutes River.

TRAIL	21.5 miles; paved
STEEPNESS	Level
OTHER USES	Bicycles; horses north of S Bay Road and south of Fir Tree Road
DOGS	On leash
CONNECTING TRAILS	Olympia Woodland Trail (Walk #114), Woodard Bay Natural Resources Conservation Area (Walk #106), Yelm to Tenino Trail (Walk #120)
PARK AMENITIES	Restrooms, benches, picnic areas, viewing platforms
DISABLED ACCESS	Trail, restrooms

Immerse yourself in rural Western Washington just minutes from shopping-center madness on Martin Way. Walk a paved trail where the woods and wetlands replace the gunning of engines with the sweet chirping of crickets. Horses come to the fence to greet you, and raptors may be soaring over the meadows in search of mice. Small ponds and wetlands add more tranquil greenery. Near Shincke Road, a large marsh-rimmed pond hosts the usual colorful assortment: kingfishers, red-winged blackbirds, marsh wrens, and great blue herons. Recent construction on the trail now allows users to safely bridge the gap from the northern section (north of I-5 and Martin Way) to the southern section of this 21.5-mile thoroughfare without interruption.

Farmlands, scrub forest, and meadows rim the trail as it journeys southward. New viewing platforms overlook ponds and wetlands. Several trailheads exist south of I-5; the northern one at Chambers Lake is the most popular, with amenities on the edge of the lake. Other trailheads are located at 67th Avenue, Fir Tree Road, and 89th Avenue.

The final stretch south of 103rd Avenue follows the Deschutes River upstream before intersecting the Yelm to Tenino Trail.

ADDRESS: *Northern trailhead:* 7204 Woodard Bay Road NE, Olympia; *Chambers Lake trailhead:* 3795 14th Avenue SE, Olympia; *67th Avenue trailhead:* 4430 67th Avenue

GETTING THERE: *Northern trailhead:* From I-5 southbound, take exit 109 (Martin Way/ Sleater-Kinney Road N). Go north on Sleater-Kinney Road about 3.7 miles. Turn left onto 56th Avenue NE and go 0.5 miles. Turn right on Shincke Road, then turn left on Woodard Bay Road and drive until you reach the junction with Lemon Road. Park on the right.

Chambers Lake Trailhead: From I-5 northbound, take exit 108 (Sleater-Kinney Road S). Turn right on Sleater-Kinney. Cross Pacific Avenue and turn right onto 14th Avenue. The

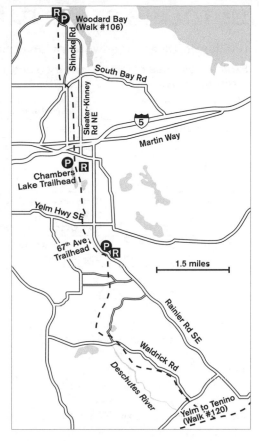

entrance is after the trestle on the left. From I-5 southbound, take exit 109 (Martin Way/College Street SE), head south on College Street SE, and proceed as above.

67th Avenue Trailhead: From I-5 northbound, take exit 108 (Sleater-Kinney Road S). Turn right at Sleater-Kinney Road. Turn left at 14th Avenue SE, then right onto College Street SE. Cross the Yelm Highway and stay on College Street, which becomes Rainier Road SE. Turn right onto 67th Avenue and follow it to the end. From I-5 southbound, take exit 109 (College Street). Turn left on College Street SE and proceed as above.

CONTACT: Thurston County Parks and Recreation Department, (360) 754-4371, www.co.thurston.wa.us/parks

<u>108</u> TOLMIE STATE PARK

11 miles northeast of downtown Olympia

Explore 105 acres of forests, salt marshes, and beaches along the Nisqually Reach.

TRAIL	4.3 miles; natural surface, paved
STEEPNESS	Level (beach) to steep
OTHER USES	Pedestrians only in forest; bicycles on paved trails
DOGS	On leash
CONNECTING TRAILS	None
PARK AMENITIES	Restrooms, amphitheater, picnic shelters, underwater park; park closed Mondays and Tuesdays from October 1 to March 31
DISABLED ACCESS	Restrooms, edge of marsh, picnic area, some trail sections

Jellyfish, sculpins, and rock crabs share the saltwater marsh with eelgrass and pickleweed. On the tidal flats, young geoducks have been planted in plastic tubes to protect them from crabs and seagulls until they are a year old. Divers head offshore to explore the sunken barges that have created an underwater reef. You can explore the beach or head inland for miles of forest walking.

The upper parking lot offers the best views across Puget Sound to the Olympic Mountains. From there, a steep trail with railroad-tie steps leads to the beach and the lower picnic areas. As at other recreational beaches on the Sound, the best time for quiet and solitude is any day but a hot, sunny one. If the tide is in, you can stop on the footbridge over the marsh for a view of the inhabitants. Offshore the usual waterfowl gather—more during fall and winter migration than in summer.

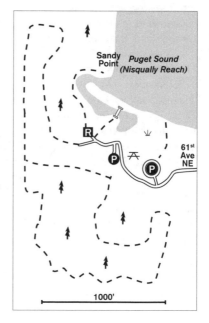

From the beach, a long loop trail takes you west into the forest of lichen-covered trees. A boardwalk keeps your feet dry while letting you examine the plant life along the way. Benches make good snack stops or resting points. A shortcut about halfway through the trail brings you back to the parking lot.

The park honors Dr. William Fraser Tolmie, a pioneer physician with the Hudson's Bay Company who served for 18 years at Fort Nisqually, just east of the present-day park. Married to a daughter of a Hudson's Bay Company chief factor, John Work, Tolmie was instrumental in returning peace to the region after the Indian Wars of 1855–'56. The park is closed on Mondays and Tuesdays, and from October 1 to March 31.

ADDRESS: 7730 61st Avenue NE, Olympia

GETTING THERE: From I-5, take exit 111 (WA 510/Yelm/Marvin Road) and head west on Marvin Road NE. Go about 3.5 miles and turn right on 56th Avenue NE. Go 0.4 miles, turn left on Hill Street NE, then left again on 61st Avenue NE, where you will find the park. A Discover Pass is required for parking.

CONTACT: Washington State Parks, (360) 456-6464, www.parks.wa.gov

OLYMPIA

<u>109</u> NISQUALLY NATIONAL WILDLIFE REFUGE

9.5 miles northeast of downtown Olympia

Walk through green forest by ponds and a river, or stroll the miles of level boardwalk crossing this 3,000-acre protected estuary.

TRAIL	1-mile loop, plus 3-mile round-trip boardwalk
STEEPNESS	Level
OTHER USES	Pedestrians only (no jogging)
DOGS	Not allowed
CONNECTING TRAILS	None
PARK AMENITIES	Restrooms, interpretive center (open Wednesday to Sunday), nature walks, observation decks
DISABLED ACCESS	Twin Barns Loop, Nisqually Estuary Boardwalk Trail, restrooms, interpretive center

Completing its journey from the heights of Mount Rainier, the Nisqually River releases its pent-up energy into the broad expanse of the estuary. The air is rich with the scent of salt from Puget Sound and freshwater from the river. The open meadows and wetlands are vast, inviting exploration.

In winter, snow geese and white-fronted geese huddle into the receding tide line. Year-round, dozens of great blue herons stand like sentries of the wetland, some intent on the fish that dart between their stilt-like legs, others staring as though trying to comprehend the human forms with binocular eyes. Green-belted

kingfishers hover above their prey, while over the grasslands immature bald eagles practice soaring and diving. Most visitors to the refuge come for the birds: there are more than a hundred species of resident waterfowl, raptors, and songbirds, as well as more than twenty thousand migratory birds that gather here during fall and winter.

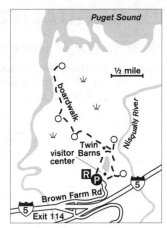

But you needn't be a keen birder to appreciate a walk around the 1-mile Twin Barns Loop on either natural surface or boardwalk. This shorter stroll takes you through moss-draped forest and to viewing platforms and observation decks where interpretive signs explain the lives of muskrats and beavers.

For those wanting a longer sojourn, the Nisqually Estuary Boardwalk Trail continues as a spur from the barns and meanders to the north, with the salt-water tidal estuary to the northeast and the freshwater wetlands of McAllister Creek to the south. In recent years the old Brown Farm Dike was removed to allow the waters of Puget Sound to mingle with the river water and improve habitat. Along the new obstacle-free boardwalk you'll find benches, viewing platforms, and a viewing blind. On clear days Mount Rainier highlights the skyline to the east, and from the Twin Barns Loop you can get views of the Olympics to the west.

The Nisqually Reach Nature Center offers a free summer-evening lecture series, and in the warm season there are free daytime guided walks focusing on the birds, plants, or history of the area.

ADDRESS: 100 Brown Farm Road, Olympia

GETTING THERE: From I-5, take exit 114 (Nisqually). Turn west at the end of the ramp and go under the freeway. Turn right (following signs) into the refuge. Holders of a Senior Pass or an Interagency Annual Pass are exempt from the $3 per vehicle admission fee.

CONTACT: Nisqually National Wildlife Refuge, (360) 753-9467, www.fws.gov/nisqually

OLYMPIA

<u>110</u> SEQUALITCHEW CREEK

DuPont, 15 miles northeast of downtown Olympia

Huge moss-bedecked maples tower above a 38-acre watershed canyon where the clear stream makes its last journey to the waters of Puget Sound.

TRAIL	1.5 miles one way; gravel, paved
STEEPNESS	Gentle to moderate
OTHER USES	Bicycles
DOGS	On leash
CONNECTING TRAILS	None
PARK AMENITIES	Restrooms, interpretive guide, map
DISABLED ACCESS	None

In a mighty forest of green canopy, green trunks, and green undergrowth, you can stroll gently downhill next to a murmuring creek on its last mile and a half to Puget Sound. This satisfyingly rich forest is a remnant of what surrounded a trading post of the Hudson's Bay Company in the early 1830s. Nisqually Indians fished the creek for coho salmon and traded blankets, potatoes, and seeds. Now, the nearby town of DuPont is bustling with shops and schools, but they have preserved this gem of a walk.

Stop in at city hall for a trail map, then follow signage at the far end of the parking lot to cross the creek and turn north (left), downhill. Although much of the trail is a gentle gradient, there are steeper parts where the pavement has been replaced by deep gravel to combat slippage problems. Parents with strollers may have trouble here. This is a gloriously quiet walk, with

just the sound of the creek in the deep cleft of forest. Near the wetlands is an old railroad tunnel, in which kids of all ages will love hooting and yodeling to create a symphony of echoes. Emerging from the tunnel, you'll find an expansive stretch of Puget Sound beach complete with pebbles, driftwood, and bits of the old narrow gauge railway. If you want a short but heart-pumping workout, you can follow the switchbacks up a path on the south side that leaves the main trail just inland of the tunnel and wetlands.

ADDRESS: 1700 Civic Drive, DuPont

GETTING THERE: From I-5, take exit 119 (Steilacoom Road/DuPont). Turn west onto Steilacoom Road. Continue onto Barksdale Avenue. Go 0.3 miles to reach city hall on the right. To find the trailhead, park behind city hall, at the far end.

CONTACT: DuPont Parks and Recreation Department, (253) 912-5245, www.ci.dupont.wa.us

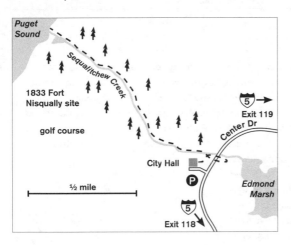

OLYMPIA

<u>111</u> PRIEST POINT PARK

2.5 miles north of downtown Olympia

Meandering woodland trails through 341 acres lead out to the bluffs and shoreline of southern Puget Sound.

TRAIL	6 miles round-trip; natural surface
STEEPNESS	Gentle to moderate
OTHER USES	Pedestrians only
DOGS	On leash
CONNECTING TRAILS	None
PARK AMENITIES	Restrooms, picnic shelters, playground, wading pool
DISABLED ACCESS	Restrooms, picnic areas

Warm sun filters through the summer canopy of big-leaf maples and Douglas firs. The air feels cool and then warm, and is fragrant with the delicious, almost imperceptible scent of blackberry blossoms. Ellis Cove Trail, the primary walking trail of Priest Point Park, meanders for 3 miles through woodland magic, passing creeks and ravines and then traversing bluffs above southern Puget Sound. Sword ferns, huckleberry, and salal weave a lush green carpet beneath towering western red cedars. This forest so well cocoons you in a sylvan spell that it's hard to believe urban Olympia lies just minutes away.

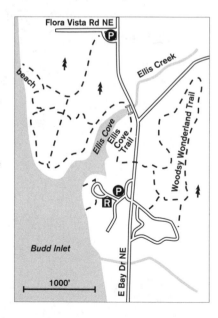

The wide, soft, wood-chip path is easy on the feet and quiet, as bicycles and horses are prohibited. The sculptured wooden trail signs are imaginative and playful. At one junction, a carved squirrel shows the way out, and elsewhere a sea otter perches on the trail post. Look for the unexpected sculpture of the small black bear climbing a trunk high above the trail.

More forest trails can be found in the northwest quadrant of the park, accessed from parking on Flora Vista Road, or by footbridge over Ellis Creek itself. Here you'll find paths leading to the pebbled beach of Budd Inlet, and more walking possibilities at mid- to low tide. Deep in the woods, the paths meander and turn, but there's no fear of getting lost, what with all the wooden animals to give directions. Sturdy wooden walkways lead you down into the cool ravine where Ellis Creek ends in a tidal estuary.

Interpretive signs explain the life of the estuary and the native peoples who traveled to this point on Budd Inlet to trade. A French missionary lived here from 1848 to 1860. After he left, the virgin forest was reduced to stumps within 40 years. In 1905 the City of Olympia bought Priest Point Park and 75 years later created Ellis Cove Trail and the Woodsy Wonderland trails in the eastern portion of the park. This is one park to savor over and over again.

ADDRESS: 2600 E Bay Drive NE, Olympia

GETTING THERE: From I-5 northbound, take exit 105 (City Center/Port of Olympia); from southbound, take exit 105B. Follow signs for the Port of Olympia, staying right toward Plum Street. Follow Plum Street (which becomes E Bay Drive, then Boston Harbor Road NE) north for about 2 miles. The park entrance is on the right. To reach Ellis Cove Trail, enter the park and pass over Boston Harbor Road NE to get to another parking lot.

CONTACT: Olympia Parks, Arts, and Recreation Department; (360) 753-8380; www.olympiawa.gov/city-services/park

<u>112</u> MCLANE CREEK NATURE TRAIL

7 miles southwest of downtown Olympia

Boardwalk trails lead past beaver ponds, over wetlands, and through 150 acres of temperate rain forest alive with wildlife.

TRAIL	2 wetland loops (0.6 miles and 1.1 miles), plus a 1-mile forest loop; natural surface, paved
STEEPNESS	Level to gentle
OTHER USES	Pedestrians only
DOGS	Not allowed
CONNECTING TRAILS	None
PARK AMENITIES	Restrooms, viewing platforms, picnic shelter, demonstration forest, interpretive signs
DISABLED ACCESS	Trail sections, restrooms

Enter a temperate rain forest in healing, more than 75 years after loggers took out the giants. Huge stumps show the scars of springboards but now serve as nurse logs for new saplings. Beavers maintain their ponds, and black-tailed deer and coyotes roam the open grassland at dawn and dusk.

Starting the loop either way leads you past active beaver ponds. These elusive but energetic rodents may not be easy to see, but you can observe the evidence of their work: freshly gnawed alders and cottonwoods lie tumbled along the water's edge. In winter the pond is full, almost overflowing, and alive with ducks, geese, herons, frogs, otters, muskrats, and salamanders. Sometimes fall floods wash the dam

---

It's a Bird, It's a Plane . . .

Well, most of us can tell the difference. But can you tell one bird from another? If you're a beginning birder, start by learning general shapes and sizes, and obvious color patterns. A bird's habitat is also a clue to its identity, whether you find it in a forest, meadow, wetland, or Puget Sound beach. The longer you study birds, the better you'll get at the specifics, such as telling one gull from another (they're tricky, though, with several years of plumage changes!) or one duck from another and moving past the LBJ (little brown job) category for all the smaller songbirds. Learn more by walking with more experienced birders, such as on National Audubon Society outings or ranger-led interpretive walks.

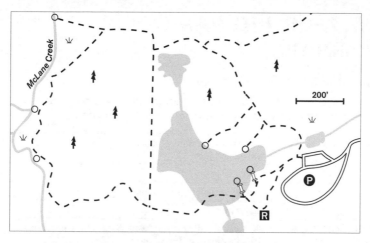

out and the pond drains, but within six months the beavers can rebuild and refill the pond.

A cutoff trail, the Old Grade, makes a shorter loop or can be explored as a side trip from the main trail. This is a remnant of old logging days, when locomotives chugged through here on their way to the Mud Bay Timber Company on Puget Sound, just 5 miles away.

On the southern edge of the loop, you walk in a forest of western red cedar and Douglas fir. Moss and lichen adorn the massive limbs, and woodpeckers leave their markings where they have bored for insects. Sparkling-clear McLane Creek is home to spawning chum salmon. Interpretive signs along the trail help you envision the creek and surrounding habitat in all their seasonal changes.

ADDRESS: 5042 Delphi Road SW, Olympia

GETTING THERE: From I-5, take exit 104 (US 101 N/Aberdeen). Go 4 miles and take the Mud Bay/2nd Avenue exit. Turn left at the stop and go over the freeway. Take the first left onto McKenzie Road (which becomes Delphi Road). Go about 3 miles to the sign for McLane Creek Demonstration Forest and Nature Trail, and turn right to reach the trail parking. A Discover Pass is required for all vehicles.

CONTACT: Washington State Department of Natural Resources, (360) 577-2025, www.wa.gov/dnr

<u>113</u> WATERSHED PARK (OLYMPIA)

1 mile south of downtown Olympia

Immerse yourself in 153 acres of a moss-draped temperate rain forest cut by whispering Moxlie Creek, where salmon come to spawn.

TRAIL	2.8 miles total; natural surface, boardwalk, wooden bridges
STEEPNESS	Gentle to steep
OTHER USES	Pedestrians only (no jogging)
DOGS	On leash
CONNECTING TRAILS	Olympia Woodland Trail (Walk #114) at the Eastside Street pedestrian trailhead
PARK AMENITIES	Portable toilet at Henderson Boulevard parking lot
DISABLED ACCESS	Short section of gravel trail from 2829 Henderson Boulevard trailhead

For nearly 100 years this temperate rain forest basin supplied the drinking water for all of Olympia. Saved from logging in the 1950s, Watershed Park now encircles you with a rich scent of wetland forest and the soothing sounds of birds and water. Bracken, horsetail, maples, and alder line G. Eldon Marshall Trail, which stretches from the rim to the streambed of Moxlie Creek and back. Trees tumbled by winter's windstorms lie like giant matchsticks, their roots exposed like pinwheels.

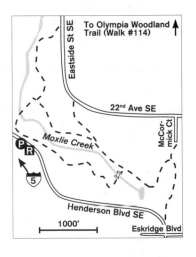

From the Henderson Boulevard parking lot, descend into the forest, taking the loop in either direction. Steps lead down to marshes where, in summer, green algae create an impressionist painting on the water's surface. Sword ferns, bracken, and maidenhair ferns line the trail. In this deep, shady forest of Douglas fir, big-leaf maple, and alder, be ready for banana slugs and skunk cabbage, natural inhabitants of so wet and lush a place.

This is a popular walk, despite its ruggedness—or perhaps because of it. Young families come with children in tow, teaching them the wonders of the streambed, where salmon spawn and tadpoles scoot about like tiny bumper cars gone crazy. Dogs are welcome, but only on leash, to protect the fragile habitat and sensitive replanting areas. Boardwalks, too, protect the wetlands and help you keep your feet dry; sturdy wooden bridges offer vantage points above the clear, sandy-bottomed creek. Good trail maintenance has kept this rain forest walkable even on wet winter days.

ADDRESS: *Parking:* 2500 Henderson Boulevard SE, Olympia; *Pedestrian:* 2829 Henderson Boulevard SE; 1605 Eastside Street SE; 1201 22nd Avenue SE

GETTING THERE: From I-5 northbound, take exit 105 (City Center/Port of Olympia). Stay hard right, following Port of Olympia signs. At the end of the ramp, turn left (onto unmarked Henderson Boulevard) and go 0.25 miles to the trailhead on the left.

From I-5 southbound, take exit 105B. Follow signs for the Port of Olympia, staying left for Henderson Boulevard. Go under the freeway, and shortly after the roundabout the trailhead parking will be on the left.

CONTACT: Olympia Parks, Arts, and Recreation Department; (360) 753-8380; www.olympiawa.gov/city-services/parks. To volunteer to help maintain or enhance this park, call the Park Stewardship Program at (360) 753-8365.

OLYMPIA

<u>114</u> OLYMPIA WOODLAND TRAIL

1 mile south of downtown Olympia

A level, accessible trail follows an old railway line for miles through a forest of towering maples and firs.

TRAIL	2.5 miles one way; natural surface, paved
STEEPNESS	Level
OTHER USES	Bicycles; horses on parallel natural trail
DOGS	On leash
CONNECTING TRAILS	Olympia's Watershed Park (Walk #113), Chehalis Western Trail (Walk #107), Lacey Woodland Trail (extension to the east)
PARK AMENITIES	Restrooms, benches, map signs, picnic area
DISABLED ACCESS	Paved trail, restrooms, picnic area

Birdsong rings brightly in this emerald thoroughfare of old Olympia forest. Huge maples, dressed in soft green moss-velvet, stand sentinel over the smoothly paved trail, and deep in a green cleft a stream rushes through a canopy of ferns. Just over 0.5 miles from the trailhead, near the Frederick Street trailhead (pedestrian only), a spur trail leads to a waterfall along East Indian Creek. Other small natural-surface nature trails have been built by volunteers and lead into the creek canyon or onto the surrounding ridges. Although never far from the interstate highway, the traffic blurs to white noise, and, surprisingly, the sound of birdcalls and the rushing stream can be clearly heard.

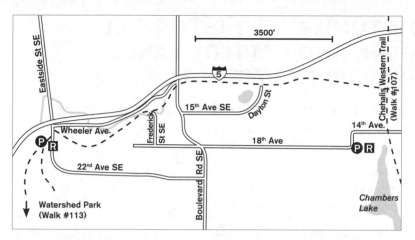

Over 25 years ago, this abandoned railway line began tempting Olympia's residents with the dream of creating an accessible trail from Olympia to Lacey and beyond. The trail opened in 2007 and now extends almost 5 miles from the State Capitol. Hundreds of volunteers of all ages have planted over fifteen thousand shrubs and saplings to help restore native flora. The idea of "green" is a theme with the trail: the parking lot is porous pavement, the restrooms are lighted with solar tubes, and the entire roof of the restroom and picnic shelter at the Eastside Street trailhead is covered in plants.

The entire trail runs from Watershed Park in Olympia to central Lacey, for a total of 4.75 miles. Although the eastern trailhead is in Lacey's Woodland Creek Community Park, with a pond and meadow trails, the 2.3 miles of interim trail traverse the business district and shops. For bicycling, the whole trail is a dream, but walkers seeking a natural venue should stick to the 2.5 miles between Olympia's Eastside Street and the Chehalis Western Trail, or take short strolls at the Lacey end near Woodland Creek Community Park.

ADDRESS: 1600 Eastside Street SE, Olympia. Pedestrian trailheads at Frederick Street and Dayton Avenue.

GETTING THERE: From I-5, take exit 105 (Port of Olympia); from I-5 southbound, take exit 105B (Port of Olympia). Go straight through the light onto Plum Street. Go 0.1 miles and turn right onto Union Avenue SE. Go 0.2 miles and turn right onto Eastside Street SE. Cross the bridge and look on the left for the parking lot and a low building with plants on its roof.

CONTACT: Olympia Parks, Arts, and Recreation Department; (360) 753-8380; www.olympiawa.gov/city-services/parks. To volunteer, contact the Woodland Trail Greenway Association: www.wtga.org.

OLYMPIA

<u>115</u> TUMWATER HISTORICAL PARK AND CAPITOL LAKE INTERPRETIVE TRAIL

Tumwater, 2 miles south of downtown Olympia, to Olympia

Wander 35 acres along the Deschutes River to Capitol Lake wetlands and an interpretive trail.

TRAIL	1.5 miles; natural surface, paved
STEEPNESS	Level
OTHER USES	Bicycles
DOGS	On leash
CONNECTING TRAILS	Capitol Lake; Tumwater Falls Park (Walk #116) via sidewalk
PARK AMENITIES	Restrooms, playground, picnic shelter, interpretive trail, fishing docks, viewpoints
DISABLED ACCESS	Paved trail, restrooms

Nestled in a pocket of marsh and greenery beneath the ramparts of I-5, tiny Tumwater Historical Park may not be a long-distance destination in itself unless you're a Washington State history buff. Numerous interpretive signs tell of life along the river, the old Olympia Brewery, and the early settlers. After strolling the garden-like setting of wild roses and marsh walks to the edge of the river, you can head north under the freeway to the shores of Capitol Lake, where a dock provides viewing access to the lake and a chance to get closer to the ducks and geese or to spot birds in the reeds that adorn its edges.

In this wild corner of Capitol Lake (created in the late 1970s when the lake was dredged) you may hear the blackbirds whistle *tse-er, tse-er* or spot a great blue heron studying the water for lunch. The trail splits here, with the paved portion following the

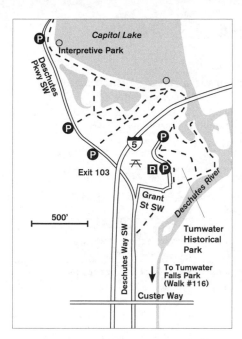

lake toward the Capitol Lake Interpretive Center and another viewing and fishing dock. Dozens of botanical markers dot both sides of the trail for those interested in what grows along the lakeshore.

If you stay left and follow the fence line on a natural surface path, you can loop around a wetland, pass near road parking on Deschutes Way, and circle back to the paved lake trail. Despite its proximity to the freeway, this stretch of trail is surprisingly quiet except for the undulating song of robins and the chirps of wrens.

The lake was first proposed in 1911 as a means of trapping sediment from the Deschutes River, but was not created until 1951. Today this lake is home to migrating and resident flocks of, among others, western grebes, red-winged blackbirds, juncos, pied-billed grebes, scaups, ruddy ducks, and swallows. In recent years New Zealand land snails have colonized the water, and due to their invasive nature, the lake is closed for swimming and boating.

ADDRESS: *Tumwater Historical Park:* 802 Deschutes Way SW, Tumwater; *Capitol Lake Interpretive Trail:* 300 Deschutes Parkway SW, Olympia

GETTING THERE: From I-5 northbound, take exit 103 (Deschutes Way). Continue straight from the ramp through one stop sign, then turn right on Grant Road, which leads into the park.

From I-5 southbound, take exit 103 (2nd Avenue). At the light, turn left on Custer Way to cross the freeway. Immediately after the overpass, take a sharp right, curving down to Deschutes Way. Turn right, then right again onto Grant Road into the park. Parking is available along Deschutes Way to access the interpretive trail.

CONTACT: Tumwater Parks and Recreation Department, (360) 754-4160, www.ci.tumwater.wa.us/departments/parks-recreation. Washington State Department of Enterprise Services maintains the interpretive trail; call them at (360) 902-8881 or visit www.des.wa.gov.

116 TUMWATER FALLS PARK

2.5 miles south of downtown Olympia

The whoosh of cascading falls promises a sense of wilderness on this short jaunt into 15 acres of historical Washington.

TRAIL	Less than 1 mile; paved, natural surface
STEEPNESS	Level to steep
OTHER USES	Pedestrians only
DOGS	On leash
CONNECTING TRAILS	Tumwater Historical Park (Walk #115) via 1 block of sidewalk
PARK AMENITIES	Restrooms, picnic area, playground, viewing platforms, interpretive signs, salmon ladders, guided tours, native garden, historical site
DISABLED ACCESS	Salmon ponds, interpretive kiosk, restrooms

Walk the banks of the wild and tumbling Deschutes River as it makes the final leaps toward Puget Sound in three pounding cascades. A loop trail of paved pathways leads from the upper falls to the lower falls, and historical replicas of bridges span the river. So wonderfully noisy is this river that it blocks all sound of the nearby freeways and leaves you with a sense of having stepped out of the urban world into the mountains.

This small park is not only a great place for a short walk but it is full of information about the historical setting. It was here that Leopold Schmidt started the Olympia Brewery (visible across the river), and there were mills and logging ventures as well. In spring and summer the native-plants garden flourishes, and the maples create patterns of light and shadow over the well-maintained trails and footbridges. In winter the paths are kept clear and dry, and the rain-swollen river rages beside you.

In autumn, though, the park portrays its best character, with a colorful palette of fall leaves on the deciduous trees and the excitement of seeing the salmon run as the fish make their way up the ladders flanking the falls. A Washington Department of Fish and Wildlife facility is located on the grounds, and here you can learn about the spawning of the salmon and how the fish eggs and milt are harvested to be placed in hatcheries throughout the state.

Owned privately by the Olympia Tumwater Foundation, the park is free and open to the public daily. Side paths parallel the river on the old railroad grades, allowing for more exploration. Tumwater Falls Park is located immediately upriver from Tumwater Historical Park, and the two parks beg to be united. Until then, you can walk the 800 feet of sidewalk between the two, or drive for 1 minute and continue your walk and tour of historical Tumwater.

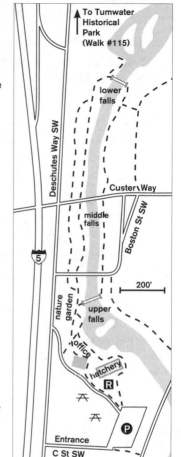

ADDRESS: 110 Deschutes Way SW, Tumwater

GETTING THERE: From I-5 southbound, take exit 103 (2nd Avenue) and follow 2nd Avenue to Custer Way, which will cross the freeway and river by the old Olympia Brewery. Turn right immediately onto Boston Street SW, then left onto Deschutes Way SW. In 0.2 miles turn left onto C Street SW into the park.

From I-5 northbound, take exit 103 (Deschutes Way). Continue north on Deschutes Way for 0.3 miles. Turn right onto C Street SW into the park.

CONTACT: Olympia Tumwater Foundation, (360) 943-2550, www.olytumfoundation.org. Donations to the park, which is a 501(c)(3) charity, may be tax deductible.

117 PIONEER PARK

Tumwater, 4 miles south of downtown Olympia

Stroll meadows and grasslands along the banks of the Deschutes River in this 85-acre community park.

TRAIL	1.5 miles total; gravel, natural surface, paved
STEEPNESS	Level
OTHER USES	Bicycles
DOGS	On leash
CONNECTING TRAILS	None
PARK AMENITIES	Restrooms, picnic areas, playground, playing fields
DISABLED ACCESS	Paved trail, restrooms

This spacious community park with a rural feel and open meadows lies only minutes south of downtown Olympia. Here you can walk well-defined trails through open grassland or explore the banks of the Deschutes River. A trail system completed in 1996 has enlarged the park, and now it appeals not only to playground users and ball players but also to walkers, joggers, and birders.

Nestled in a curve of the Deschutes River, the meadow hosts rabbits and shrews, food for the hunting hawks overhead. From the parking lot, turn south from the playing fields and cross the natural meadow. The row of cottonwoods and alders defines the riverbank, where you can wander the sandy edge or picnic on the graveled bar. No swimming is allowed, but you can stop and throw a fishing line. Free-to-borrow life jackets are available to allow parents some peace of mind as their children play on the riverbanks in summer. Back in the meadow, take a different loop to return to the cars. If it's a clear day, look for the white crown of Mount Rainier to the east. Winter rains swell the river to dangerous levels, so it's not a time for exploring too close to the banks.

ADDRESS: 5801 Henderson Boulevard SE, Tumwater

GETTING THERE: From I-5 northbound, take exit 101 (Tumwater Boulevard). Turn east and follow Tumwater Boulevard to its end (about 1 mile). Turn left on

Henderson Boulevard and go about 0.6 miles. The park is on the left just past the Deschutes River.

From I-5 southbound, take exit 103 (2nd Avenue). At the flashing light, turn left on Custer Way, which crosses the freeway. Continue on Custer Way through one light, then turn right at Cleveland Avenue. Go 1.2 miles and turn right on Henderson Boulevard. Go 0.5 miles, across Yelm Highway and the railroad tracks. The park is on the right at the bottom of the hill.

CONTACT: Tumwater Parks and Recreation Department, (360) 754-4160, www .ci.tumwater.wa.us/departments/parks-recreation

<u>118</u> MIMA MOUNDS NATURAL AREA PRESERVE

10 miles south of downtown Olympia

Stretch your legs and your imagination in 625 acres of grassland where the earth mounds into a bubbled landscape.

TRAIL	3 miles; paved and natural surface
STEEPNESS	Level
OTHER USES	Pedestrians only
DOGS	Not allowed
CONNECTING TRAILS	None
PARK AMENITIES	Picnic tables, restrooms, viewing platforms, interpretive signs
DISABLED ACCESS	Paved 0.5-mile loop trail, interpretive kiosk, restrooms

Leave your car in the embrace of the forest, and step into a rare and magical land of undulating prairie grasses and ground cover. In spring and summer the prairie glows with blue and yellow flowers, and butterflies flit between the blossoms. In fall and winter the grasses give way to low orange and brown ground cover, and clumps of frothy white reindeer lichen brighten the undulating mounds. Year-round, raptors circle overhead searching for voles and mice, and on clear days Mount Saint Helens rises above the forest to the southeast.

Unique in heavily forested western Washington, this natural grassland hides a geological mystery: How were these hundreds of acres of rolling mounds formed? Naturalists and scientists have long been pondering the origins of these mounds

of glacial rocks and loam, and since 1841 more than thirty theories have been proposed, from burial grounds to gophers. Today, scientists generally agree that the mounds were formed after the last glaciers retreated 16,000 years ago and that they may have been the result of melt-water or earthquakes.

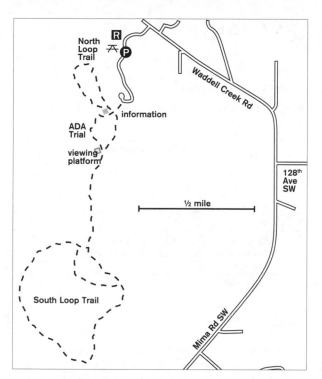

This unique prairie has long been known by the Native Americans who came here to find herbs and camas root, important plants used for healing and food. They maintained the health of the prairie by burning each year to keep the encroaching forest at bay. This practice also provided an open hunting ground and made traveling easier. Today, the DNR also does controlled burns to reduce the invasion of the forest and nonnative plants.

If you choose the long southern loop trail, you can see remnants of the stumps removed by the DNR. In fall and winter patches of controlled burns may be unsightly, but it is in these areas that the spring flowers flourish each year.

ADDRESS: 12470 Waddell Creek Road SW, Olympia

GETTING THERE: From I-5 northbound, take exit 95 and stay left to merge onto Maytown Road SW. Go toward Littlerock, where the road jogs slightly and becomes 128th Avenue SW. Continue west to the T-junction with Waddell Creek Road and Mima Road SW. Turn right onto Waddell Creek Road SW. The park is on the left in about 0.7 miles. A Discover Pass is required for parking.

CONTACT: Washington State Department of Natural Resources, (360) 577-2025, www.dnr.wa.gov

OLYMPIA

<u>119</u> MILLERSYLVANIA STATE PARK

10 miles south of downtown Olympia

Walk through miles of old-growth forest and over lakeside wetlands in this 843-acre park.

TRAIL	8.6 miles; boardwalk, natural surface
STEEPNESS	Level
OTHER USES	Bicycles
DOGS	On leash
CONNECTING TRAILS	None
PARK AMENITIES	Restrooms, playground, picnic areas, beaches, campgrounds, fitness trail, nonmotorized-boat rentals
DISABLED ACCESS	Restrooms, campgrounds, paved trails

Stroll under immense old Douglas fir and western red cedar trees on miles of soft, needle-lined trails. Cross a wetland on a puncheon boardwalk. Enjoy the quiet of this state park forest in a section far from the bustle of the beaches (the park has 3,300 feet of lakefront). Here you may see pileated woodpeckers or their dainty cousins, the downy woodpeckers. Even if the birds elude you, you'll see evidence of work in the large holes pecked into snags throughout the forest.

For those with a mind for exercise besides walking, follow the blue-and-white arrows to the 1-mile fitness trail. Millersylvania's trail uses natural stumps for steps and logs for balance, an interesting (but possibly slippery) version of the normal exercise equipment found on other fitness trails.

Those arriving early or staying in the campgrounds might find scat or tracks of martens, raccoons, or coyotes. Around the borders of Deep Lake you may see evidence of muskrats or otters. Birdlife is prolific. On and over the lake, look for ducks, geese, ospreys, and eagles. In summer, hummingbirds frequent bushes by the orchard and lakeshore.

The land was homesteaded in 1855, and remnants of the narrow-gauge railroad and skid roads can still be found. In 1921

Anyone Home in the Alder Cone?

Alder cones may be tiny, but they harbor tasty food. Chickadees fly from cone to cone listening for a meal. If they tap and hear a hollow sound, it means there's a tasty bug burrowed in the cone. Oh yum!

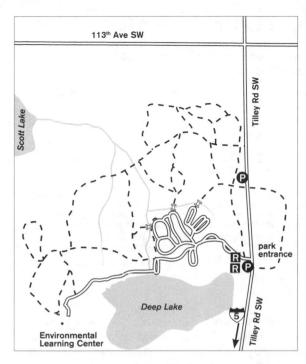

the Miller family, who had dubbed it Mill-ersylvania, donated the land to the state, stipulating it was to be held forever as a park. The park's structures were built almost entirely by hand in 1935 by the Civilian Conservation Corps. There is a separate parking lot for walkers on Tilley Road, in an old orchard north of the main entrance.

ADDRESS: 12245 Tilley Road S, Olympia

GETTING THERE: From I-5 southbound, take exit 99 (93rd Avenue S/WA 121 S).

Turn left on 93rd Avenue S/WA 121 S. Drive 1.5 miles and turn right on Tilley Road S/WA 121 S. The park entrance is on the right in 2.9 miles. A Discover Pass is required for parking.

CONTACT: Washington State Parks, (360) 753-1519, www.parks.wa.gov

120 YELM TO TENINO TRAIL

Tenino, 13 miles south of downtown Olympia, to Yelm,
20 miles southeast of downtown Olympia

*Walk past historic towns, farmland, forest, the Deschutes River, and
McIntosh Lake on this rural rails-to-trails pathway.*

TRAIL	14 miles one way; paved
STEEPNESS	Level to gentle
OTHER USES	Bicycles; horses on parallel trail
DOGS	On leash
CONNECTING TRAILS	Chehalis Western Trail (Walk #107)
PARK AMENITIES	Restrooms at all trailheads, picnic tables at Yelm trailhead, historic interpretive signs
DISABLED ACCESS	Paved trail

Walk through historic Yelm, and then into the countryside with great views of
Mount Rainier. One of the newest rails-to-trails conversions in Western Washington, this bicyclers' paradise (and walkers' long-distance challenge) connects the
rural towns of Yelm, Rainier, and Tenino along the route followed for more than
100 years by the Burlington Northern Railroad. Although the trail parallels WA 507
fairly closely, it is pleasantly quiet. You pass orchards, farms, and backyards.

Now fully paved, the trail from Yelm goes southwest through the town of
Rainier's Wilkowski Park. Restrooms and a trailhead can be found here. West
from Rainier, you cross the Deschutes River near the Chehalis Western Trail (Walk
#107), then skirt the borders of Lake McIntosh for 0.75 miles, with some good
birding. The trail passes under historic trestles and traverses tranquil sections of

Douglas fir forest and agri-
cultural land. The trail ends
at Tenino City Park, which
has parking and restrooms.
Parts of the trail cross driveways and small roads, so
keep kids and pets close.

ADDRESS: *Tenino trailhead:*
Washington Avenue, Tenino;
Yelm trailhead: 105 W Yelm
Avenue, Yelm

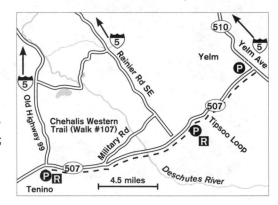

GETTING THERE: *Tenino trailhead:* From I-5, take exit 101 (Tumwater Boulevard). Stay on Tumwater Boulevard through the traffic circle. Turn right onto Capitol Boulevard SE/Old Highway 99 SE. Go about 9.8 miles. In Tenino, turn left onto Sussex Avenue, then right onto S Frost Street. Follow S Frost as it becomes O'Brien, then turns sharply left to become Washington Avenue. The trailhead is in the park.

Yelm trailhead: From I-5 north- or southbound, take exit 111 (Marvin Way/WA 510). Go 13 miles southeast on WA 510 into Yelm. Before the first stoplight in Yelm, turn right into the city hall parking lot on W Yelm Avenue.

CONTACT: Thurston County Parks and Recreation Department, (360) 786-5595, www.co.thurston.wa.us/parks

OLYMPIA

ACKNOWLEDGMENTS

This fourth edition marks the twentieth anniversary of *Take a Walk: Seattle*, and for that, I want to thank all my readers, who have kept the book alive. Many friends and family members have helped with my research by walking dozens of miles with me, and their help and friendship are greatly appreciated. For this edition, special thanks go to Chip Muller, Angela Ginorio, Clare Meeker, Dan Grausz, Jules and Erik Still, and Amanda Hacking for providing a bed and office space while I did the research. Also, a big thanks to Gary Luke, Em Gale, and all the staff at Sasquatch Books for their help in creating a great fourth edition.

INDEX OF WALKS AND PARKS

ABOUT THE AUTHOR

Born to a family of incurable travelers, Sue Muller Hacking has dusted her boots on the trails of Asia, Africa, South America, the United States, and Canada. An award-winning photojournalist and freelance writer, she is a resident of Seattle when not sailing around the world or trekking in Nepal with her husband and (now-adult) children.